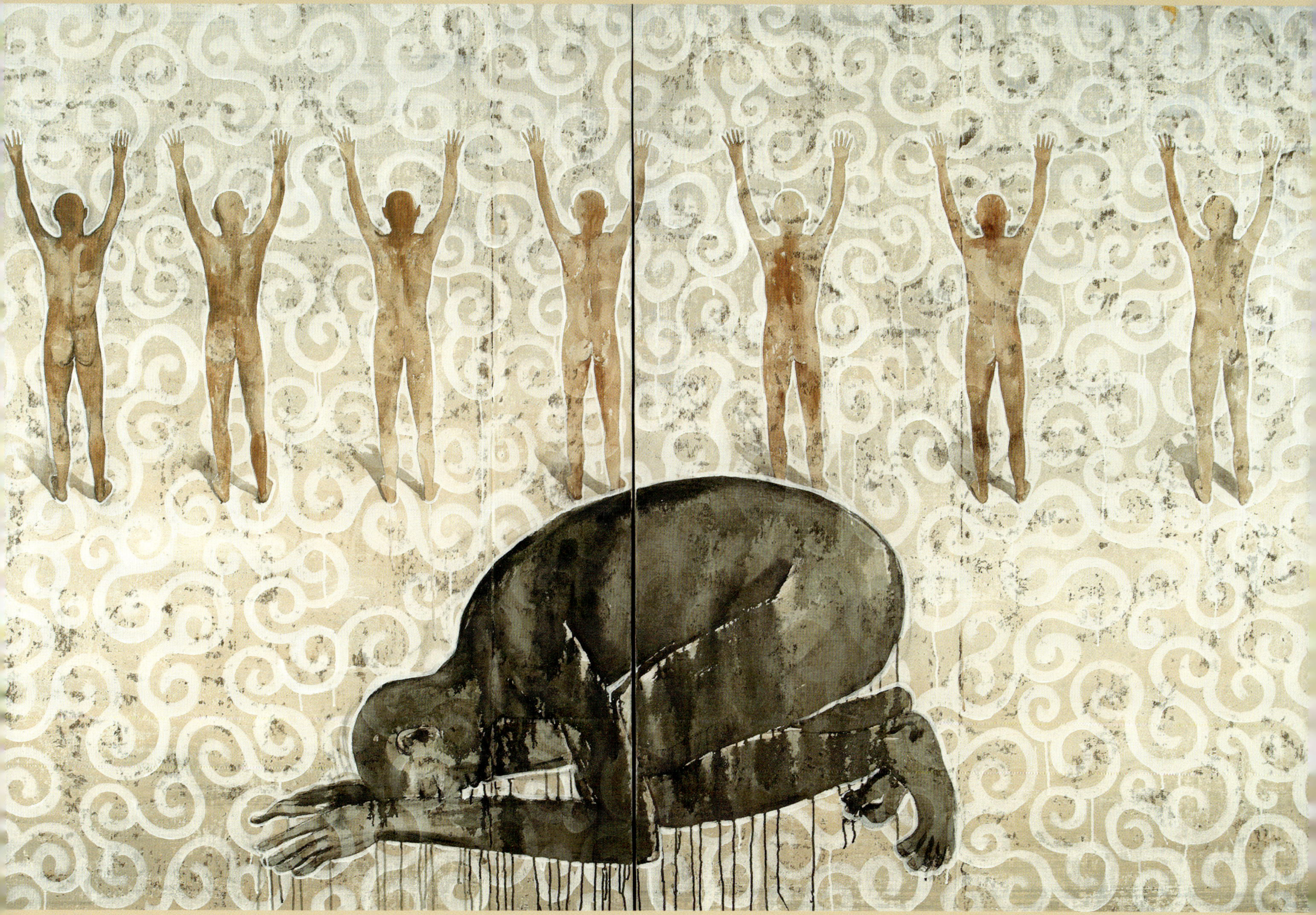

The Dancer on the Horse

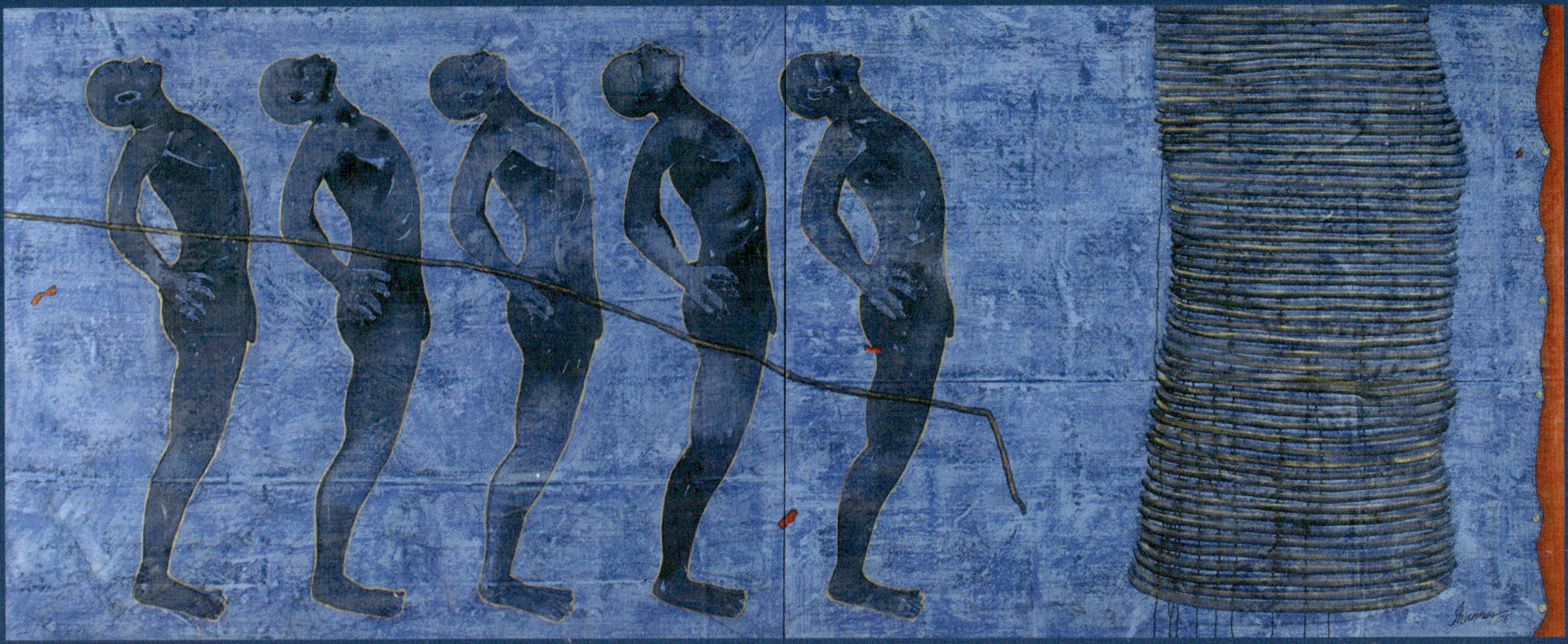

CONTEMPORARY INDIAN ARTISTS SERIES

The Dancer on the Horse
Reflections on the Art of Iranna GR

Ranjit Hoskote

Mapin Publishing | Lund Humphries

First published in 2007 in India by
Mapin Publishing Pvt. Ltd.
10B Vidyanagar Society Part I
Usmanpura, Ahmedabad 380 014 INDIA
T: 91 79 2754 5390/2754 5391 • F: 91 79 2754 5392
E: mapin@mapinpub.com • www.mapinpub.com

Also published in 2007 by

Lund Humphries
Gower House, Croft Road
Aldershot, Hampshire GU11 3HR
United Kingdom

and

Lund Humphries
Suite 420
101 Cherry Street
Burlington VT 05401-4405
USA

Lund Humphries is part of Ashgate Publishing
www.lundhumphries.com

By arrangement with Grantha Corporation, USA
E: mapinpub@aol.com

Distributed in the Indian subcontinent by
Mapin Publishing Pvt. Ltd.

Distributed in the rest of the world by
Lund Humphries

ISBN: 978-0-85331-965-8 (Lund Humphries)
ISBN: 978-81-88204-92-2 (Mapin)
ISBN: 978-0-944142-38-7 (Grantha)

Library of Congress Control Number: 2006940423
British Library Cataloguing-in-Publication Data
A catalogue record for this book is available from the British Library

Designed by Revanta Sarabhai / Mapin Design Studio
Edited by Diana Romany / Mapin Editorial
Processed by Reproscan
Printed in Singapore

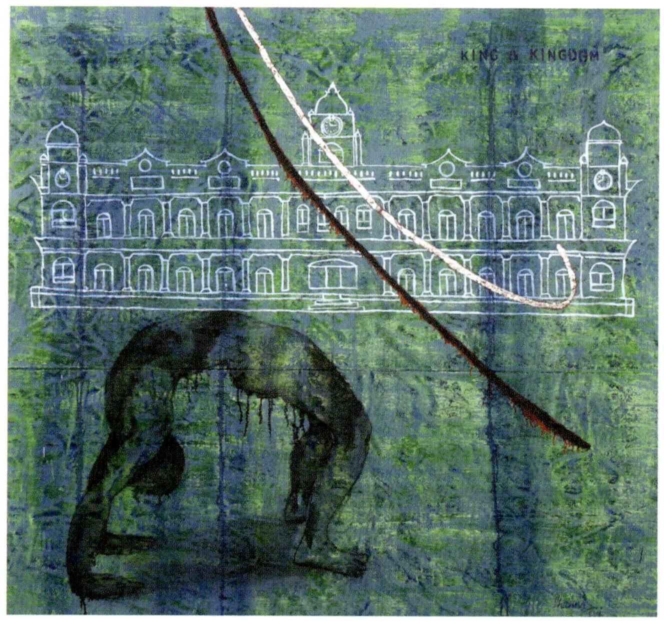

Page 1: *Prayer*, acrylic on tarpaulin, 108x66", 2006
Page 2: *The Story of Five Gentlemen - II*, acrylic on tarpaulin, 132x52", 2006

The book is dedicated to my guru, Shri Channaveer Swamiji, Sarangamath

During the last twenty years of my journey there have been many important people who have contributed to my artistic growth:

I would like to thank my present guru, Shri Prabhu Sarang Dev Shivacharyaru, for his help on the path to divinity.

To my grandmother, who shaped the values of my life and my father and mother, for being there when I needed them most.

My sincere gratitude to Professor Rajeev Lochan and Professor VG Andani for their guidance. To fellow artists Himmat Shah and Shobha Broota, who helped me from time to time see where I'm going wrong.

A special thank you to my artist wife, Pooja Iranna, for her love and support, and to my children, who give beauty and meaning to each day of my life.

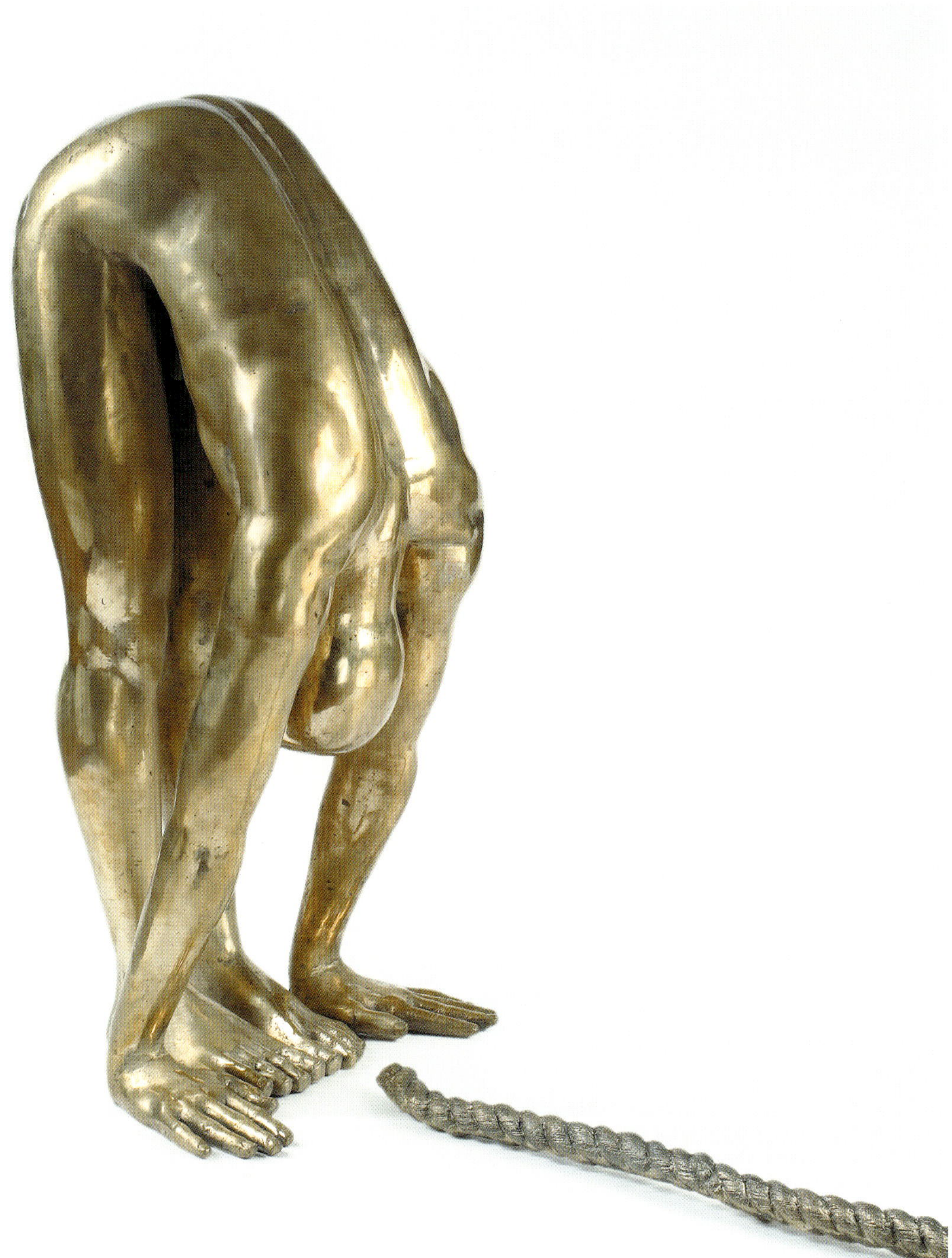

Departure, bronze, 36x12x75", 2006

Foreword

Iranna's paintings are a visual delicacy; an indulgence that that is never unexciting and an experience that is enduring yet ostensibly precise - that is, till you have caught a glimpse of his bronzes, which are a luxury for the senses as his sculptural installations render his process exponentially by adding a third dimension to the human figure that constantly appears in his painting.

I have always enjoyed living with Iranna's paintings and consider him a truly exceptional human being of strong moral fibre and impeccable character - a trait that manages to find its way to the artist's work. Iranna as a person is uncomplicated and modest; he is as delightful as his work and incredibly easy to get along with. A remarkably positive influence and support structure in Iranna's life is that of his wife Pooja who has contributed much to his unprecedented success in recent years.

The Dancer on the Horse, illustrated on the cover, is a painting that is currently owned by my three-year-old son Abhivardhan Berry and even though his interest stems essentially from the fact that there is a horse in the picture and the background is his favourite colour, I hope that his attachment with the work will remain even after he gets over his fondness for farm animals and everything that is red.

My brother Saman Malik and I take great pleasure in collecting Iranna's work. We are pleased that some paintings from our collection have been documented in this publication along with a cross-section of his work that covers key periods of his career. We expect that this book will only be the first of many that will be published on Iranna's work in the coming years as the diversity and skill that he possesses is sure to place him among India's leading contemporary artists.

Tanuj Berry & Saman Malik
November 2006
New Delhi

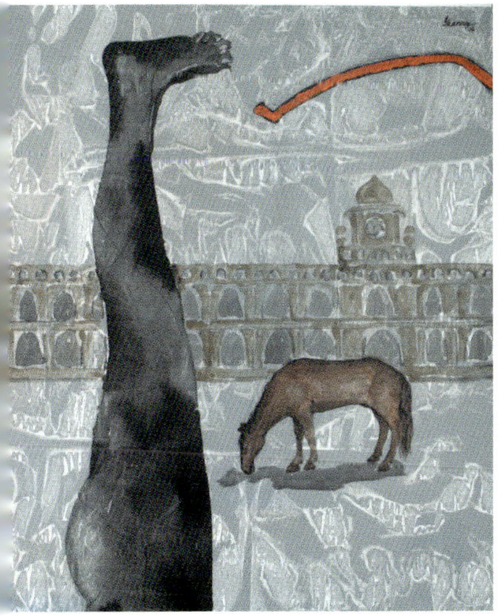
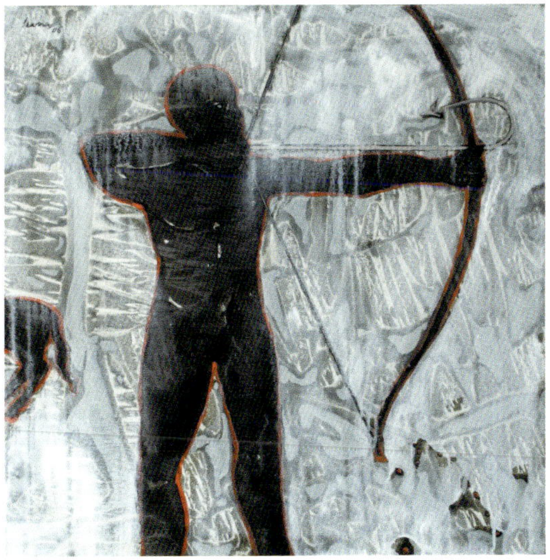
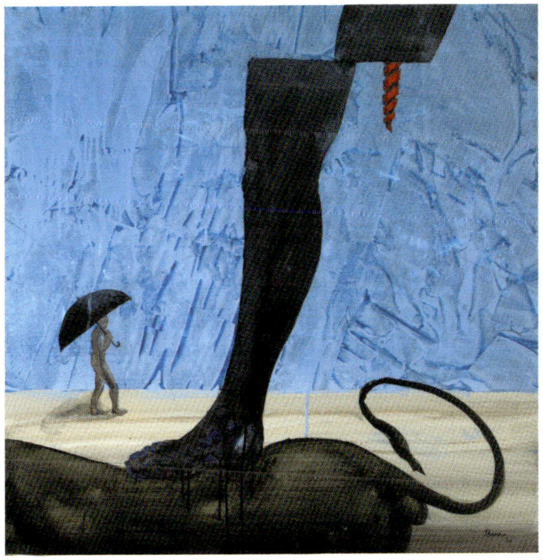
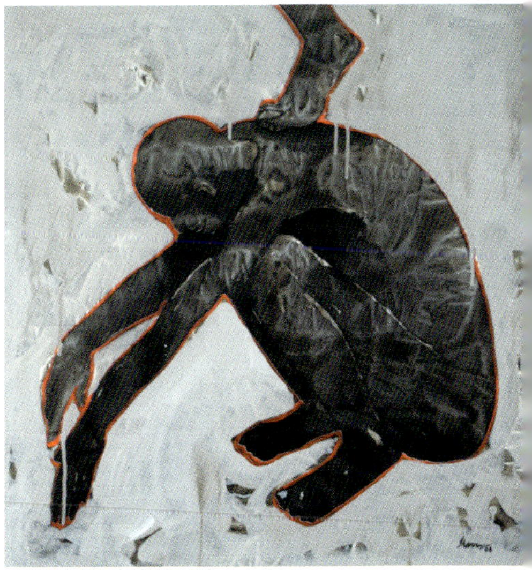

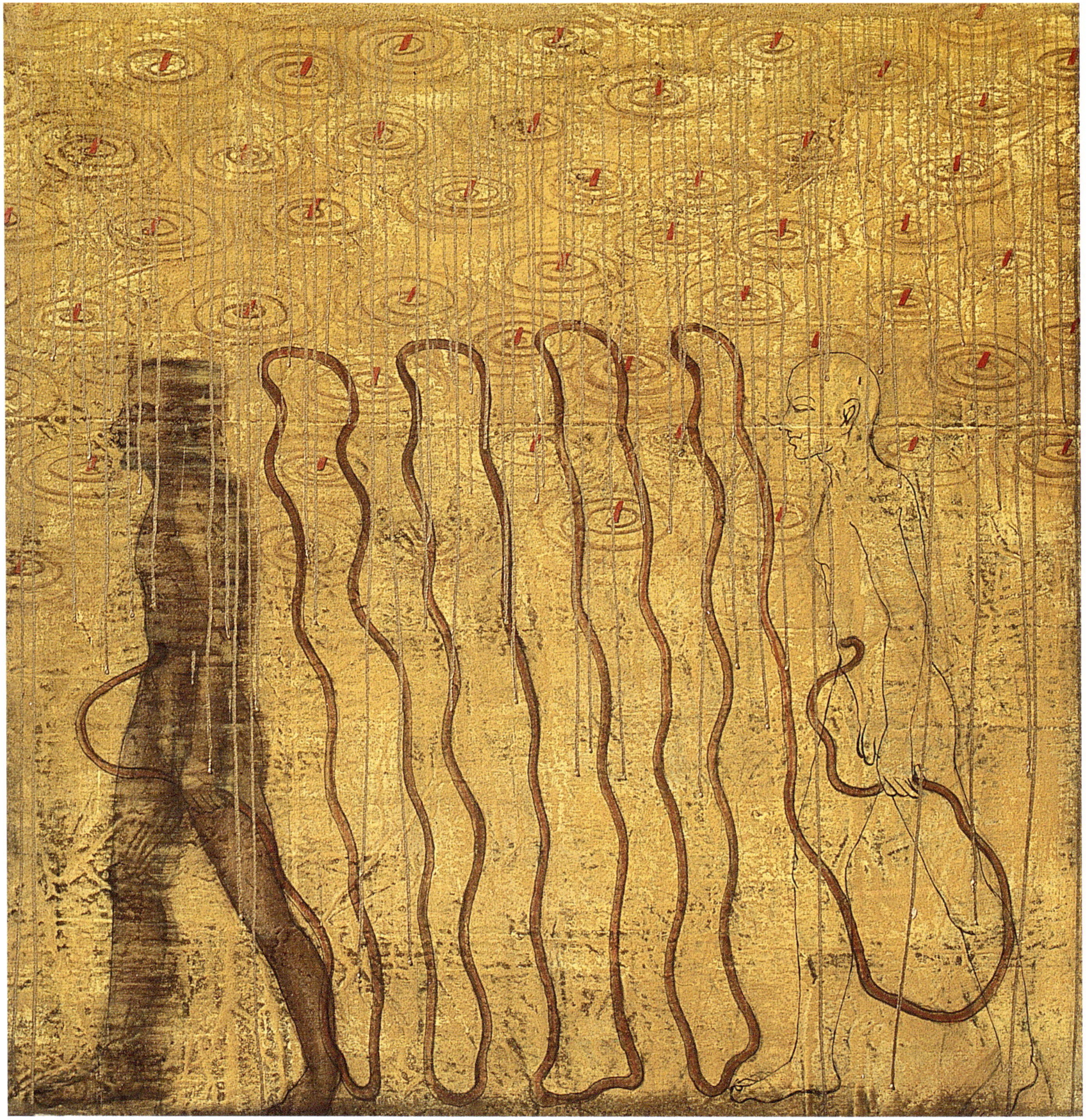

Generation, acrylic on tarpaulin, 66x66", 2003

The Dancer on the Horse
Reflections on the Art of Iranna GR

The Artist as Nostalgist and Futurist

From the small pastels and drawings that he essayed at the beginning of the 1990s to the magisterial large-format diptychs that have engaged his attention in recent years, Iranna GR has consistently displayed a measure of audacity in the range of his subjects and the manner in which he addresses them. Iranna has never fought shy of unlocking the ancestral cabinets of the guild. He has repeatedly confronted the grand narratives of myth and improvised elliptical allegories from the raw material of history: in his work, he alludes to the sketchbooks of Renaissance masters and to the iconography of the late-medieval Vijayanagara Empire; to the manuals of Yoga and to footage from the wars of the early 21st century. In a painting pointedly titled *Creation: Not After Michelangelo* (oil on canvas, 1995), which he produced soon after graduating from the Delhi College of Art, the artist summarily recast the scenario of Adam's advent, as enshrined on the ceiling of the Sistine Chapel and in the global popular imagination.

Rejecting the patriarchal gesture of beatific touch by which the current of life passes from the fingertips of the Supreme Being into those of his creature, Iranna endowed his primordial Man with a greater degree of independence, yet also a greater degree of vulnerability and agitation. Not for Iranna the heroic Adam awakening to his destiny in a sublime serenity yet untouched by the anguish of Fall and Expulsion: the young Indian artist (whose experience of European art was confined, at that time, to colour reproductions) chose to picture his Adam lying on his back, waking from the deep sleep of potentiality into a state of uncertainty, kicking in the air, plucking at cones of phallic ectoplasm that swirl in the air above him.

Creation has the air of a manifesto: it is almost certainly phrased as a polemic against the Renaissance-to-Postmodernism curriculum that most of India's art academies work with, centred as it is on a static account of Euro-American art history that offers emerging artists no means of adapting this inheritance to their own experience of the world, their specific cultural environment and political circumstances. Placed close to the beginning of Iranna's artistic career, this painting dramatises the boldness of Iranna's painterly investigations; and it is important to hold in mind the fact that, for him, a painting is not only an expressive occasion that permits the exercise of his sensuous talents, but also a critical inquiry into the philosophical and political questions that preoccupy him.

Iranna's student years (1990–94) coincided with a period of tumultuous change in Indian society as well as a period of fierce debate on the Indian art scene. At the collective level, the Indian economy, long controlled by the State, was opened up to private initiative and foreign investment; while this transformation extracted its toll in the agricultural sector and in small-scale industry, it opened up experiential horizons that had been withheld for several generations, allowing far more Indians than ever before to explore a new and amplified sense of the world, to travel, to form connections across national borders. Technological changes, such as those that ushered in 24-hour satellite television and the Internet, assisted in this upheaval in consciousness. Yet there was also a darker, more sinister side to the early 1990s: disruptive tendencies within the polity exploded in the form of a bitterly revanchist Hindu-majoritarian movement, whose aim was to correct supposed historical wrongs enacted on the Hindu population centuries before by invaders acting in the name of Islam or Christianity. This ideology may be viewed as a grotesque neo-tribalism, an outcome of modernity in its use of mass-mobilisation techniques, communications technology and the apparatus of propaganda dissemination. It arose partly in defensive response to the vast openness generated by the globalisation process, and partly as a vehicle for a newly emergent and highly aggressive class of political actors that had no sympathy for the inclusive and secular nature of the Indian Republic. It expressed its resentment and expansionism through a long cycle of oppression and violence against the Republic's Muslim and Christian minorities.

During the years that Iranna spent studying art - first in the small town of Gulbarga in peninsular India, and then in the national capital, New Delhi - India went through an epic churning marked by bitter irony, a piquant sense of liberation, and tragic paradox. On the one hand, the country found itself participating more actively in transnational exchanges of ideas, personnel and resources; powerful new technologies of communication, imaging and representation became available, triggering off a popular feeling of empowerment while also fuelling a revolution in the artistic imagination. On the other hand, India suffered new asymmetries of social opportunity and entitlement, ethnic violence, the legitimisation of brute force as an instrument for the expression of group interests. The classical left-of-centre perspective, to which India's intellectual class and most postcolonial Indian artists have subscribed, was no longer adequate as an instrument to explain or cope with these changes. Those sensitive to the scope and magnitude of the sweeping transformation of the 1990s found themselves considerably uncertain with regard to gauging the country's future and their own.

Indian artists were divided between those who wished to retrieve traditional resources of myth and narrative for contemporary purposes, and those who viewed these with scepticism as elements of a reactionary world-view, tainted by association with the religious imagination, best discarded or abandoned to the Right. While a number of artists announced the demise of painting and gravitated towards open forms such as video art, assemblage, performance and installation, others insisted on the primacy of pictorial space and set about devising means of revitalising painting. Abstraction, with the exception of a few committed non-representational artists, seemed to have faded away into epigonic repetition or quasi-mystical vagueness; it opposed, not the sociality of language, but the straw man of figuration. And as for figuration, this tendency within postcolonial Indian art appeared to have run aground on the opposite shoals of feeble narrative and exhausted solipsism.

The situation was redeemed within years, though, with the emergence of a new generation of artists, seemingly inexhaustible in their tactical energy, voracious in their appetite for formal and conceptual resources, and magisterial in their command of mythic resonance, detail, scale and artistic proposition. While many of these artists were in their mid-30s at this time - Atul Dodiya, Surendran Nair, Baiju Parthan, Nataraj Sharma, Rekha Rodwittiya, Ravinder Reddy and Anandajit Ray spring to mind - a phalanx of younger artists also seized the momentum of the period to launch themselves into a future that was uncharted but vibrant with the hope of experiment. Iranna may accurately be seen as one of these young artists, whose sensibility was formed in the febrile crucible of early-1990s India.

Indeed, Iranna's own journey could have been patterned on one of the templates of radical transformation that globalisation-era India specialises in. Born Iranna G Rukumpur (he has used several variations of his name in print, before settling on Iranna GR) in 1970 in the village of Sindgi, on the northern border of the peninsular Indian state of Karnataka, the future artist grew up on his father's farm, working in the fields and studying at the Sarang Math, a school whose practice bridged traditional learning and the demands of modernity. He discovered his gift for image-making very early. His father encouraged him in the appreciation of religious icons, whether votive images or the inventively rendered figures of divinities, midway between iconography and science-fiction, which recur in Indian calendar art. As a boy, Iranna delighted in drawing large chalk figures on the asphalt surface of a new road, especially the epic figure of Hanuman, the demigod who manifests himself in the form of a monkey. Iranna found his true calling when his guru gave him the freedom to follow his own imagination while decorating a temple.

In response to a question that the present writer put to him, about the recognition of his artistic abilities as a child, Iranna described the excitement of the years - between the ages of nine and fifteen - when he studied at the Sarang Math. "Discipline in everyday routine was a new experience for me, under the loving grace of my Guru. There, I had the first-hand experience of total freedom, while deciding upon the decoration of the Ashram and the temple," he writes. "This was in connection with a celebration, where I was

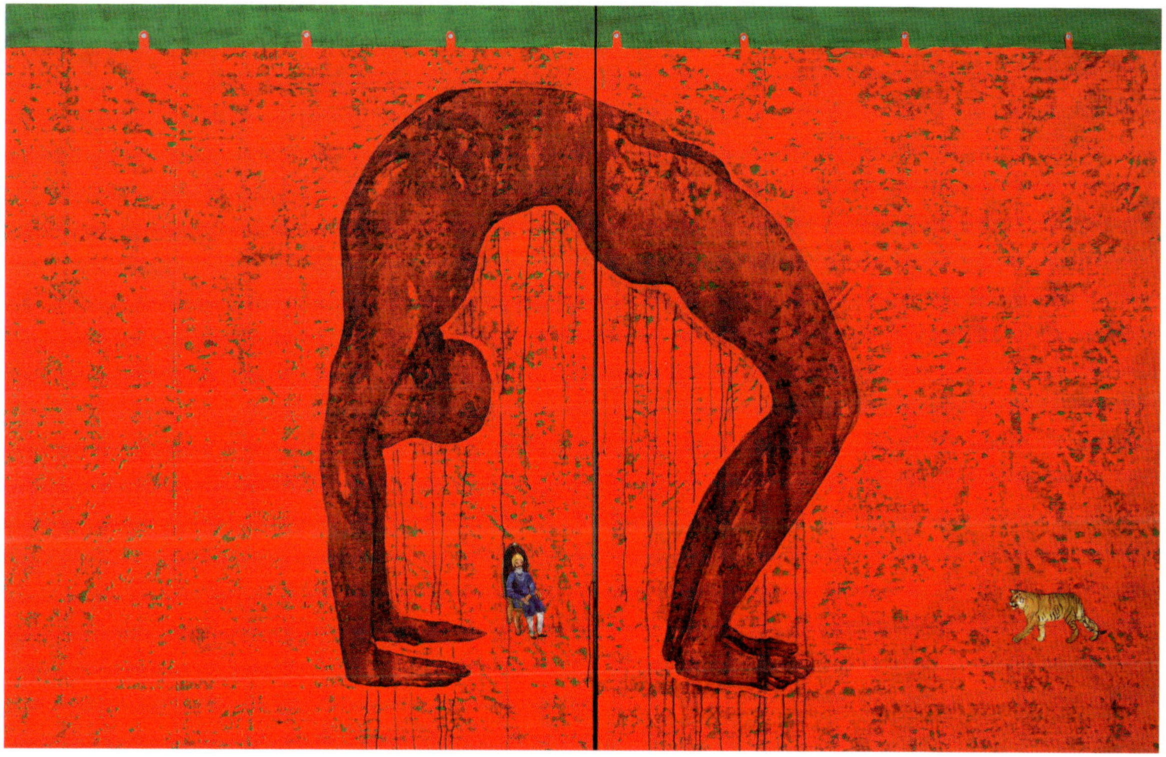

Retired King - III, acrylic on tarpaulin, 108x66", 2006

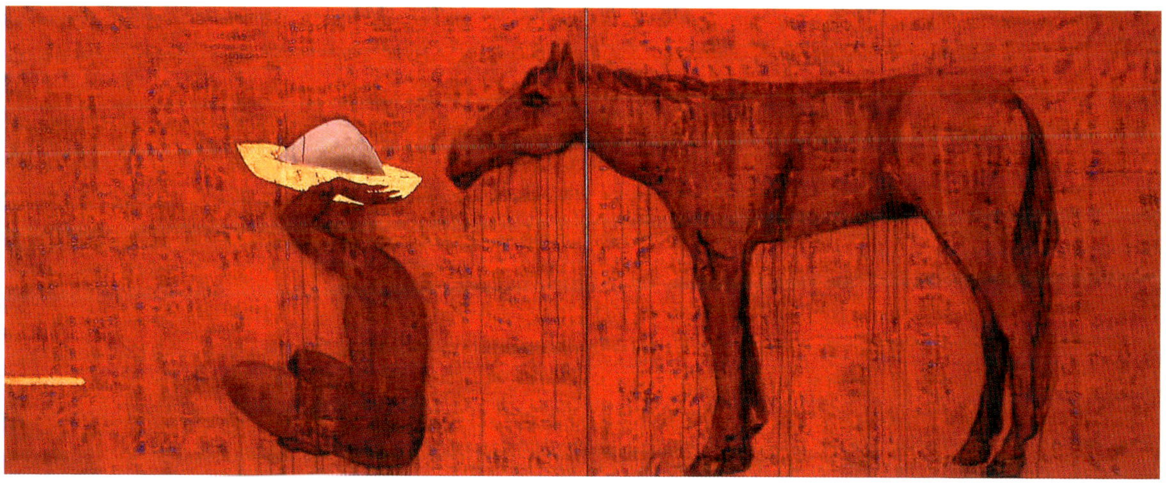

Ashwadana, acrylic and gold foil on tarpaulin, 132x52", 2005

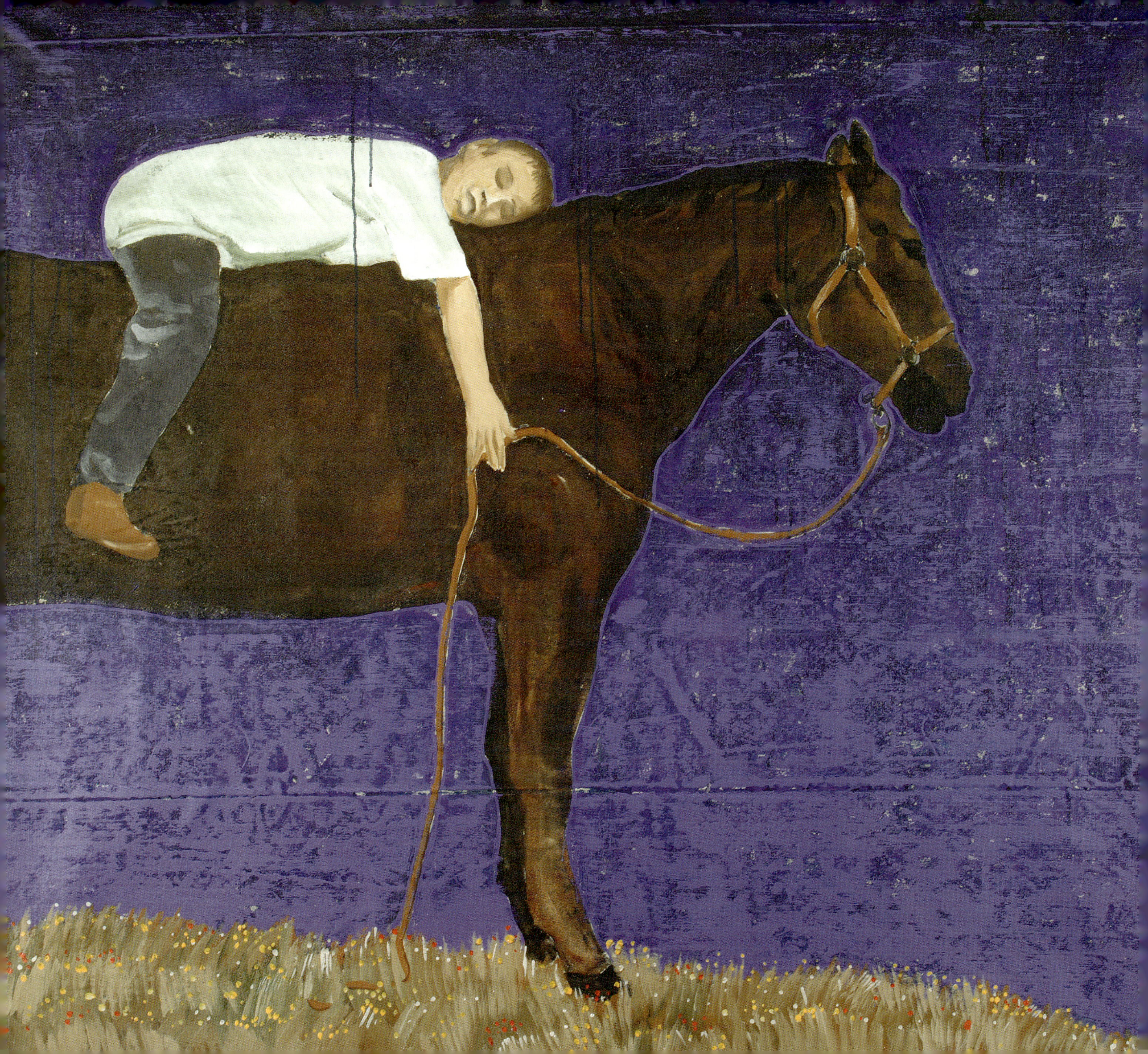

given full charge. I explored enamel paints. It took me a month and a half to complete the painting of the temple, which was appreciated by everybody in the village, and my efforts were mentioned in the Sabha meeting. This was unbelievable and gave me a lot of confidence. It was the major turning point for me. It was the first memorable taste of recognition. This recognition confirmed my decision to go in for the arts as a career. My father was not so happy about my decision but there was no other option for me. At this point every material became an excuse to create, every situation helped me towards creativity and I was very happy."[1]

With resolute persistence, and despite the reluctance of his family to let him pursue the uncertain vocation of art, Iranna moved beyond the ambit of his rural background. He put himself through the Foundation Course for Art in Bijapur, a prerequisite to qualify as an art teacher; visiting various places with a group of fellow students, he painted 300 landscapes during the two-year duration of this programme. He then enrolled at the College of Visual Arts in the district headquarters of Gulbarga, where he earned a Bachelor's degree in Fine Arts (1990–92), following this up with a two-year period of residence at the Delhi College of Art, from where he graduated with a Master's degree in Fine Arts and a firm grasp of the national as well as the international art scene (1992-94).

The sacred bond of trust and affection between the teacher and the disciple, a key motif in traditional Indic pedagogy, informs Iranna's relationship with the academic institutions through which he has passed; at each point of transit, he recalls the importance of having received the appropriate gesture of instruction from the right teacher. At the Sarang Math, his Guru convinced his father to let him be guided by his inclinations and study art; in Bijapur, MS Jati introduced the young student to the magic of colour, by demonstrating how a branch of bougainvillaea could be rendered in watercolour. At the art college in Gulbarga, Professor Andani saw the small-town boy's landscapes and paintings of divinities, and foresaw his potential for growth. And in Delhi, Iranna points to his experience as Professor Rajeev Lochan's student. Lochan, now Director of India's National Gallery of Modern Art, did not outline a syllabus for Iranna; he simply asked him to paint 50 paintings in a specified span of time, choosing only one of them as successful while rejecting the others. Iranna says that this gesture, redolent of the silent teaching of a Zen parable, pointed him in the direction of his actual painterly strengths, and away from his indulgences.[2]

Infinity Night, acrylic on tarpaulin, 66x52", 2006

Subsequently, after having practised as an independent artist and worked at the Garhi Artists' Village on a National Academy of Arts/Lalit Kala Akademi grant, Iranna spent a year as artist-in-residence at the Wimbledon School of Art, London, on a Charles Wallace Scholarship awarded by the British Council (1999–2000). Succeeding one another in rapid succession as they did, these shifts of location, ethos and activity must surely have called up the young artist's reserves of adaptability: they enriched his consciousness yet also generated an existential unease. We may justifiably interpret the recurrent single figure that negotiates an estranged and estranging environment in many of Iranna's paintings as an oblique self-portrait.

This self-surrogate confronts obstacles and practises new reflexes; it assumes the likeness of a child or a figure modelled on the ageing warrior Bhishma from the epic *Mahabharata*, lying on a bed of springs instead of the original arrows. During the late 1990s, no doubt reflecting his own passage through a multiplicity of choices and decisions, Iranna also attended to the formal problem of establishing a significant relationship between this compelling figure and its ground; he activated that ground, variously, as a theatre of operations, an illusionist backcloth or an allegorical landscape.

In recent years, Iranna has travelled widely across the globe, exhibiting in three continents and piloting a course through the complex terrain of global art. A cosmopolitan who is at ease in various regions and with various cultures, he chooses to live and work in New Delhi. In the course of fifteen years, he has extended his practice from painting to sculpture, while also marking his engagement with a variety of media including lithography and drawing; he calibrates his career with periodic exhibitions, each testifying to the remarkable degree of evolution that takes place in his perspective and methods from one suite of works to the next. If he records a continuity of preoccupation with the fate of the bodied self, his interest also shifts between the tight space of the single-occupancy chamber and a landscape that is large enough to accommodate a continent alive with people and machinery. The deepening of his quest for an understanding of humankind's liberation from its political predicaments is matched by the extension of his formal capabilities from the inwardness of pictorial space into the force field of the three-dimensional object.

Iranna's chosen vehicle of articulation is the allegorical tableau: an idiom that offers its contents to the viewer with disarming candour, even as it withholds many of the subtexts that would render them readable - so investing its protagonists and situations with the quality of enigmatic presence. Iranna takes advantage of the critical and even adversarial stance that allegory permits, while also nourishing its potential for all that cannot be decoded, cannot be named: the expressive and the sensuous. It is a tribute to his ingenuity and tireless self-questioning that he has perfected his allegorical art, for its roots lie in artistic choices that were widespread to the point of being formulaic during his student years. At that date, the styles of the Italian Transavantgarde had won considerable favour with the votaries of the narrative and allegorical options in Indian figuration; they had percolated to his generation through the work of their immediate predecessors, many of them associated with the influential Faculty of Fine Arts at the Maharaja Sayajirao University, Baroda.

By a quirk of circumstance, then, the visions of Sandro Chia, Enzo Cucchi and Francisco Clemente found many apostles in Delhi, Baroda and Bombay between the mid-1980s and the mid-1990s; indeed, the early and often self-repudiated work of many prominent contemporary artists owes much to these exemplars. Looking back over the exhibition catalogues of young artists who first showed twelve or thirteen years ago, for instance, we would be surprised at the frequency with which the apocalyptic visions of the Transavantgarde turn up, replete with flame-tongues, hybrid spaces fused from interior and landscape, and buoyant dream figures. Iranna's early work indicates this lineage clearly, but he very swiftly and confidently moved away from it, infusing his images with his own dilemmas as a migrant several times over, his oscillation between the roles of nostalgist and futurist, his love of solitary exploration and his awareness of being one of innumerable dancers in a vast social choreography.

With the advantage of hindsight and on the evidence of nearly two decades of his activity, we may observe that Iranna's art has developed through a dynamic and overlapping interplay of binaries at three levels. *First*, as I have said earlier in this essay, Iranna is at once a nostalgist and a futurist; neither role cancels the other out, but rather, each sustains the other in an attempt to conjure away the linearity of time on a composite scale of interwoven periods. So that, while elaborating a rich pictoriality by revisiting the vivid impressions of childhood and allowing a polyphony of traditional cultural resonances to sound in his paintings, Iranna also incorporates the signs of the present and a science-fictive future in his work.

Second, Iranna is a figurative artist who does not renounce the abstractionist imperative. He dwells on the fate of the figure and articulates his philosophical reflections on the nature of the bodied self, the contexts of its being and expression; but he also attempts the vivid retrieval of the decorative by means of abstraction. In his most recent work, especially, he explores the nature of power, authority and their implications for the definition of selfhood; and yet, he also imbues his paintings with a sensuous opulence and takes a marked interest in motif, pattern and non-representational surface for their own sake, visual assonances from the treasury of India's textile heritage.

Third, and with this we unpack the aims of his figuration, Iranna attends to the interiority of the spiritual quest, deploying the sleeping or levitating figure to explore dream, meditation, reality and epiphany as alternative states in a widely inclusive spectrum of consciousness; at the same time, crucially, he also focuses on the predicament of the political subject, voicing a range of concerns about the individual and the group, binding relationships and constricting structures, the seesaw of power games and the shifting balance of power by allusive means, gathering a vocabulary of symbols and metaphors together and modulating them into contemporary fables. What is permanent, his figures seem to ask,

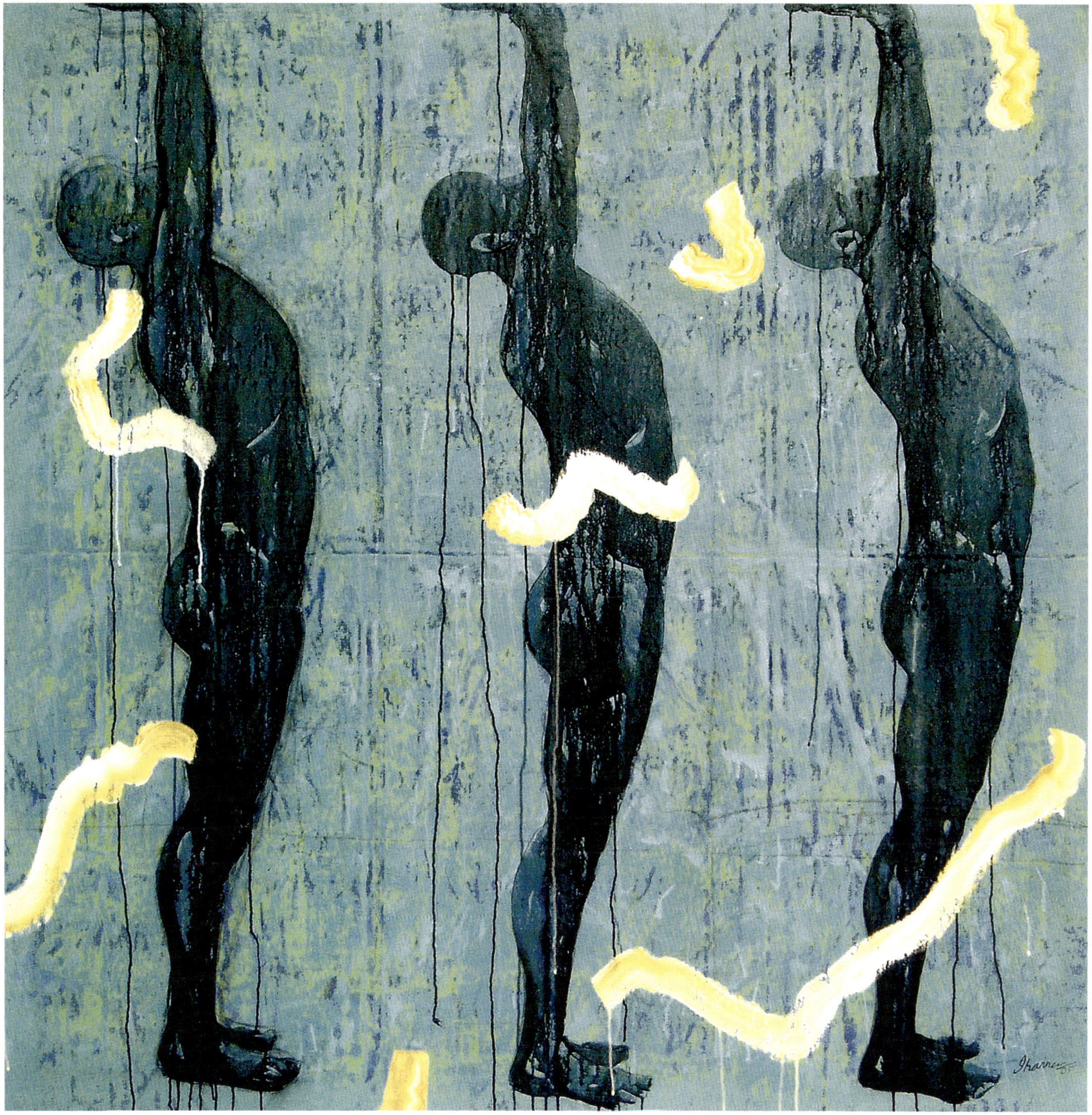

The World is Too Small, acrylic on tarpaulin, 54x66", 2005

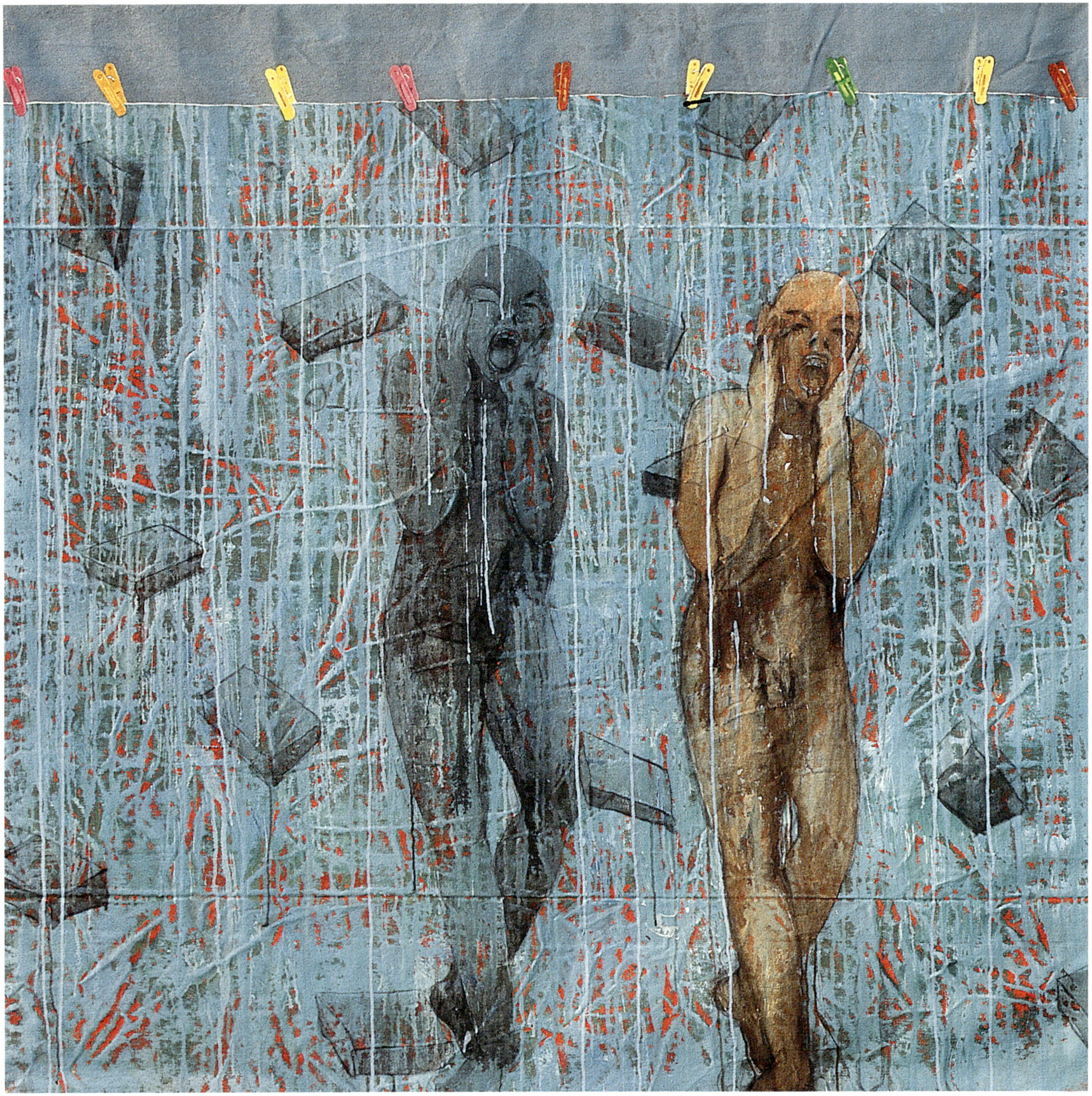

Chorus, acrylic on tarpaulin, 66x66”, 2003

and what is transient; what part of the self becomes inextricably entangled in the apparatus of control, surveillance and security, and what part of the self escapes this fate by evaporating through thick walls or dodging through a grid of photographs?

An Ecology of Loss and Redemption

It is a forgivably human tendency to hold on, in the form of images or narratives, to what we have lost by growing up and going away. Iranna's achievement in his paintings of the 1990s is to have threaded this private impulse through the larger fabric of ecological struggles in India. Working across a range of materials, processes and surfaces - including pastels, oils on canvas and paper, acrylic on canvas, and lithographs - Iranna attested to the lifeworld of the village, of farm work and the routines of the seasonal cycle. He drew and painted the implements, devices and animals that populate the farmer's everyday life: all the familiarities that he was in the process of leaving behind, as he individuated himself into an emigrant sensibility, carrying his past with him as a freight of mental residues, heirlooms to sustain him in the new metropolitan existence that he would have to shape for himself.

Among these mental residues were the sensuous immediacies of a rural childhood. In the course of an email conversation with this writer, Iranna writes: "From the tender age of six, I was pushed into working on my father's farm, with various kinds of vegetation. I was attracted towards the movement of dug-out earth while ploughing, the texture of plants, mud, leaves. My habit of observation had already begun. I would pick up thrown out materials like boxes, batteries, reeds, and make toys by putting them together, and forget about my work in the fields. It was a joy to watch the carpenter make wheels and ploughs, giving form to the wood. At that age, I also developed a bond with various animals in the village. By caring for them, taking them on their rounds, feeding them, milking them, and even decorating them, I became sensitive towards them."[3]

The architecture of the villages, towns and cities that Iranna knew as a child also surfaces powerfully in his paintings of the 1990s. The artist's birthplace, Sindgi, is located in the Bijapur area: today an outlying district of the modern state of Karnataka, Bijapur was once counted among peninsular India's greatest political and cultural centres. The capital of the Adilshahi dynasty, which flourished between 1489 and 1686, it was home to a distinguished school of Deccani painting, an Indo-Persian idiom that combined a scientific exactitude with delicacy of rendering in its portraiture and its evocations of nature. Long eclipsed by the grander visibility accorded to the Mughal and Rajput schools of northern India both by academics and tourists, the Adilshahi atelier has only recently come to be appreciated for its unrivalled command over a mode of representation set on the cusp between courtly stylisation and exquisite realism.

Bijapur also possesses a refined tradition of Islamic secular and sacred architecture. The graceful domes of its mosques and tombs, the ramparts of its forts and the arcades of its palaces have long inspired observers, both Indians and foreigners. Indeed, the domes, filigreed screen-walls and crenellations of such Bijapuri masterworks as the Gol Gumbaz and the Ibrahim Rouza served as points of departure for the colonial-period experiment now known as the "Indo-Saracenic style" developed by architects such as George Wittet in early-1900s Bombay (the General Post Office and the Prince of Wales Museum in the west-coast metropolis are examples of this marvellously strange recovery of Adilshahi forms by British practitioners, across the gulf of several centuries).

Between the 15th century and the 17th, Bijapur also hosted a vibrant confluence among the Deccani Muslim, the Carnatic Hindu, the Maratha Hindu and the Goan Hindu-Catholic cultures that variously exerted their influence in this region. The Muslim warrior-saints known as the Ghazi Sufis were a powerful presence, and found acolytes among Muslims and Hindus alike. And Bijapur was - and continues to be - a great centre of the Lingayat stream of Shaivism, to which Iranna's family belongs. The Lingayats revere Shiva in the form of the sacred phallus, the *linga*, but do not privilege temple worship over ethical practice. The Lingayat poets celebrate the body as the worthiest temple, to be purified by responsible living and turned into a monument to the Divine. Iranna grew up reading the compositions of Basavanna, the reformer of the Lingayat stream, and quotes him: "Your conscience is Shiva, your body is a temple: the legs are its columns and the head is its finial."

The Lingayat world-view is premised on the communion of Shiva and Shakti, the male energy and the female generative principle of the universe; they teach the virtues of focused devotion, a life refined by the perfections of thought, attitude and conduct. The *linga-yoni* symbolism that recurs in Iranna's paintings is traceable to this source, but it is not embalmed in the stasis of inherited iconography; rather, it assumes various valencies along a gamut that stretches from tenderly sentimental regard to awe and terror. In his recent works, which draw a parallel between mud and flesh, and contemplate the transience of bodily existence, Iranna invokes the Lingayat vision of the world as a theatre of appearances in which the seeker must learn to distinguish between that which is solid and enduring and that which is merely fluid and transitory.

In the paintings that Iranna executed between 1990 and 2000, we find certain obsessively recurrent images. Among these is the *deepastambha* or column of lamps in a temple courtyard in western India, an architectural form derived from the campanile, brought into India by the Iberian architects who were active in the Portuguese territories on the west coast. There is also the *mall-khamb* or greased maypole, a survival from ancient festivities that continues in usage today, as a device for athletes to demonstrate their prowess as they clamber up and master its slippery, treacherous height. There is Nandi, the bull attendant of Shiva; and the elephant, which could be the trumpeting symbol of Sri-Lakshmi, goddess of abundance, or Airavata, the many-tusked cloud-elephant on which Indra, Lord of the Rain, rides out. Some of these elements of sacred architecture and temple statuary were implanted in Iranna's consciousness in childhood; others suggested themselves during the study tours that he undertook to such heritage sites as Hampi, Halebid and Belur, as an art student.

Some observers have wondered whether the recursion of such elements in his work implies a reactivation of the signals of a fossilised tradition. Iranna responds with the trope of the mantra, the sacred word or phrase that is repeated until it grows in intensity, elaborating itself into a route to deeper levels of awareness and becoming a talisman that protects the serene vitality of the meditator. "The deeper impressions of form come through your seeing in childhood. This is one reason why I repeat images from my observations in childhood. Anything that you truly *see* for the first time gets deeply rooted in your consciousness. For example, when one chants a mantra, the sound of it creates an ocean of energy in space. This repetition has nothing to do with reviving lost traditions," the artist says. "I repeat these forms of the *deepastambha*, of Nandi and the elephant, as symbols coming from the subconscious. Yet each time, I look at them from a different perspective. In childhood they were as I saw them. Now they have a different meaning for me. The plough, the wheel and the utility items had a different meaning then. Now I see them with a different meaning as a form, as energetic objects."[4]

An unmistakeably autobiographical note sounds through Iranna's works of the late 1990s, especially in the series titled *Shadows of the Real*, where he introduced such protagonists as the questor traversing landscapes punctuated by furrows, ploughshares, lamp columns, tree-stumps, chain-hooks and phallic horns springing from trapdoors. *Shadows of the Real - I* (oil and gold foil on canvas, 1998) is dominated by a ploughshare, the object cast as a breathing portrait of something inanimate; elsewhere on the picture surface, literally translated into a picture field, the pointed tip of another plough seems to cut through.

In *Shadows of the Real - II* (oil and silver foil on canvas, 1998), the artist arranges an army of cattle in a grid, figured as though in a *pichchwai* from the Vaishnava temple-town of Nathadwara in southern Rajasthan; some of the animals stray from the alignments of row and column. A *yogi* meditates among them, a sharp tongue-shaped implement thrusting up near his folded legs. The business end of a giant plough, shaped like the broken prow of a boat, lies stranded in a slaughtered forest of tree-stumps in *Shadows of the Real - IV* (acrylic on tarpaulin, 1998). A man stands on the plough/prow, stunned by the emptiness of what he sees, by the ecology of loss that spreads around him in all directions.[5]

Updating MF Husain's canonical painting, *Zameen* (1955), Iranna substitutes the master's idyllic folk-Romanticism with an awareness of the catastrophes of ecological degradation and peasant immiseration; the fragmentation of rituals and the erosion of routines; the destruction of thriving communities, fertile environments and entire lifeworlds by the advancing engines of discompassionate progress. As the art historian Roobina Karode

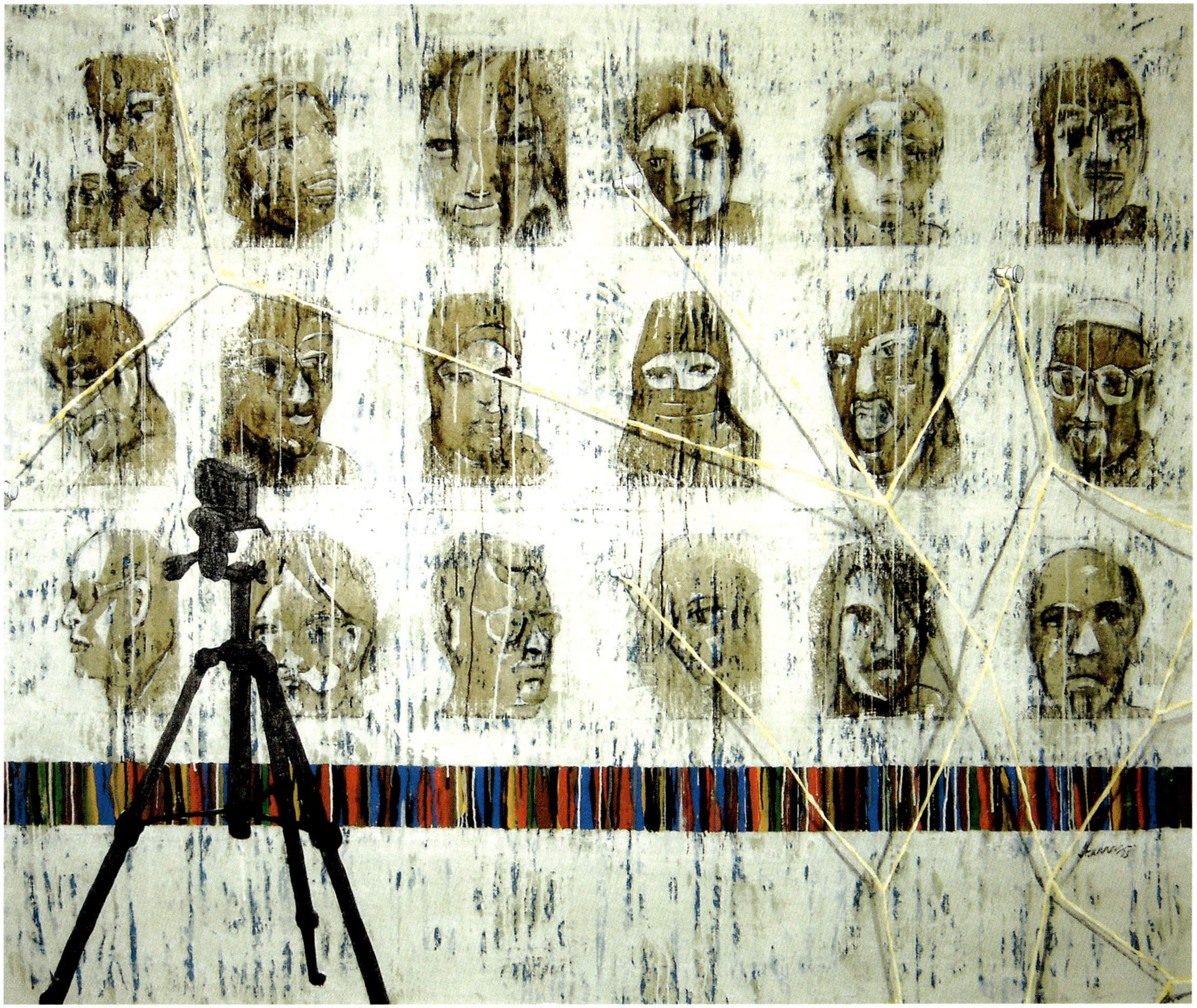

No One's Face, acrylic on tarpaulin, 82x66", 2005

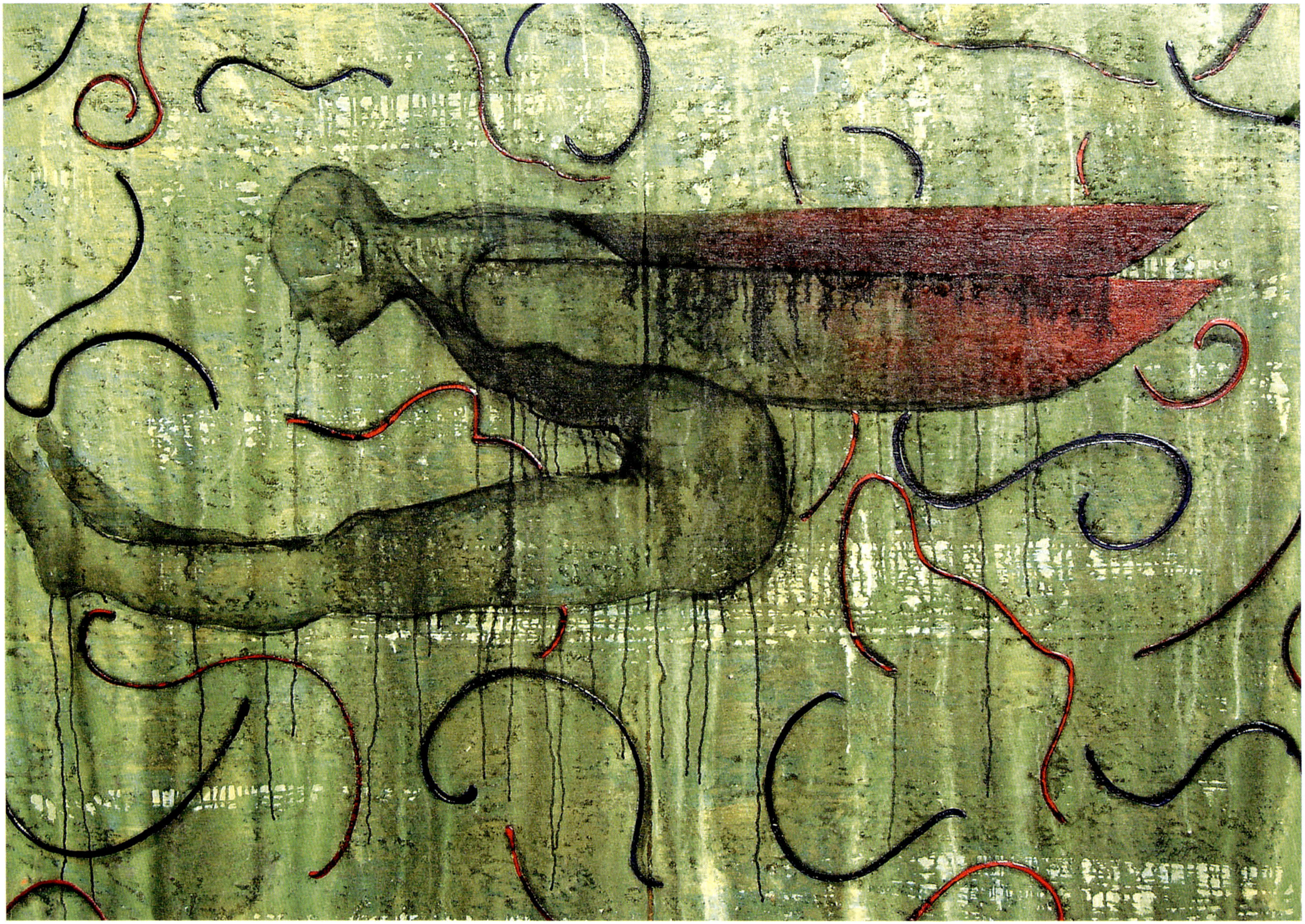

Wind beneath my Wings, acrylic and tarpaulin, 66x52", 2005

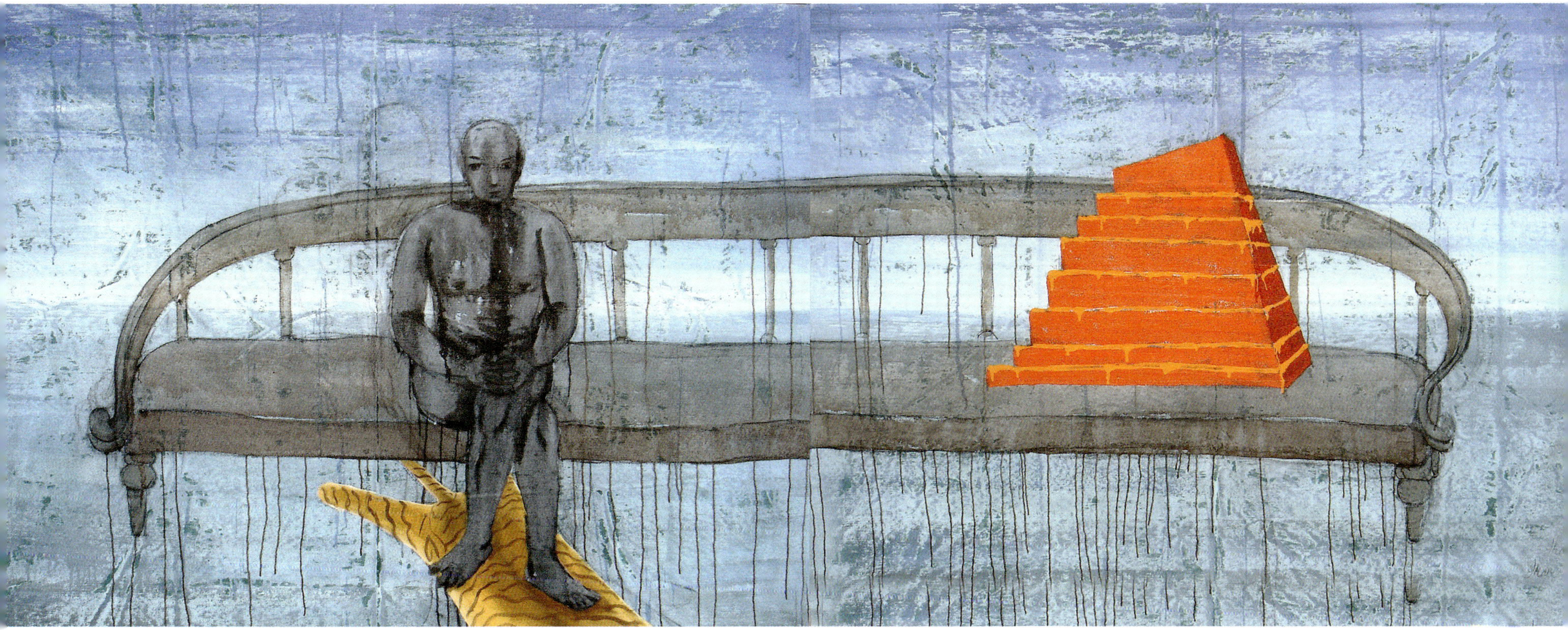

The Retired King - II, acrylic on tarpaulin, 132x48”, 2005

reminds us, Iranna has never forgotten his Lingayat farming background; of this phase of his art, she writes: "The plough is the most sensuous tool for Iranna as it splits open the body of the earth to participate in the regenerative process. It is as the farmer's son perhaps that he realises the importance of fertility more than others, worshipping both the fertile land and the tools of his livelihood."[6]

We must clarify, though, that Iranna's impulse was never to document these forms as an ethnographer or to memorialise them as a runaway inheritor; the premise of his work was not so much to create elegies for a lost utopia, as to propose a ground for political action, even if at the basic level of recognising the scale of India's environmental tragedy. But this ecology of loss is also an ecology of redemption: the farmer's son nourishes the field of his canvas, his acreage of pigment and surface. He embraces the erotic tactility of paint and approaches the tarpaulin as a coarse, textured, resistant surface, treating these materials as living organisms; he applies his colours in a palimpsest of layers and overlayers, its plenitude evocative of the density of a world in which the cycles of human activity run in consonance with the cycles of nature, instead of violating and poisoning them with discordance. In indicative, metaphorical form, Iranna manages to record an individual's small-scale transcendence, the visual mantras through which he attempts the exposure and overcoming of a brutal history.

The Multiple Fates of the Bodied Self

From 2000 onwards, Iranna's paintings have focused sharply on the centrality of the human subject; on the existential predicament of the bodied self as a transformation-oriented spirit twinned with a vulnerable body that is subject to time, strain, failure and violence. Iranna has produced ever more sophisticated versions of this bodied self, their assurance apparently reflecting his own. Athletic and well-muscled, these new protagonists seem ready for the multiple fates that await them. Iranna's current figures are far more complex in their anxieties and exhilarations than their predecessors in his work of the 1990s; formally, too, these archetypal beings are many generations ahead of the brushily conceived, near-diagrammatic figures that inhabited Iranna's frames a decade ago.

The naked and tonsured figure that has long served Iranna as his key image is compacted from many ancestries. It fuses the *yogi*, the *bhikshu*, and the *tirthankara*, exemplars of transcendence drawn from Indic culture's three major sacred traditions, the Hindu, the Buddhist and the Jaina. In more secular key, it also encodes references to the figurative practices of Gauguin and Bacon; to the work of the exponents of the Tagore circle in Jorasanko; and to the android martyr-saviours of science fiction.

Such intertextuality is integral to Iranna's logic of figuration, which engages vigorously with the human body cast in situations at once archetypal and political, suggestive of a deep archive of ceremonial physiology but also memorialising the present. In *Generation* (acrylic on tarpaulin, 2003), foetus and pharaonic demigod morph into prisoner and refugee; the sequence of hominid evolution doubles as a scale of moral choices. Far from remaining enclosed in a heroic Modernist isolation, Iranna's single figure implies and even actively summons a sociality into being.

A figure reclines on a set of springs in *Lift* (oil on tarpaulin, 2001). The pose proposes an ironic take on *yoga-nidra*, the refreshing deep-sleep state prized by yogic practitioners; stripped of head, frame and mattress, the bed appears to have been pared down to the essentials cherished by the heralds of the life led in tune with nature. It is, we say to ourselves, a figure like Bhishma, with springs instead of arrows to support him. But then we look again, and find that the reclining figure holds a drooping lotus in one hand; as though this were the Bodhisattva Avalokitesvara-Padmapani, taking a surprising, unauthorised nap between sessions watching over the welfare of all sentient beings. Above and below - or all around, depending on how you read recession or verticality in this frame - there appear forms reminiscent of lilies floating on the surface of a pond. A light humour sparkles across the surface of this painting, livening up the evocation of Buddhist art and the homage to Monet, lightening up the solemnity of citing the grand themes and quoting the big-name ancestors.

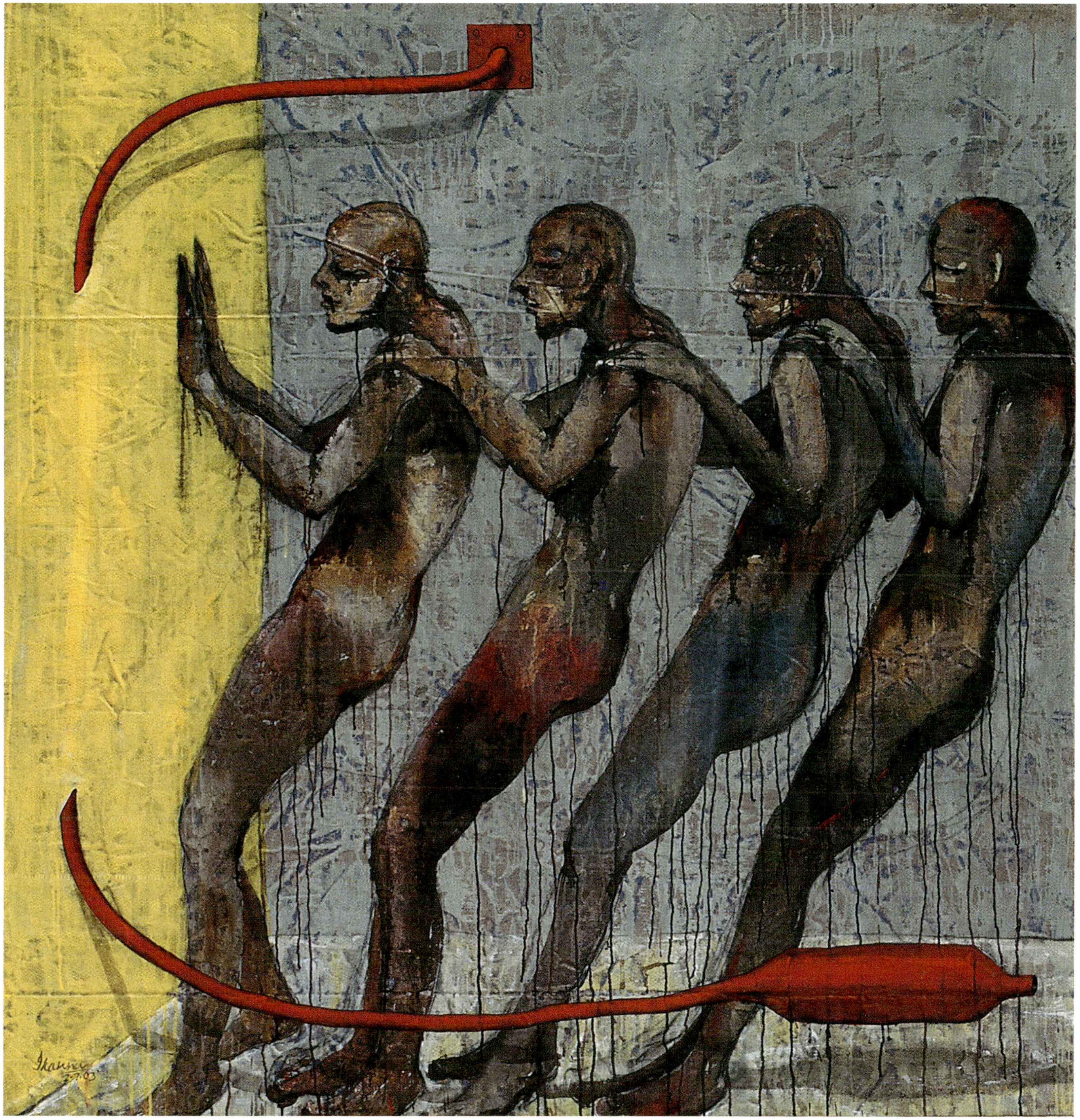

Silencer, acrylic on tarpaulin, 70x70", 1998

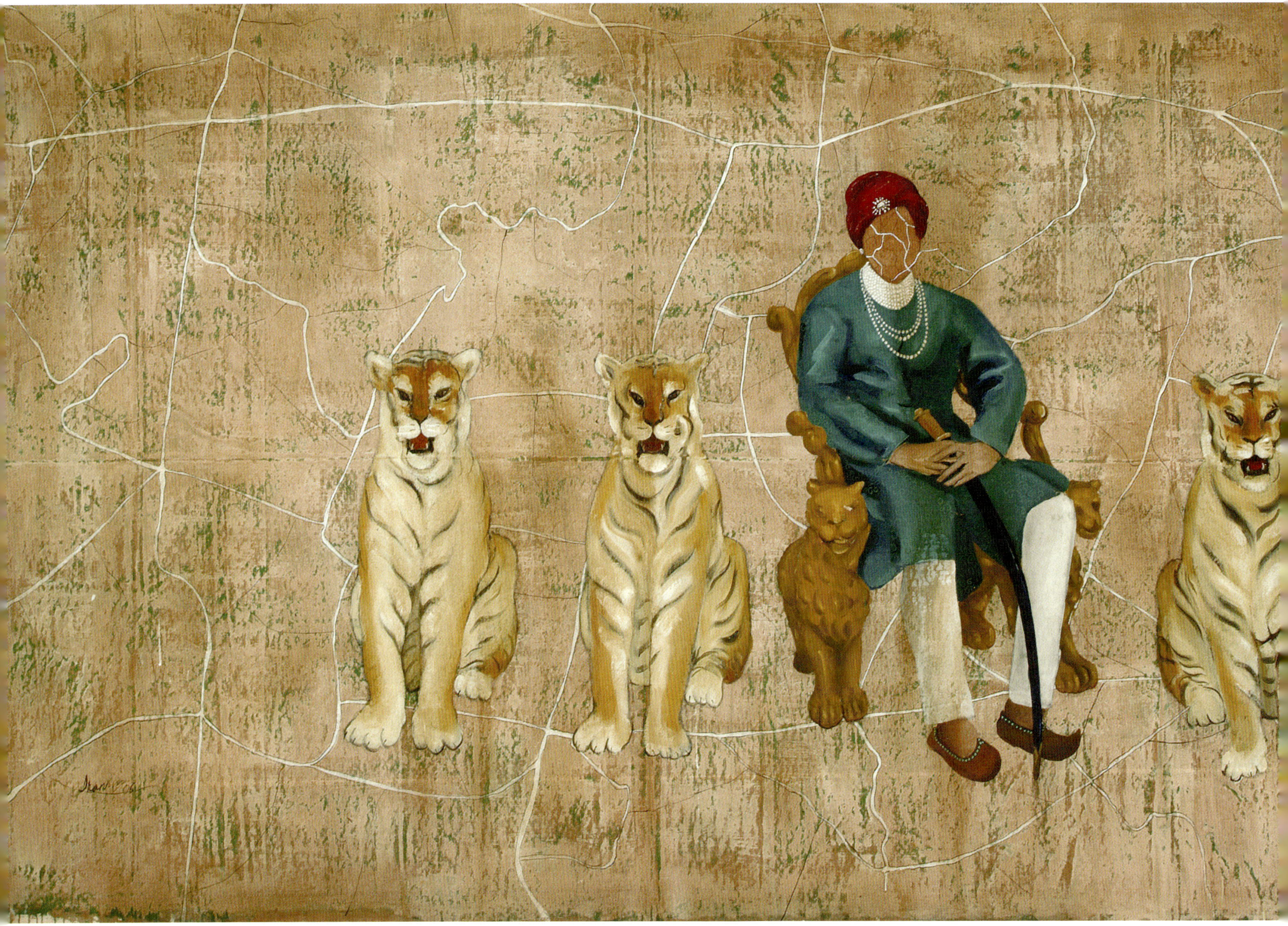

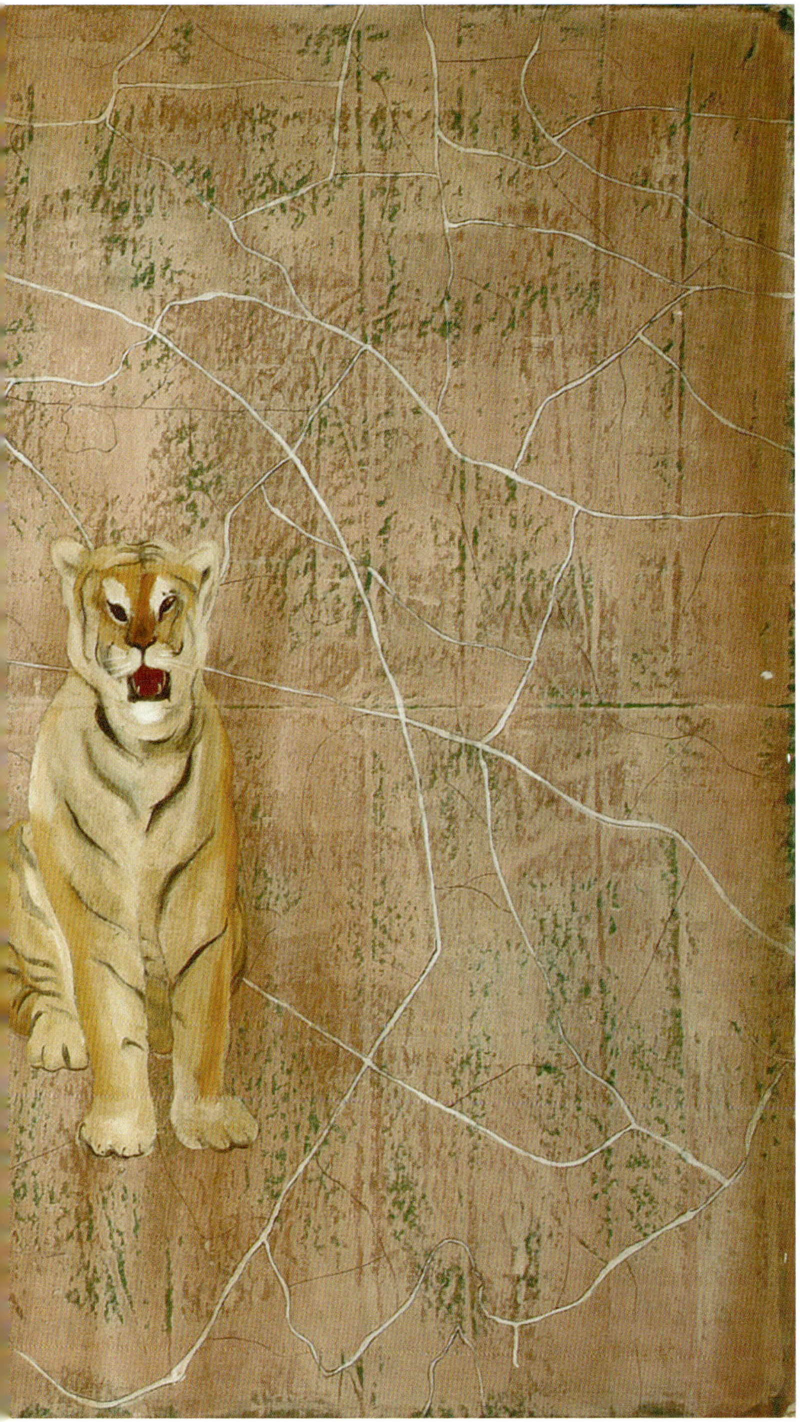

A Map for a King, acrylic on tarpaulin, 144x66", 2006

Iranna's accomplishment, in his work during the first few years of the 21st century, was to extend his investment in the figure considerably, in terms both of pictorial inventiveness and metaphorical charge. His aims were twofold: *first*, to consolidate the archetypal figure as bearer of existential crisis, and *second*, to restate the relationship between this figure and a versatile ground characterised by sensuous plenitude as well as menace. *Typically, in these paintings, the relationship between figure and landscape took the form of dream and perplexity*. Iranna's figure tested its limits, probing and gauging its surroundings, measuring the possible resistance that a wall, a water surface, the air, or a staircase might put up, wondering whether it should disturb the world's equilibrium with a sudden movement.

The protagonist of *Pendulum* (acrylic on tarpaulin, 2003), for instance, incarnates indecision, teetering at the edge of a springboard, hands clasped behind his back. His avatar in *Untitled*, likewise, stands on a springboard, offering us a three-quarter profile: he sizes up a wall striated with bands of red and gold, and studded with gravity-defying teacups and saucers, their bizarre near-realism punctured by drips of paint. Looking closely, we find further ironies of illusionism: the painting is threaded together by handles, loops of rope that thread in and out of the wall (or backcloth, or ground?), casting shadows that induce an Escherian imbalance in the viewer.

At this time, Iranna also multiplied the single figure into a dyad or a group, an ensemble that combined labour with felicity, elaborating its shared perplexity through the performance of cathartic dramatisations. In *Chorus* (acrylic on tarpaulin, 2003), we encounter two figures (or a self and its image?) screaming silently, running away from a catastrophe, as bricks explode, float and fall. This is a slow-mo echo of iconic Vietnam images, but before we can become emotionally involved, we realise that the entire scene is *maya*, a screen pegged on a clothesline, a painting fluttering in the wind within a painting.

Similarly, the format of the rogues' gallery provides the ironic model for *No One's Face* (acrylic on tarpaulin, 2003), which assembles a series of partially effaced portraits - the dreams of the figure sleeping at the base of the work, or the opportunities missed by the shadow-smeared figure climbing a flight of shallow steps. Iranna alludes here to the enforced anonymity of the collective, viewing society as a prison of roles prescribed by dominant but invisible forces (he leaves it to us to identify the habitus: the tyranny of surveillance in a command economy, or the spirit of conformism in a mediatic consumer society). In a polity of clones, what is the real; in a hall of mirrors, which of the reflections is the original; where does the object end and the shadow begin?

The artist's preoccupation with the police state continues in the sinister *Keep Smiling* (acrylic on tarpaulin, 2003), where three figures, presumably suspects or captives, stand with their backs to us, facing a wall, their feet aligned by a thin red line on the floor. Each figure holds a portrait behind its back: each shows a smiling face, which faces us. The backs of the figures' heads are marked off in squares formed from broken red lines, as though for scrutiny or execution by firing squad. *Silent Talk* (acrylic on tarpaulin, 2003) shows us a row of four somewhat androgynous figures standing like deities in an ancient Egyptian tomb panel. From both sides, a screwed clamp closes in on them; soon, we think, they will be crushed together. Above them, a toy train chugs along, a symbol that paradoxically yokes together freedom of movement and oppression by crowd, servitude to systems and protocols: captivity in the entanglements of the everyday.

Silencer (acrylic on tarpaulin, 2003) is a graceful choreography for four figures, workers turned dancers, who act out a fluid sequence of movements, each leaning back and holding on to the shoulders of the figure ahead, the lead figure pressing his hands against a yellow wall, through which is pierced a red device. The dance is rendered more complex by the captive status of the figures; the red device is a silencer, which seals the wall and shoots past their feet; no one can see or hear the dance.

Fluent and oneiric, the relationship between figure and ground in these paintings is reminiscent of the organically flowing forms of semi-divine, human, animal, chimeric and vegetal life in the sculptural programmes of the Sanchi and Bharhut *stupa*s. It is one of the subsidiary achievements of an artist such as Iranna that he should have brought, into the domain of the contemporary, this abiding sense of the play of the life energy - *lila*, which is consciousness and circumstance woven into one fabric - without lapsing into a deplorably auto-Orientalist illustration of traditional motifs.

Iranna puts the device of the shadow to salient use in this series, using it as an illusionistic trigger but also as a tenebrous cloud of doubt accompanying the outlined figure, casting its musculature and purposiveness into doubt. The mysterious *Walking on Shadow* (acrylic on canvas, 2003) appears to express the vision of the figure asleep in the upper band of the composition; its protagonist slouches, as through rain or glass, a smear of shadow and body. For a split second, when Iranna promotes such an illusion, the shadows render his beautifully painted and detailed surfaces solid. Indeed, in activating the scenario, Iranna's shadows urge us to recognise the beautifully variegated, palpably sensuous and tapestried surface, the manner in which it generates an erotic of friction, having been painted in acrylic on a base of tarpaulin - a rough trucker's medium, used to wrap goods on the long-distance coaches and trucks that link India's far-flung regions?

Iranna has always loved the sensations of surface: gloss and gleam, the feel of fabric and blood, hair and water, flesh and grass. Drawn into his work by the attractiveness of his textured, patterned surfaces, we are reminded of *pichchwai*s, jacquards, khadi; of rain smearing on glass. Would this constitute a retrieval of the decorative through the abstract? Iranna certainly refers to India's intricately patterned traditional textiles, but he also replays the flavours and textures of Klimt. In defining the ground that hosts his figures, in his works over the last six years, Iranna celebrates his Klimt-like love of pattern for itself, deploying it to rephrase the natural as a sumptuousness, the paintings clothed in a skin of jewelled gold. In his work, an abstract gorgeousness is often an imperative, just as important as the conceptual proposition it carries. Melding the abstract-decorative with the figurative-allegorical as he does, Iranna positions his art at the productive threshold of the figural – a suggestion I will build on, shortly.

"A smooth surface binds me," says the artist. "I want to extend myself, for which I need rougher surfaces. The choice of materials I use reflects my temperament. After working on various kinds of paper and canvases, I opted for the rough surface of tarpaulin. It shows the restlessness in me. I like the rusted surface of an iron sheet and old depleted walls. These surfaces excite me to create. In sculpture, I feel the need to create a delicate and fleshy surface. I create surfaces according to the demand of the creation."[7]

In Iranna's usage, such surfaces mark the transcription of desire veined with anxiety: they propose a resolution of the perennial antithesis between figure/self and ground/world, by dissolving their apparent duality in a *relational understanding*, one that places both in a circuit of continuous interplay. In *Bouncer* (acrylic on canvas, 2003), for instance, the artist orchestrates an interrelation between the self-absorbed figure bouncing on a pair of springs, and a ground detailed in a myriad floating eyes: the figure is imbricated into the ground with a rain of paint dribbles, its movements graphed over the ground in Muybridge-like flickers, its foetal crouch-and-release paralleled by the tornado-like ascension of a spiral facing it. I would tentatively describe this pictorial resolution as a *figural landscape*. No semblance of the natural, it is a trope deliberately composed from annotations: it simulates an original that is a reality of affect, not a material reality. In a period that has registered the ascendancy of critical artistic strategies that unmask and dismantle, Iranna stands apart by espousing an art of affirmation, of measured additive procedure and philosophical depth.

The Drama of *Maya* and *Lila*

Iranna has stretched himself, from 2003-04 onwards, to amplify the scale of his paintings, a significant number of which are now conceived and delivered as large diptychs. At one level, he shares this interest in an amplification of scale with many other members of his generation; but where some of his contemporaries embrace scale with enthusiasm only to find themselves overwhelmed by the difficulties of covering the vaster expanses opened up by such a formal decision, Iranna has thought out his strategies carefully. For one, he knows that large-scale paintings can hold the attention of viewers only if their surfaces are tapestries of intriguing detail, achieved through meticulous brushwork, expressive textural passages and the play of luminosity and shadow. For another, he realises that visually stimulating as such an activated surface may be, his particular idiom must push itself further in the direction of

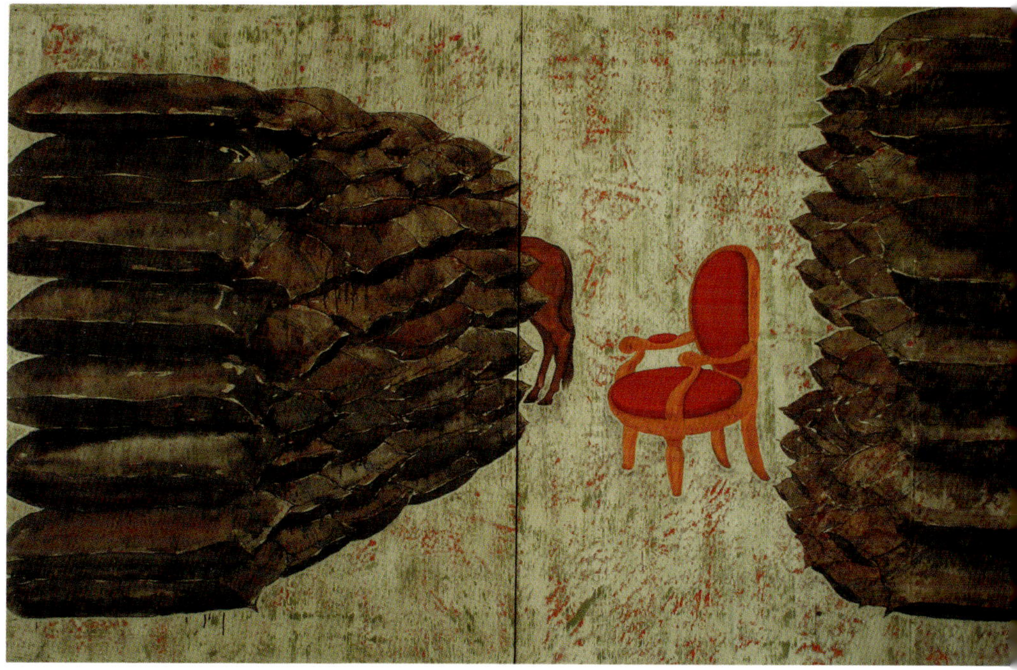

The Historical Chair, acrylic on tarpaulin, 108x66", 2006

theatre, to captivate the viewer with the enigma of occasion and gesture.

Accordingly, Iranna has extended his allegories into metaphorically fraught tableaux peopled by multiple figures, sometimes choric in their performance. Also, his human protagonists are now joined by animal figures such as the horse and the tiger, which play individualised symbolic roles rather than serving as background props (as the grouped cattle did in his paintings of the late 1990s). These new paintings indicate a fresh awareness of private and political predicaments: they often take the form of dramas of fragility and balance, vulnerability and doubt, decline and release.

In these recent works, Iranna's protagonists conduct themselves overtly as actors: some repeat lines that have lost their meaning, others are abandoned in run-down spaces, without scripts. While studying in Gulbarga, the artist and his fellow students had formed a group that would tour the neighbouring villages, staging plays to direct public sensitivity towards various social issues. Playing

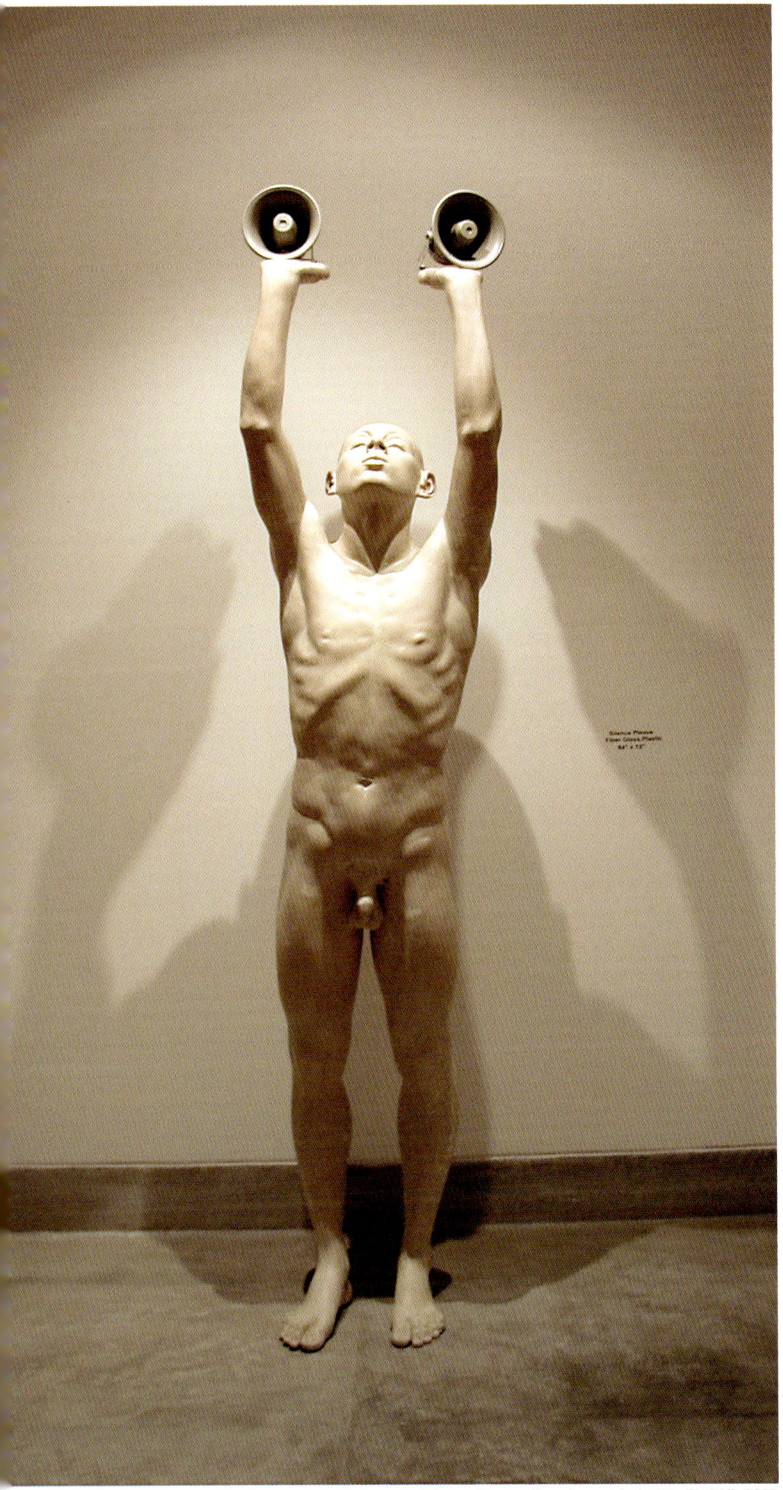

Silence Please, fibreglass and plastic, 72x72", 2005

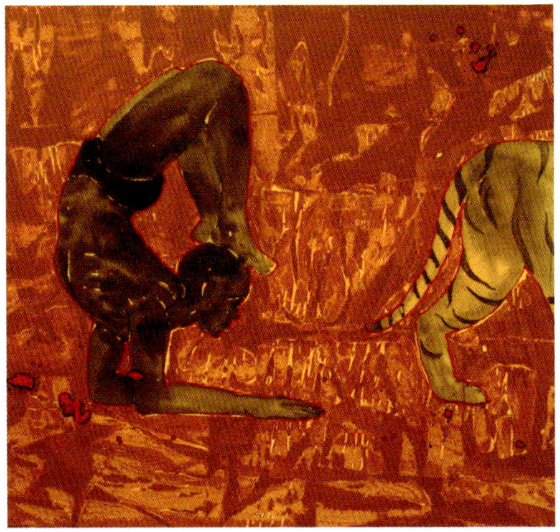

The King and the Kingdom, acrylic on canvas, 2006

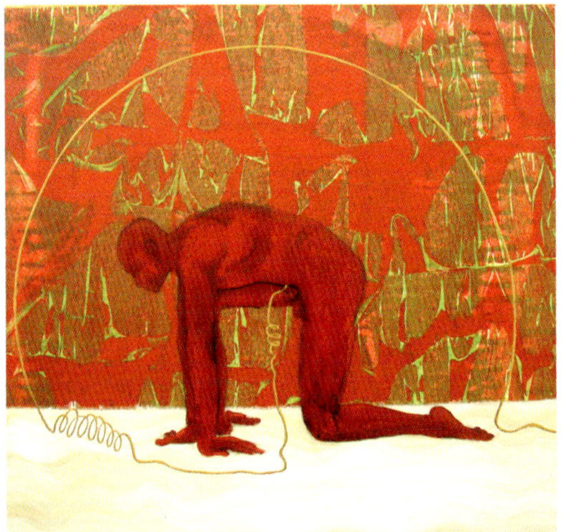

Acrylic on canvas, 30x30", 2004

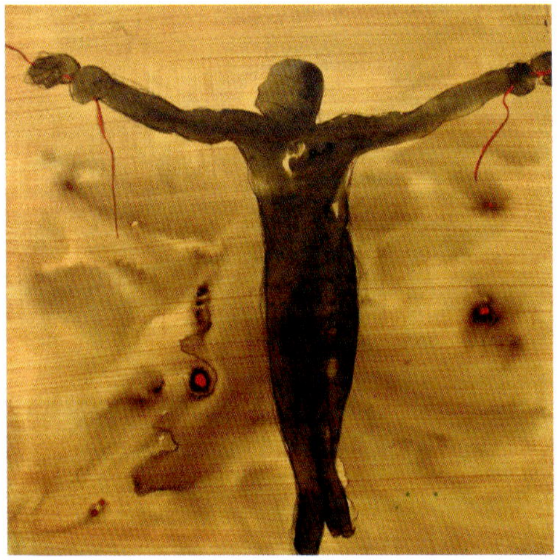

Acrylic on canvas, 30x30", 2005

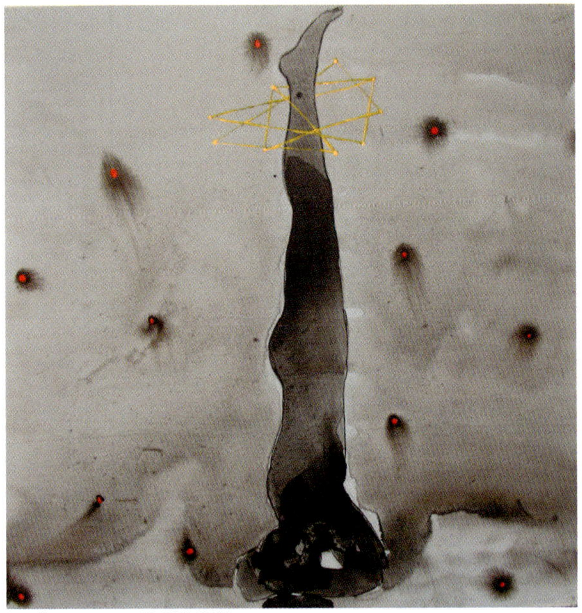

Acrylic on canvas, 30x30", 2005

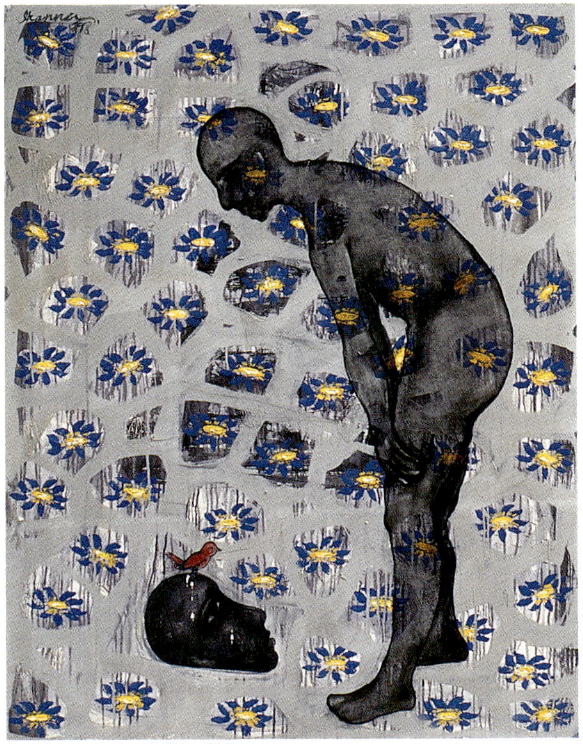

Acrylic on canvas, 48x60", 1990

other roles helped him, Iranna says, to hold his artist-persona at a temporary distance and understand the lives, choices and constraints of other people: a basic training in empathy, and in developing the position of a citizen-artist. This orientation is strongly evident in Iranna's recent sculptural work, where he creates a counterpoint between the solitude of the heroic male figure and the social meanings that the simulacrum of a human figure acquires when presented in three dimensions. While a painting tends to maintain its distance from the viewer, held back by its pictoriality, a sculpture is an object in a world of objects. And a sculpture in the shape of a bodied self is almost one of us, resonant with sociality: it speaks to us even in its silence, as an augur or shaman might summon our attention by signs; its coded address invites decipherment and conversation.

In 2005, the artist translated *Silencer* into an extremely effective fibreglass and iron sculpture, with its four figures doing their dead-end dance, up against the wall. In similar vein, he exhibited *Silence Please* (plastic and fibreglass, 2005), which proposes the paradox of inaudible proclamation: a male nude raises his arms high above his head, holding up a pair of loudspeakers. Discussing the translation of his painted images into sculptural form, Iranna notes: "My *Silencer* is a work against violence. This feeling of suffocation is better expressed through sculpture than painting. In painting, I touch through the eyes and in sculpture I touch through my body."[8]

Iranna has also renewed his commitment to an obdurate pictoriality: we must note his insistence on making images that place stringent demands on the viewer, being resonant with a mythic significance that lies beyond the parameters of everyday experience. Previously, as we have seen, Iranna has made various approaches to the heroic male figure: the body yogic and the body electric, the sublime and effulgent body, the body levitating in a trance. Now, the figure is more flexible, even more amenable to riddle-like paradox than before, even more resonant with the mandate of emancipation from circumstances.

In an untitled 2005 work, the figure pole-vaults across a metropolitan street, challenging the stability of its edifices and ornate streetlamps with the unpredictability of free play. In *The World is too Small* (acrylic on tarpaulin, 2005), three dark figures, festooned with cloud, push up at the top edge of the canvas, as though demanding release. Their stance and attitude suggests the runners on an Athenian vase, or athletes on a victory stand at the Olympics; to Iranna, at some profound level, life will always be a stadium or velodrome, where the will to triumph is always being tested, and the individual can never rest from his labours. In *Wind beneath my Wings* (acrylic on tarpaulin, 2005), he casts himself as a melancholy angel, wings pulled back and feet pointing forward, pausing for a brief aeon between a bloody past and a penumbral future.

Iranna has begun to meditate on other figures trapped between past and future, power and the loss of power. These are tragic inheritors of lost empires, deceived by cunning mapmakers and their own inability to second-guess the dark angel of history. Chief among these protagonists is the isolated figure of the dethroned ruler, as in *The Retired King - Diptych 1 & 2* (acrylic on tarpaulin, 2005). Here is a man whose power has been drained away, who sits by himself, his throne no grander than a park bench: a centre that has been left to its own devices by those who once worshipped it. The king began as a fairytale figure for Iranna, drawn from the stories his grandmother used to tell him when he was a child in Sindgi; but the figure outgrew the context of nostalgia to become a means of commenting on the harsh realities of history and political life. We find court portraits that double as maps, cracking along lines drawn by territorial disputes, with the schisms taking a toll on the king's face as well. Flanked though he is by tigers, the king in *Map for a King* (acrylic on tarpaulin, 2006) presides over a fissured land that has desiccated him as well.

The tiger appears in Iranna's paintings as an ambivalent symbol of regal power, at once magisterial and toy-like, a jubilation and a warning; in a recent pictorial parable, *Balancing Act* (acrylic on tarpaulin, 2006), a man rides a tiger in the background to an epic struggle, with two men daring each other to move while holding their precarious ground on a seesawing plank. The probable origin of the tiger image in Iranna's work lies in the talismanic, almost totemic association of that noble animal with Tipu Sultan, the 18th-century Indian ruler of the Carnatic - which included much of present-day Karnataka, the artist's home state - who came to symbolise the heroic Indian resistance against British imperial expansion in the subcontinent. A transitional figure between late feudalism and early modernity, Tipu was a progressive administrator and a much-feared warrior who was eventually overcome only by treachery; to his allies as well as his enemies, he was known as the Tiger of Mysore.

In Iranna's allegorical accounts, however, the king is often just an actor in ill-fitting costume; and the hungry tigers do not simply symbolise his exalted status, but also dominate his decisions, his moves, and even the scope of his movement. This is dramatised in a recent painting (also titled *The Retired King*, acrylic on tarpaulin, 2006), which presents us with a king and three tigers set against a sumptuous red wall. In the foreground, we see a street littered with rocks; by extension, we participate in a theatrical exposure of the false image of sovereignty by the rough actuality of protest.

Dethroned kings, actors without scripts, men trying to ram their way through walls: these powerful archetypes appear to articulate Iranna's Lingayat vision of the transitory nature of all that is gained by obsessive control, rapacious acquisition and self-aggrandisement. "The retired king is the realisation of the temporary nature of all existence. You see huge kingdoms like Vijayanagara or Delhi, where are they today? Every king is conscious of accumulations, but ultimately he has to leave. These are traditional stories that I have used to express contemporary situations," observes the artist, comparing the overthrown bearer of power to a corpse. "A body, when alive, is decorated, anointed and cared for with so much love and attention. But when it dies, it loses everything, even the respect due to it for having been flesh and blood."[9]

Power holds out the temptation of splendour, but robs its holder of dignity and peace of mind: the measures of security that surround the king turn him into a prisoner of his own making, held captive by his psychic demons and his paranoid minders. In *The Historical Chair - Diptych* (acrylic on tarpaulin, 2006), Iranna studies an empty throne, locked in by walls of heaped sandbags. A horse disappears around one of these menacing, claustrophobic palisades; the field of the painting is scumbled with red. The painting reminds us of Italo Calvino's fantastical fable, *A King Listens*, in which the ruler lives a permanent nightmare, sitting under his baldachin, balancing crown and sceptre, imagining the sounds of riot and uprising in the streets: an embodiment of pathological insecurity, he is unable to make the slightest movement without endangering his position as the focus of the political universe he has created around him, and whose creature he has become.[10]

Occasionally, Iranna resorts to humour rather than elegy, as a means of confronting the spiritual corruption of political life. In *The Last Voice* (acrylic on tarpaulin, 2006), he directs a Fascist striptease, parading a sequence of men - or rather, the same man in a sequence of moves - along a red diving board. Beginning in full military uniform, arm flung out in the Nazi salute, the figure is systematically stripped of its costume as it nears the edge; until it leaps off the plank virtually naked, a zealot to the last, its arm still frozen in the recalcitrant salute.

In another vein, Iranna also explores the hazardous border between tenderness and fear, or, to phrase it in Rilkean terms, between beauty and terror. He hunts through the archive of mythology, folklore, global art and world cinema for images that he can charge with his private experience, so transmuting them into a bridge between his imagination and the inner lives of his viewers. Consider, for instance, the recurrent image of the horse. In *Ashwadana: Diptych 1 & 2* (acrylic and goldleaf on tarpaulin, 2005), a horse stands protectively beside a child wearing a golden cap: various myths, ancient and modern, are alluded to here. We are put in mind of the Horse Sacrifice of the Vedic age, the *Ashwamedha*; and of the Indo-Aryan practice of giving horses as gifts to scholars and priests at royal sacrifices; and also of the recurring images of the white horse and the child in Tarkovsky's films, as guarantees of transcendence.

The horse is the archetypal symbol of authority, of virility and quest. In some mystical visions, as that of the Kashmiri saint-poet Lal Ded, it symbolises the cosmos, which the seeker must ride. Or, as in the Greek myth of Phaeton and his father Apollo's chariot, the horse can represent the force of crisis, which can serve the initiate well but destroy those unprepared to handle it. In *The Dancer on the Horse* (acrylic on tarpaulin, 2006), Iranna unveils a study in poise, set against a red field crimped with clothespins. And in *Infinity Night* (acrylic on tarpaulin, 2006), he composes a

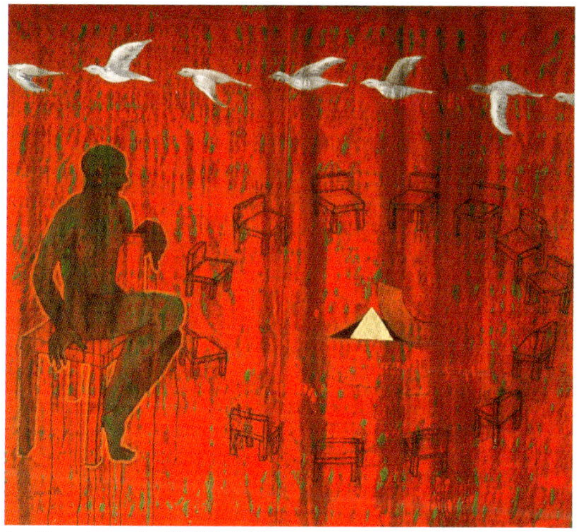

Acrylic on tarpaulin, 72x66", 2003

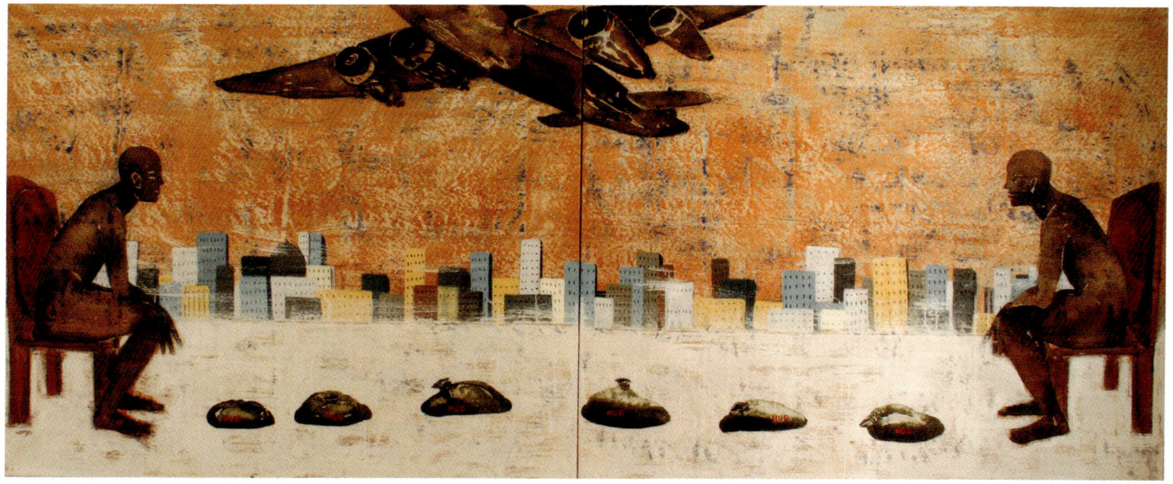

Mud Mud Mud and Mud, acrylic on tarpaulin, 132x52", 2006

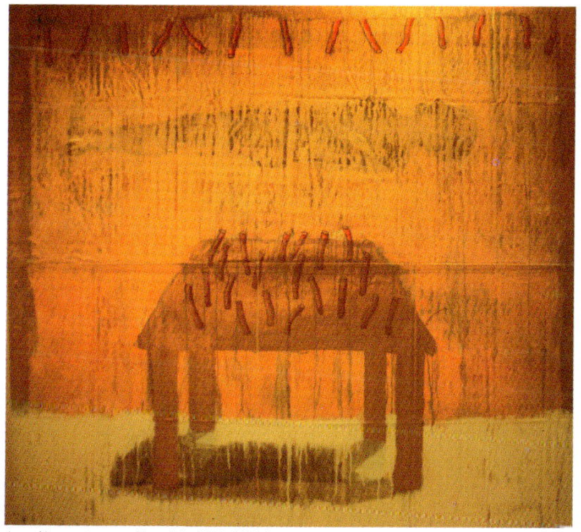

Acrylic on tarpaulin, 66x66", 2001

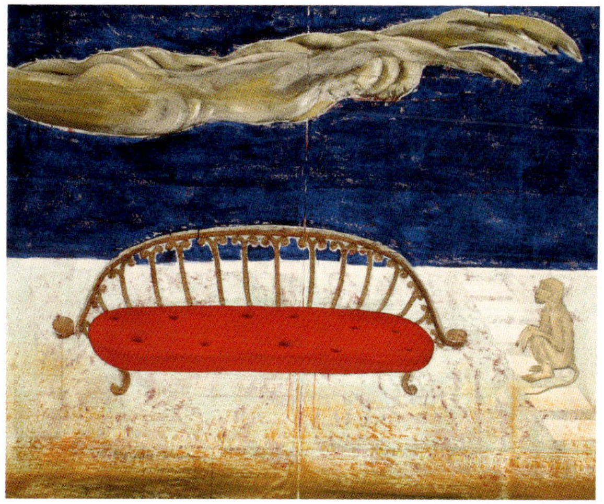

Acrylic on tarpaulin, 66x52", 2006

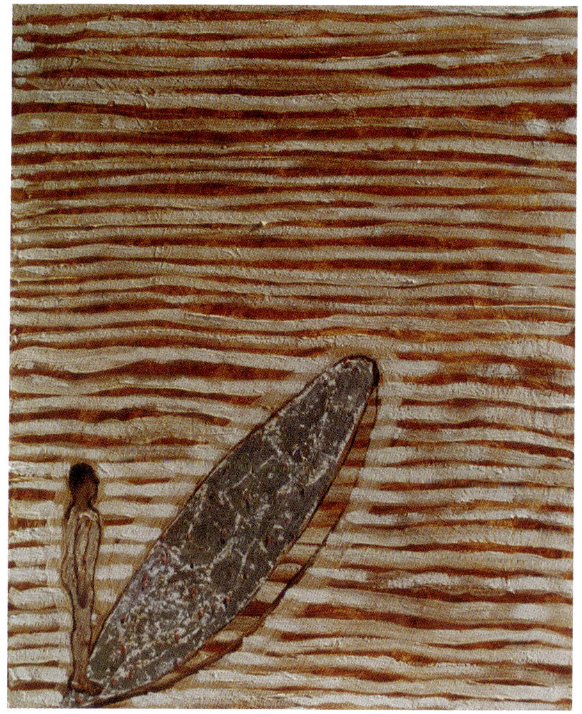

Oil, silver and foil on canvas, 40x30", 1999

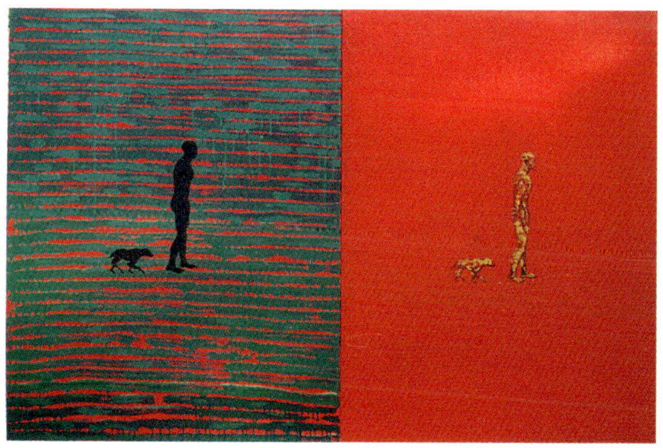

Acrylic on canvas, 72x42", 2003

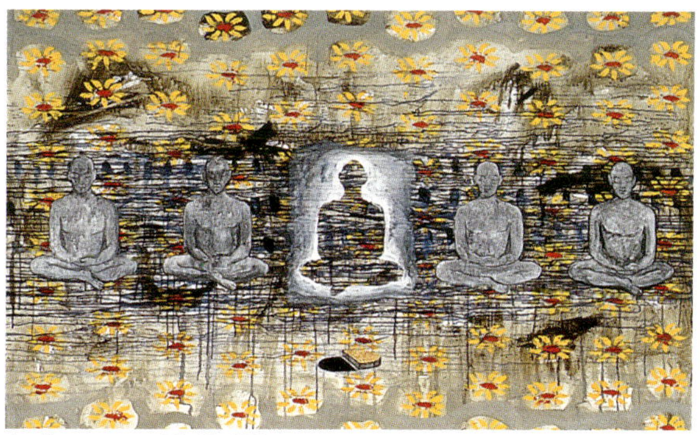

Acrylic on canvas, 72x48, 1997

tender nocturne that acquires a terrifying undertone: a boy has fallen asleep on a horse that stands in a meadow, the rein resting lightly in his hand. They have wandered to the edge of the meadow, which is the edge of the world; where the grass ends is a cliff, and we sense that immeasurable distances lurk beyond. The painting is a portrait of unquestioning trust: we are seized by the sleeping child's faith in the horse.

Here, as in many of his paintings, Iranna proposes a near-abstractionist field of textural colour, worked over with frottage-like brushwork, tuned up with crumpling and crimping. The stitch remains a key manoeuvre in Iranna's work, appearing as the cable that goes through a backcloth, or the rein that slips in and out of the grass; related to the furrow in his early paintings, the stitch underscores the role of artifice in the making and holding together of an imagined world-within-the-world. I have already described some of Iranna's surfaces as embodiments of *maya*: the backdrop that can vanish, that has to be stitched together or pinned like a cloth because it could fall or be snatched away; or because it might swaddle the figures performing before it, without warning.

To adapt the categories of Indic metaphysics for our current purposes, I would suggest that while *maya*, as the illusory appearance of reality, is the given structure of experience, *lila*, or the play that the self can enact upon reality, is the power of choice and autonomous agency. I will argue that the interplay between these opposites lies at the core of Iranna's art. When we take this perspective to his paintings and sculptures, we see that *lila* - the manner in which his figures perform or act out their agency, knowing their status as the world's captives or hostages, and subverting or protesting against this condition - is the heroic resistance to *maya*, a refusal to be subjugated by *maya*.

But *maya* is, by its nature, deceptive: the practitioner of *lila* must be able to distinguish between the delusions it promotes and the actualities it conceals. The vista that inspires beauty in one consciousness can provoke terror in another; where one person may see a cell stigmatised with the horror of prison, another may find the anchorite's healing space of prayer. In this context, Iranna refers to a teaching story told by Siddheshwara Swami of Bijapur, a spiritual guide who gives *pravachana*s or sermons to large audiences in the Sholapur and Kolhapur areas of south Maharashtra, bordering the artist's native north Karnataka. The Swami tells his listeners about two men who look after a cow: one loves the cow as a fellow sentient being, while the other is a butcher. They seem to have the same goal, but approach it with very different and indeed mutually contradictory objectives. Iranna holds on to this parable, always questioning his motives in being attached to a specific choice or idiom; his art is informed by an understanding of the bodied self and its relationship to the world, by the implications that contexts of action generate for the self and its performance of *lila*. From this sense of contextual action emerge the avatars that his protagonists assume, in response to different challenges.

Iranna's recent paintings register a turn in the direction of sacred iconography applied in secular contexts. We see, here, references to the cosmic figures that appear in the *Dasha-avatara* or the catalogue of Vishnu's ten major incarnations: in *The Myth* (acrylic on tarpaulin, 2006), a colossus strides the implied distance of pictorial space like Vamana, the Dwarf who magnifies himself to cosmic proportions; he wears the head of Varaha, the Boar Incarnation, holding the earth on his tusks. An emblematic urban skyline marks the horizon, while fragments of broken sky float in the air around this apparition. The myth of the saviour figure seems veined with intimations of catastrophe.

Not surprisingly, the metropolis becomes the site of such catastrophe, as well as of estrangement and the mutual alienation of people from one another and from themselves. In *Mud Mud Mud and Mud - Diptych* (acrylic on tarpaulin, 2006), two men occupy chairs at either end of the painting. Between them stretches a chalky ground like the floor of a coliseum, the horizon occupied by an urban profile of low-slung and high-rise buildings, even a dome. Above this scene, an aeroplane is taking off, like a giant bird of prey, its fuselage and jet engines almost within grasp. We hear the roar of the plane, sense that it must drown out the earnest effort at building a conversational bridge. Five gunny sacks spell out the gulf between the men, each stencil-marked "MUD" in red. Does every foundation prefigure a burial; must all creation begin and end in sludge?

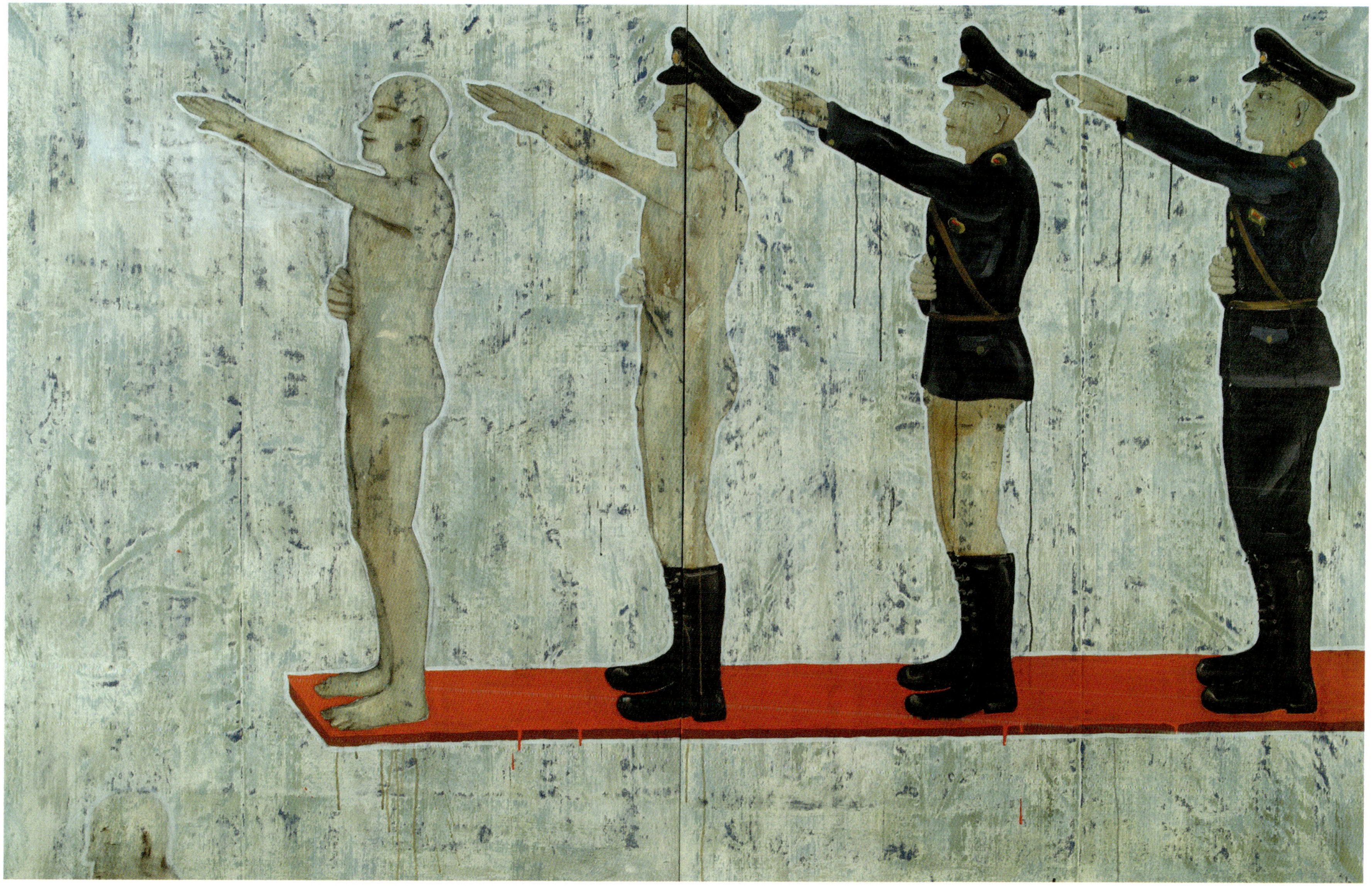

The Last Voice, acrylic on tarpaulin, 104x66”, 2006

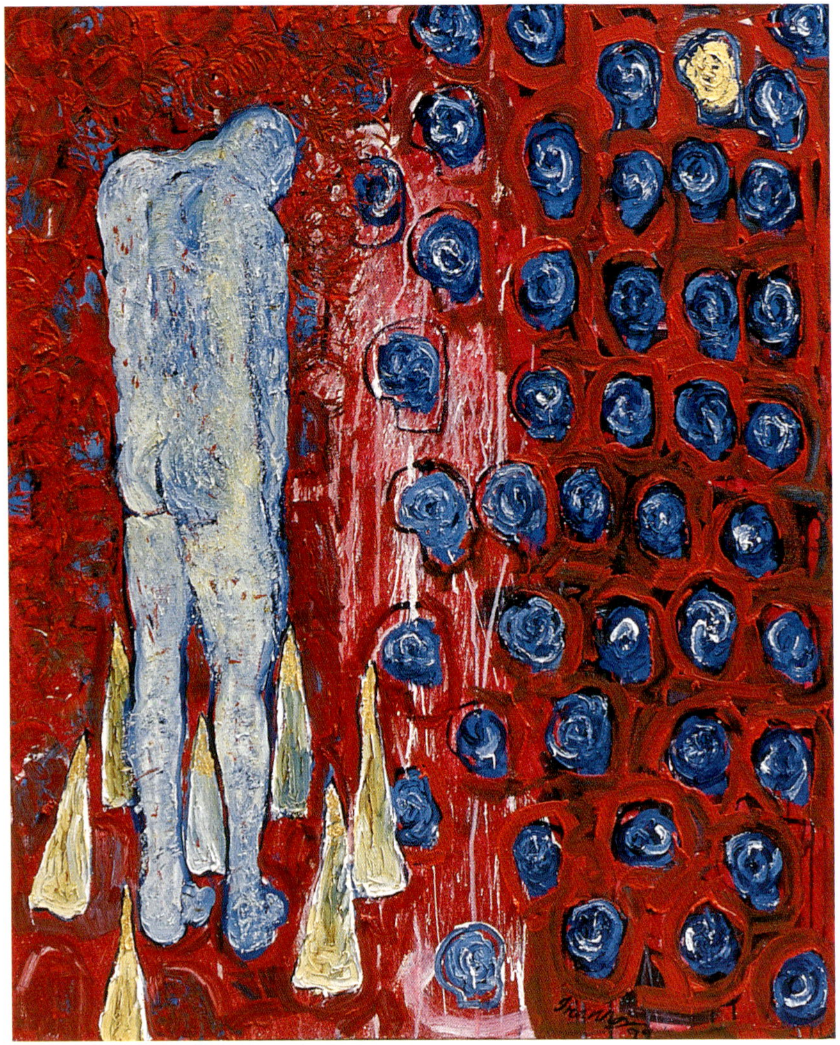

Untitled, oil on canvas, 36x48", 1996

Iranna's practitioner of *lila* has conveyed his stories in a variety of forms: *yogi* and athlete, gymnast and street acrobat, trapezist of fate and solo performer conscripted into a choric symphonics. Are these oblique, or not-so-oblique, portraits of the artist himself? Iranna concurs that they are: "I see myself in each of them, and through them, confront a society that is hostile and obstructive." Romantic as such testimony may sound; Iranna speaks from the viewpoint of an individual who has worked hard against circumstances to establish himself in his chosen trajectory. His unfailing good humour, natural courtesy and unobtrusive self-confidence should not distract us from the fact that he has had to play fate against itself to win acceptance and even acclaim in a society that did not arm him with all the necessary privileges at birth. Iranna has made his way against the current, as a person of rural background living in a metropolis; as a southerner in a north Indian setting that is often crudely intolerant of the South; as an artist in an economy that has only very recently begun to reward artists for their pains, but has more typically been indifferent to their claims.

To this writer, the most plausible self-portrait of Iranna G R is, perhaps, that of the artist as the dancer on the horse. While pursuing the logic of his own movements, the dancer must also keep track of the horse's changes of mood and direction: just as the artist must follow his own practice but also maintain a keen awareness of how the world is changing around him. The artist's perennial task is that of finding the appropriate relationship between inner and outer realities; between the fruits of solitude and the gifts of sociality; between the sanctuary-like atmosphere of the studio and the demands and opportunities of the public sphere. There is an admirable dynamism to the dancer on the horse, and also an ability to live with risk, to perform the self as a defiant figure of hazard.

Notes & References

1. Email exchange between Iranna GR and the author (January 2006).
2. *Ibid*.
3. *Ibid*.
4. *Ibid*.
5. Hoskote, 2003.
6. Karode, 1998.
7. Email exchange between Iranna GR and the author (January 2006).
8. *Ibid*.
9. *Ibid*.
10. Calvino, 1993.

Select Bibliography

Calvino, Italo. *Under the Jaguar Sun* (trans. William Weaver; London: Vintage, 1993), pp. 31-64.

Chopra, Suneet. "Iranna GR: An Art Beyond Sensation" (catalogue essay for Iranna's exhibition, "Edge Dynamics"; New Delhi: Delhi Art Gallery & Bombay: Jehangir Art Gallery, September-October 1995).

Dutta, Projjal. "Inside the Outsider: The Art and Times of Iranna GR" (conversation between Dutta and the artist, reproduced in the catalogue for "King of Clay: Paintings by Iranna GR"; New York: Gallery ArtsIndia, April-May 2006 & Palo Alto: ArtsIndia West, August-September 2006).

Hoskote, Ranjit. "Between Dream and Perplexity: Iranna Rukumpur's Modulations of the Figure" (catalogue essay for Iranna's exhibition, "Dream and Perplexity"; Bombay: The Guild Art Gallery, November 2003).

Karode, Roobina. "Shadows of the Real: Experiences of a Migrant Painter" (catalogue essay for Iranna's exhibition, "Shadows of the Real"; New Delhi: Shridharani Art Gallery & Gallery Espace, October 1998).

Koelnsperger, Ernst W. "Disorder and Early Sufferings" (catalogue essay for "Iranna GR: Selected Works"; Munich: Galerie Müller & Plate, January 2006).

Nair, Uma. "Threads of Humanism" (catalogue essay for Iranna's exhibition; Singapore: Bodhi Art, October-November 2005).

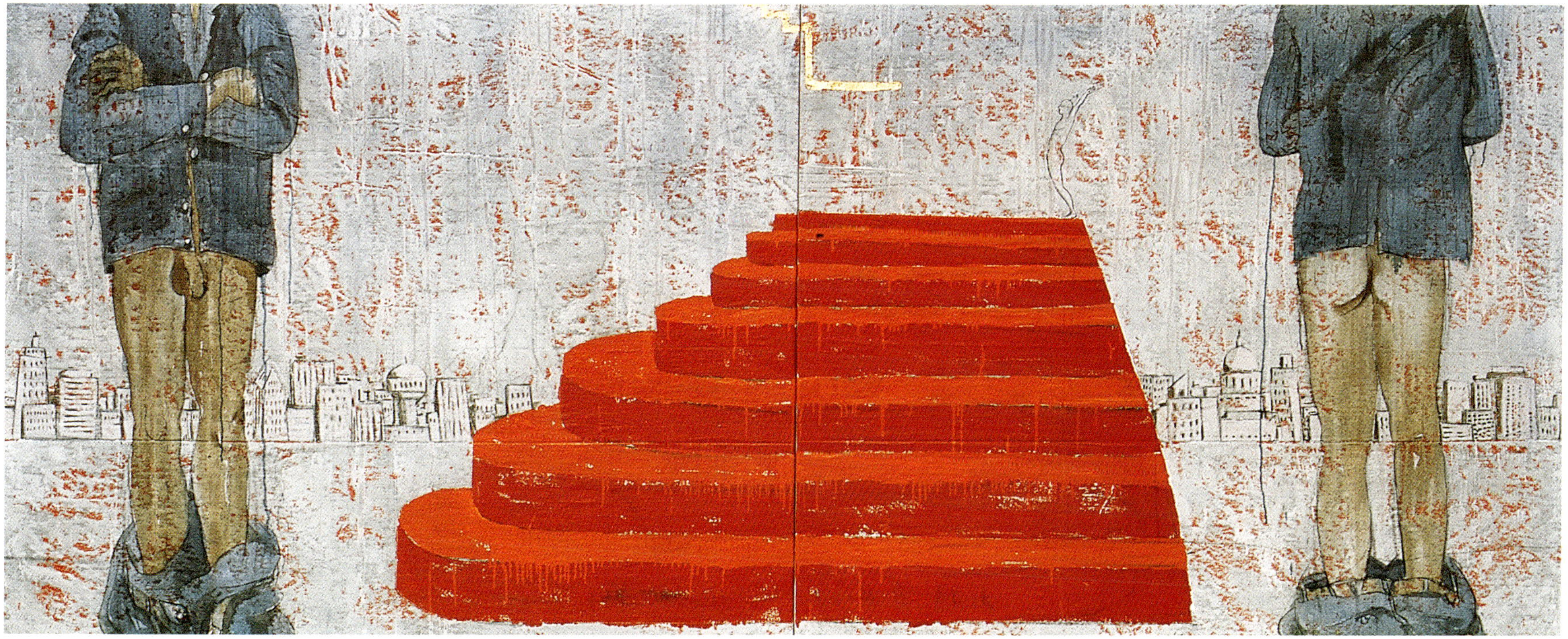

Man Made by Flesh and Bone, acrylic on tarpaulin, 132x52", 2005

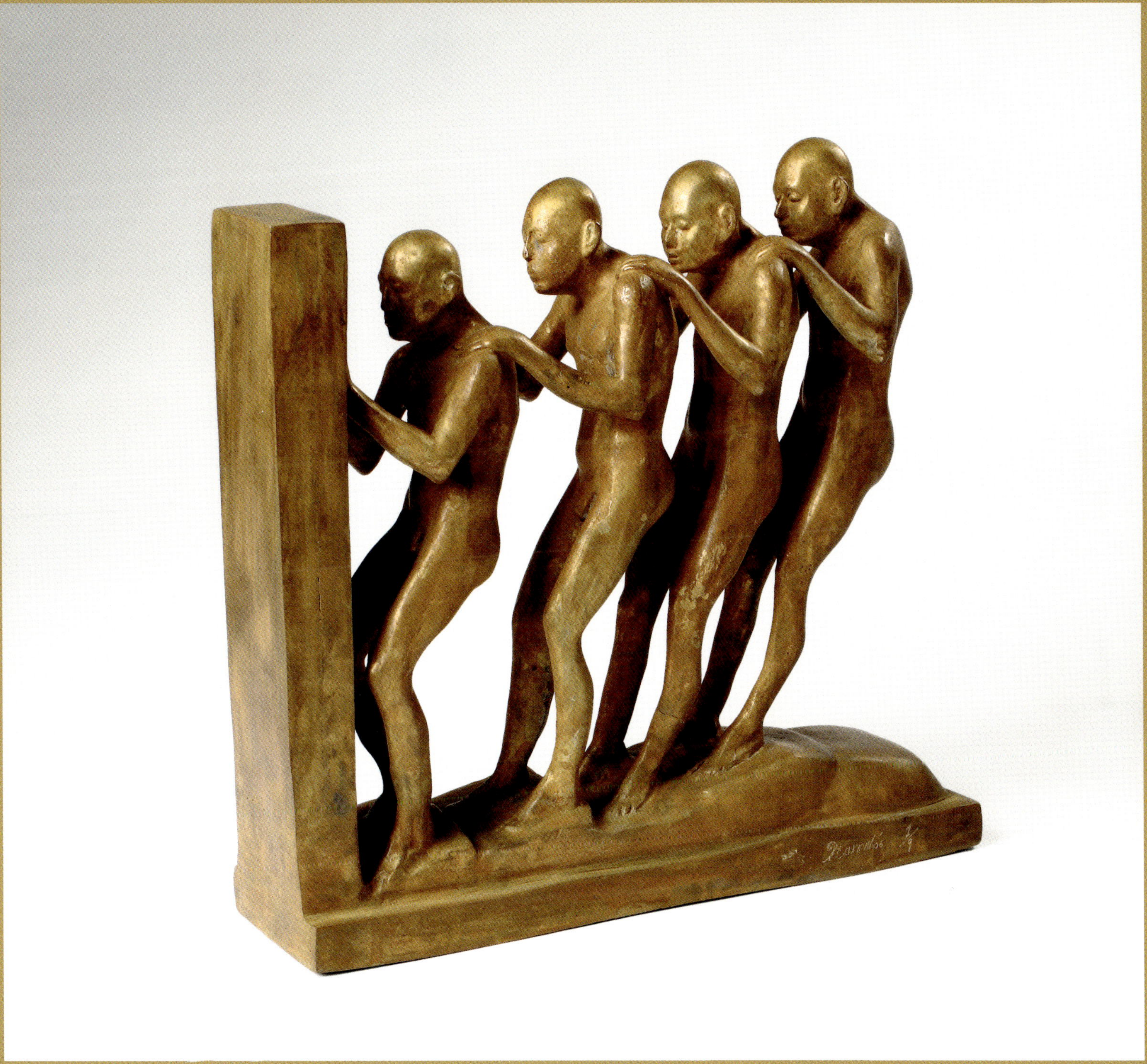

Silencer, bronze, 12x16x3", 2006

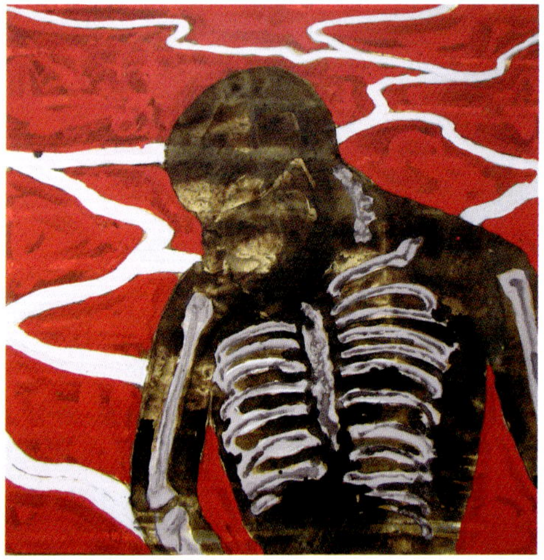
Acrylic on canvas, 30x30", 2005

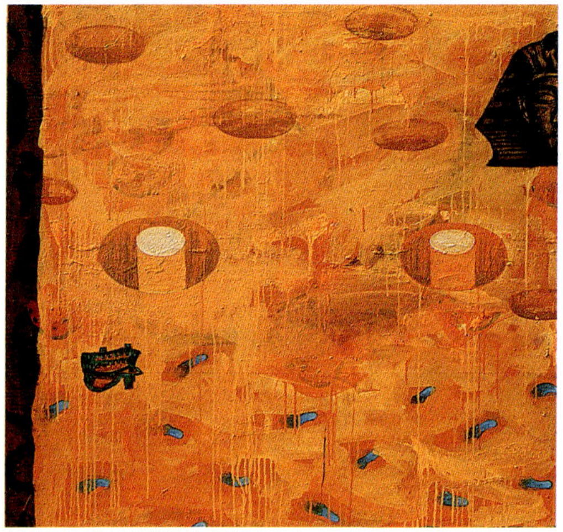
Acrylic on canvas, 66x66", 2000

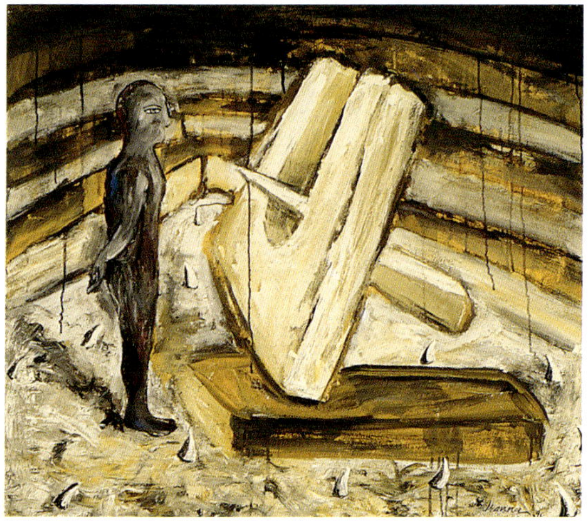
Acrylic on canvas, 42x36", 1994

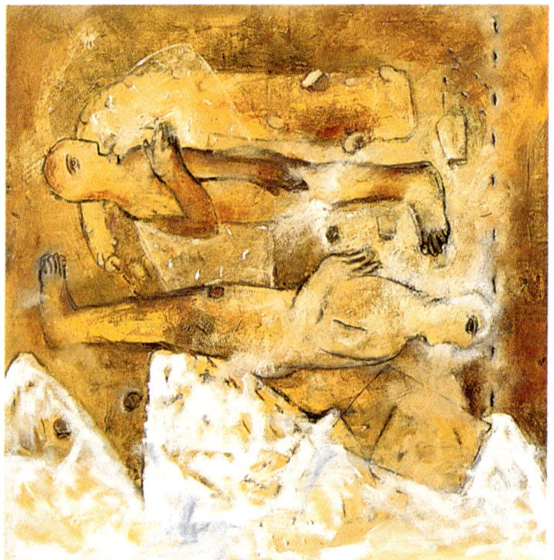
Oil on canvas, 48x48", 1995

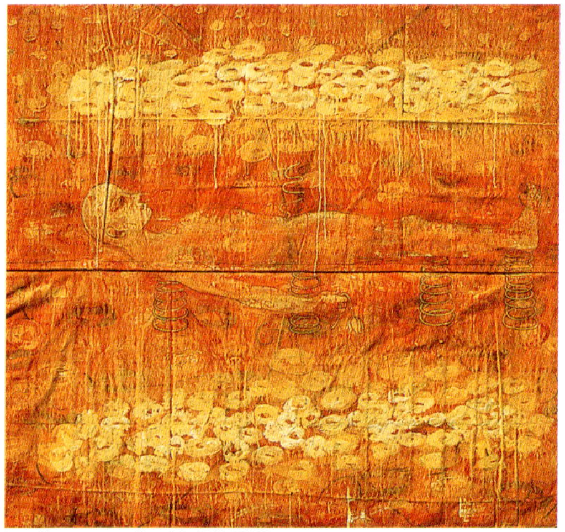
Acrylic on tarpaulin, 66x66", 2002

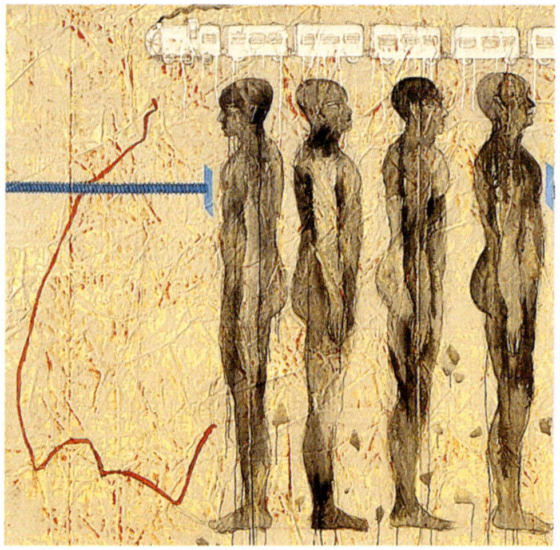
Acrylic on tarpaulin, 66x66", 2003

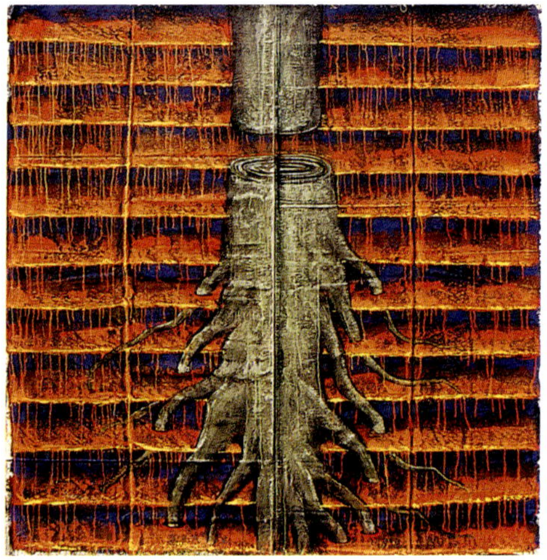
Acrylic on canvas, 63x70", 2004

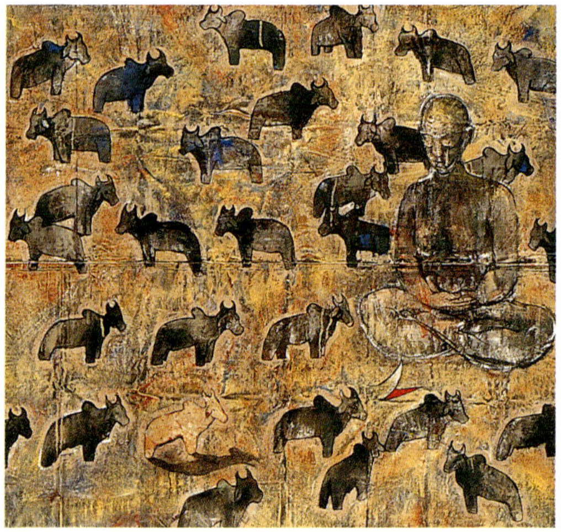
Acrylic on tarpaulin, 66x66", 1998

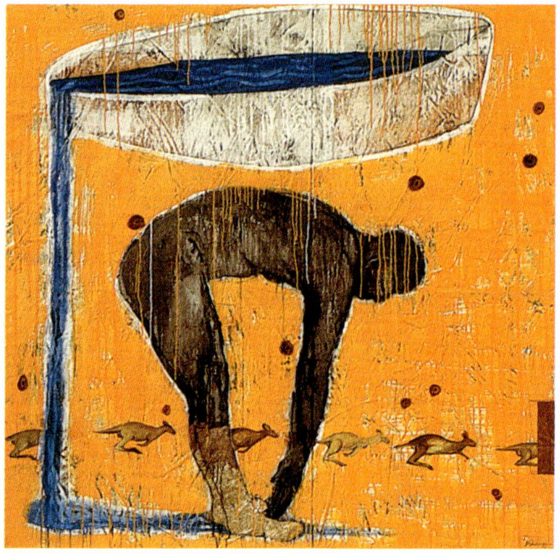
Acrylic on tarpaulin, 66x66", 2004

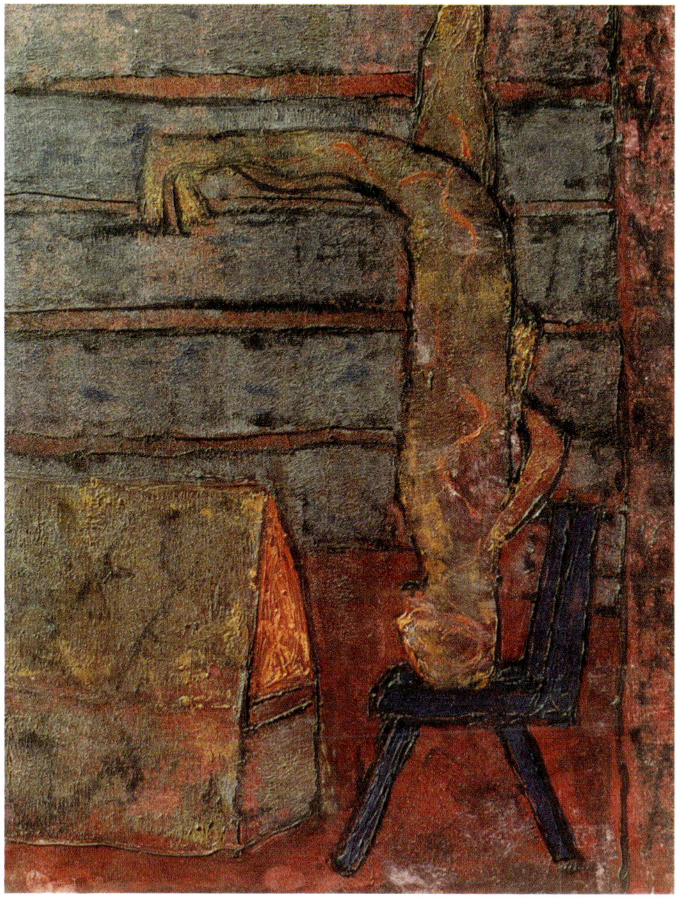

Untitled, oil on canvas, 24x30", 1993

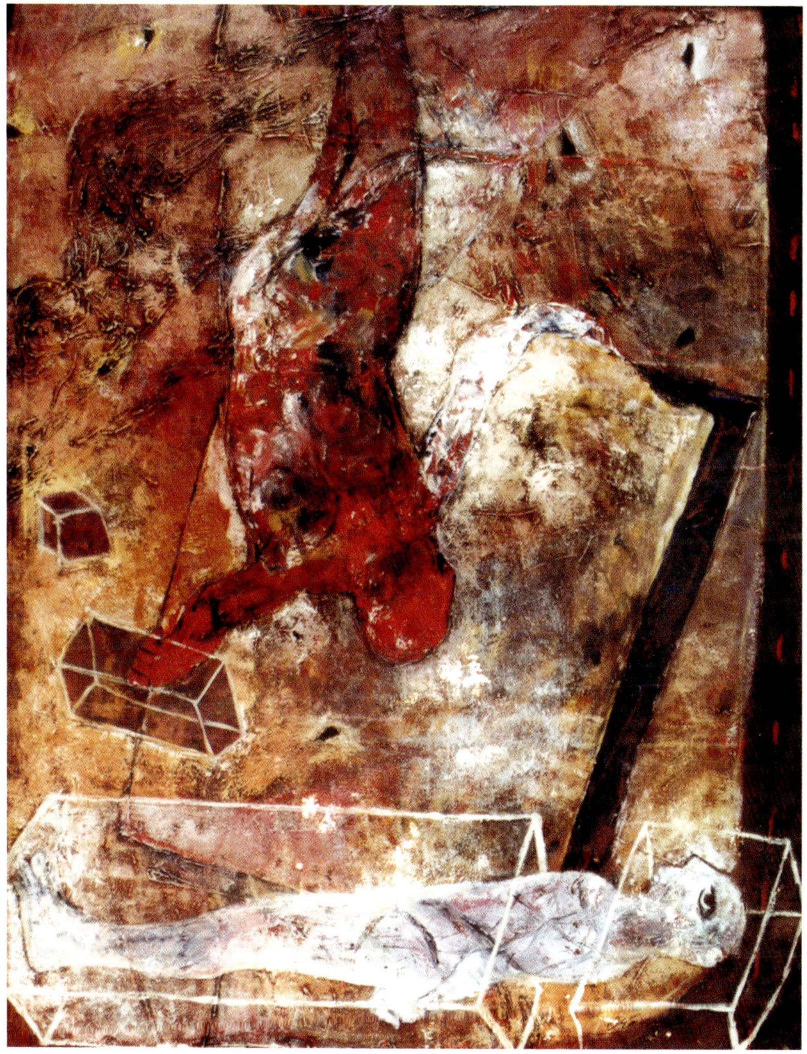

Untitled, oil on canvas, 60x70", 1994

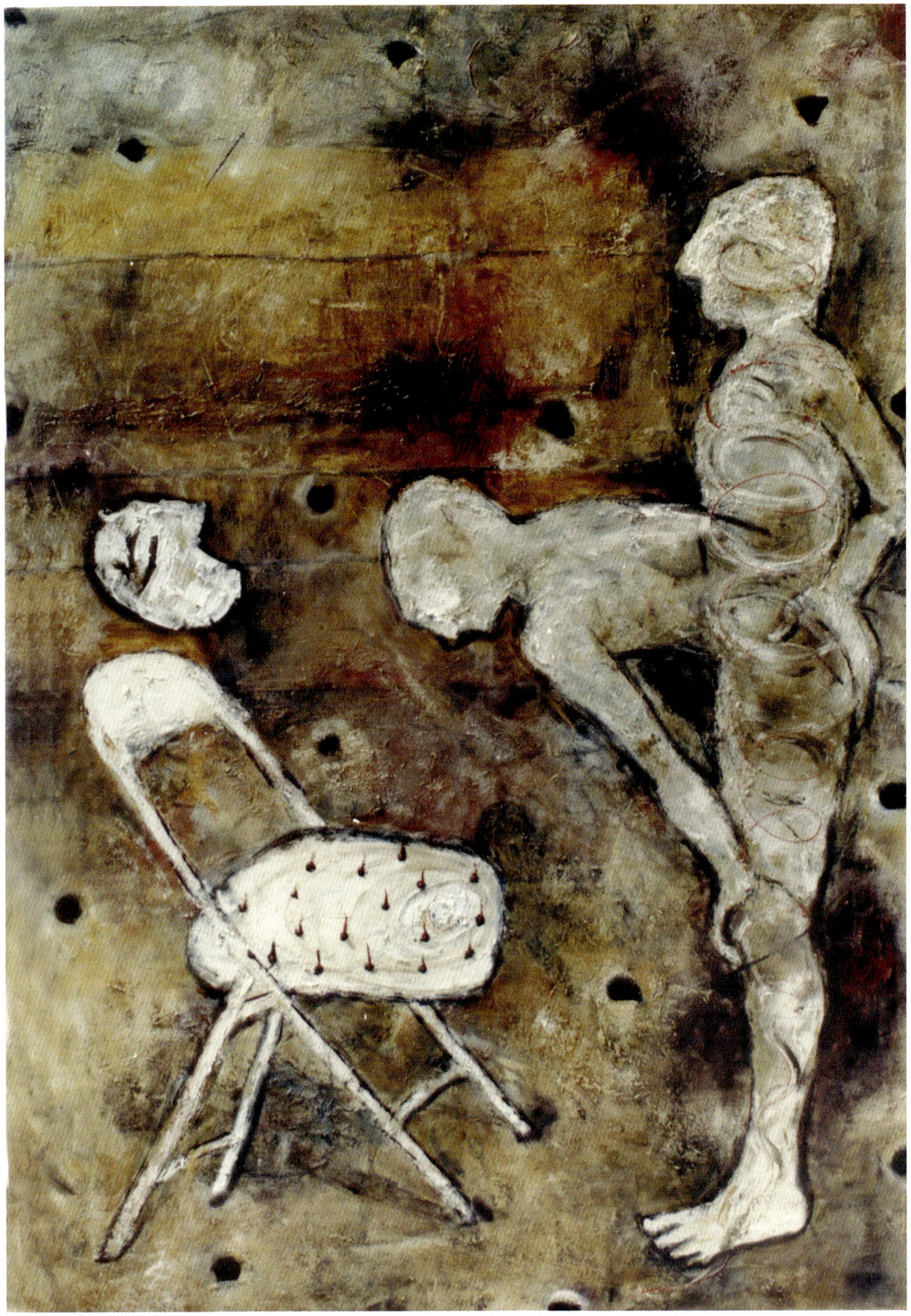

Untitled, oil on canvas, 48x72", 1994

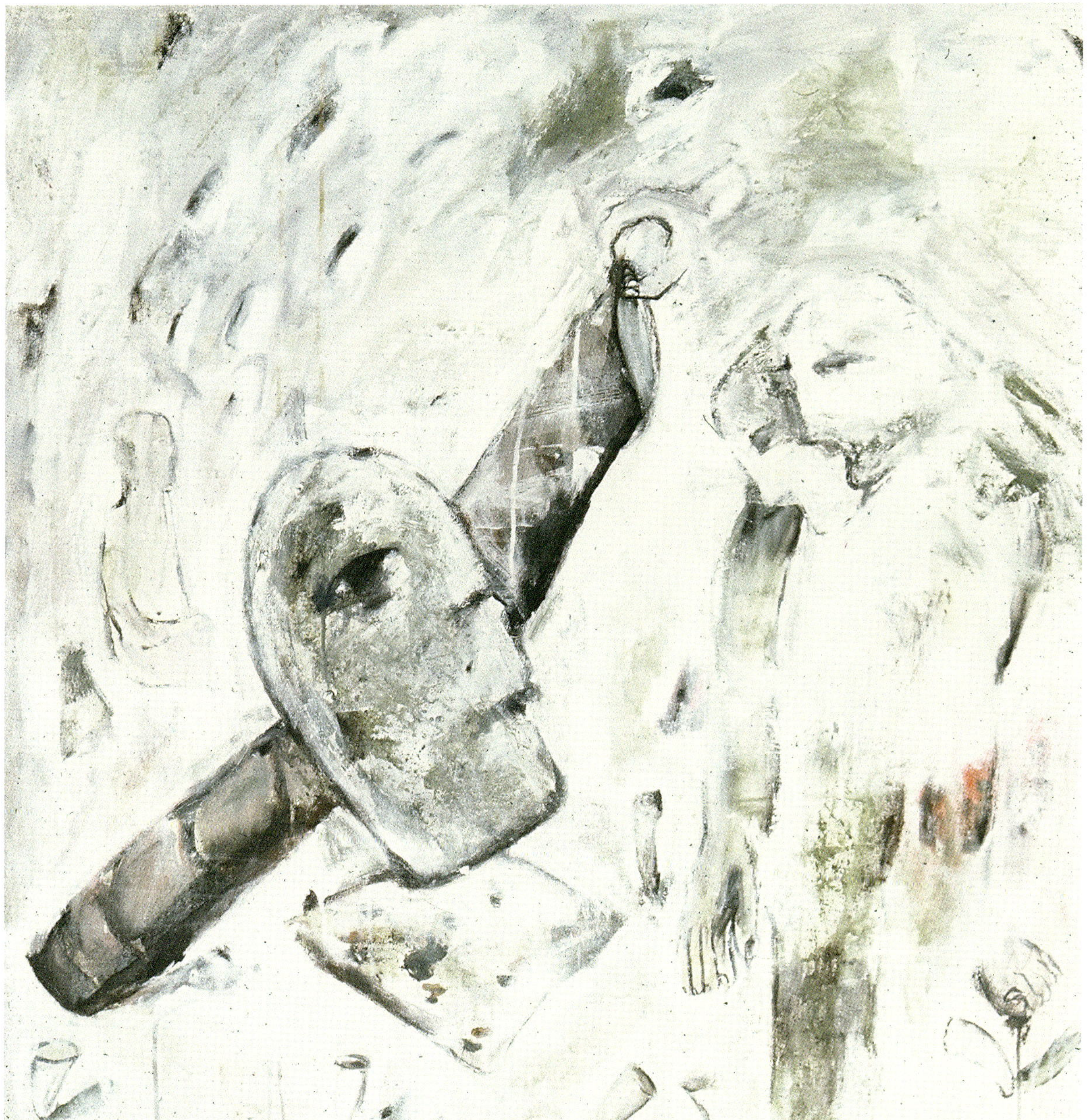

Untitled, acrylic on canvas, 30x36”, 1994

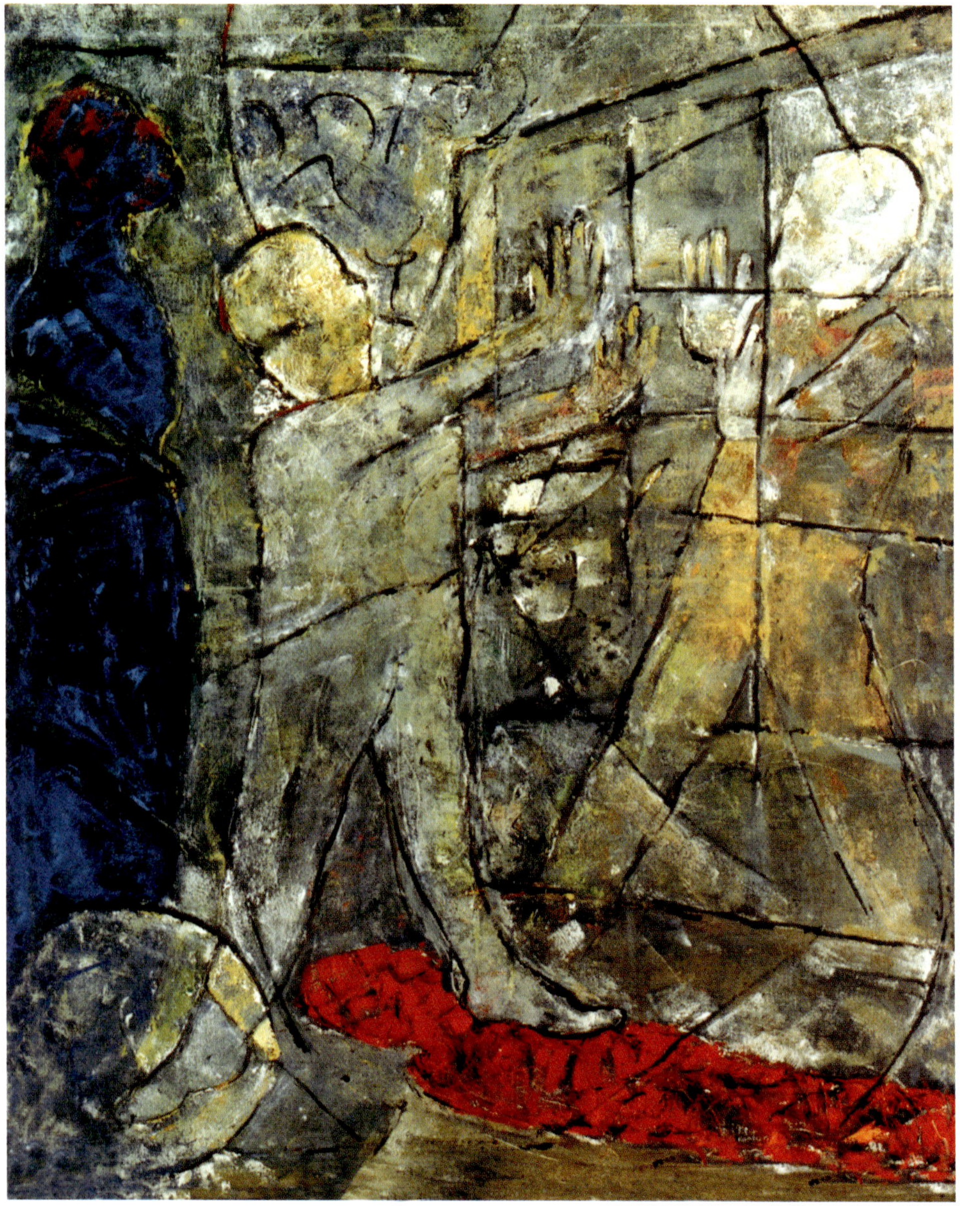

Untitled, oil on canvas, 48x60", 1994

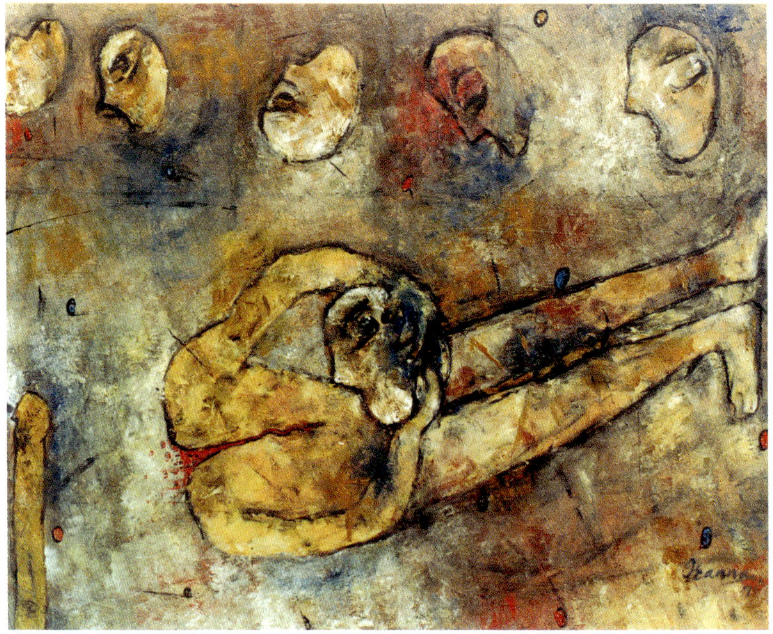

Untitled, oil on canvas, 60x42", 1995

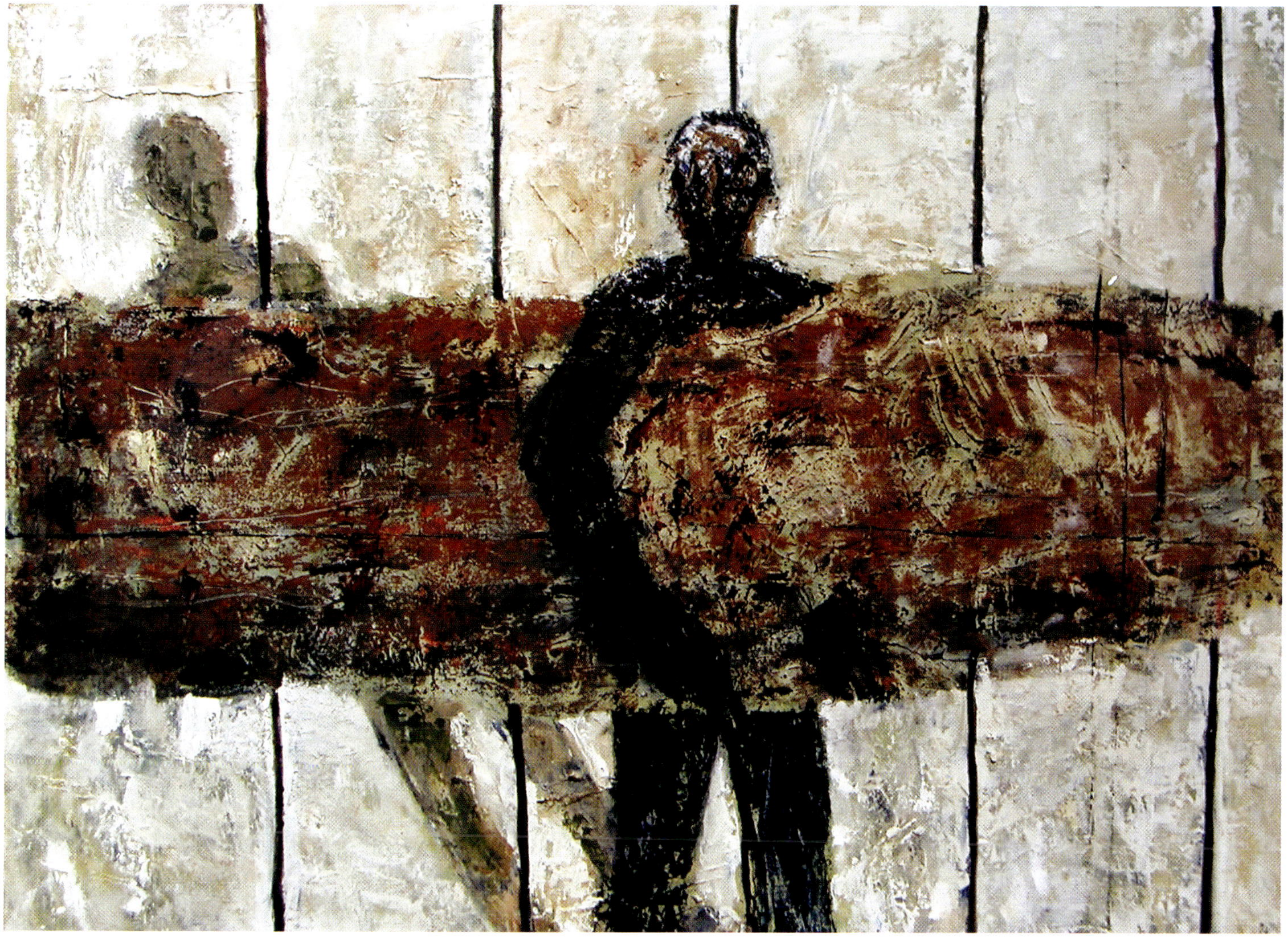

Untitled, acrylic on canvas, 48x36", 1994

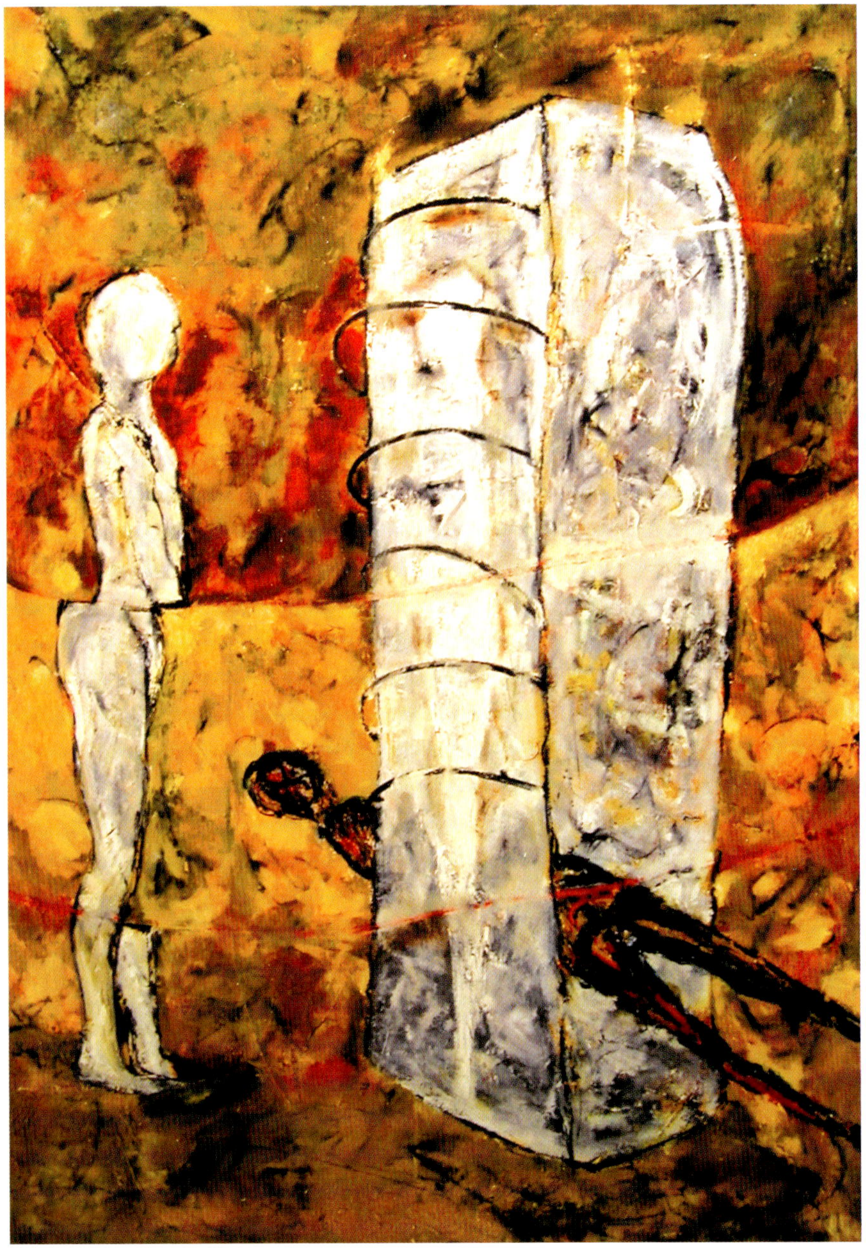

Untitled, oil on canvas, 36x42", 1995

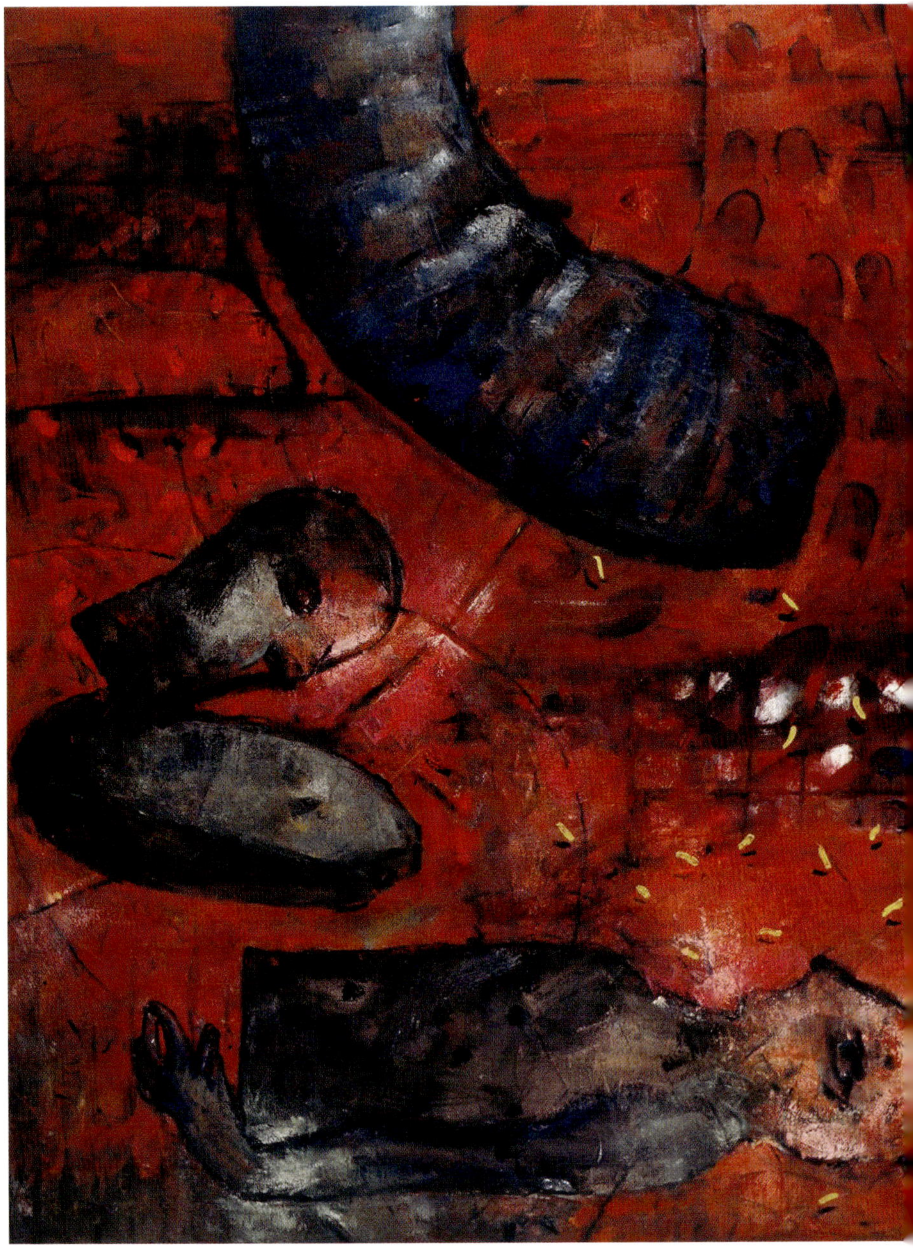

Untitled, oil on canvas, 48x60", 1996

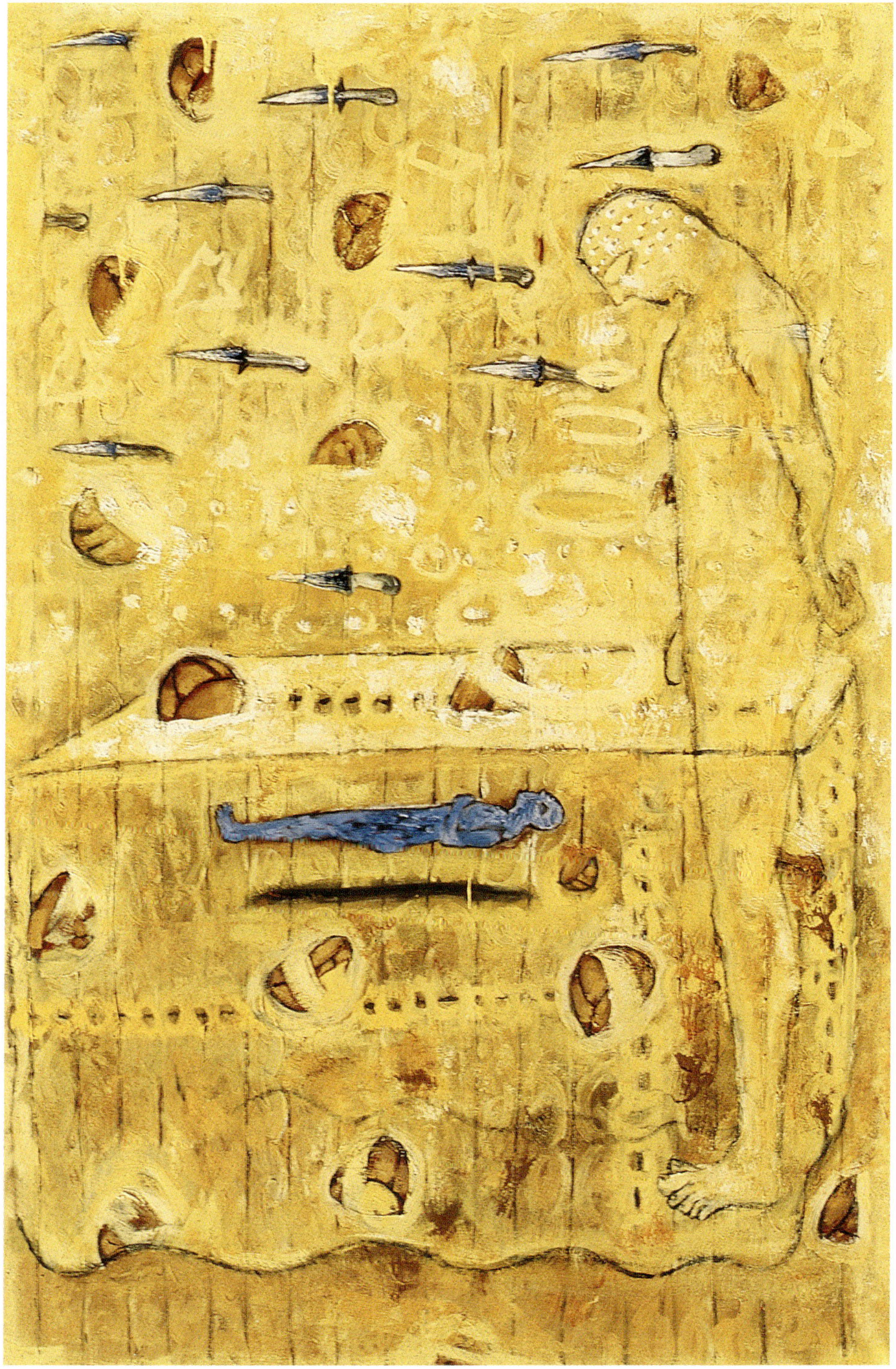

Untitled, oil on canvas, 48x72", 1995

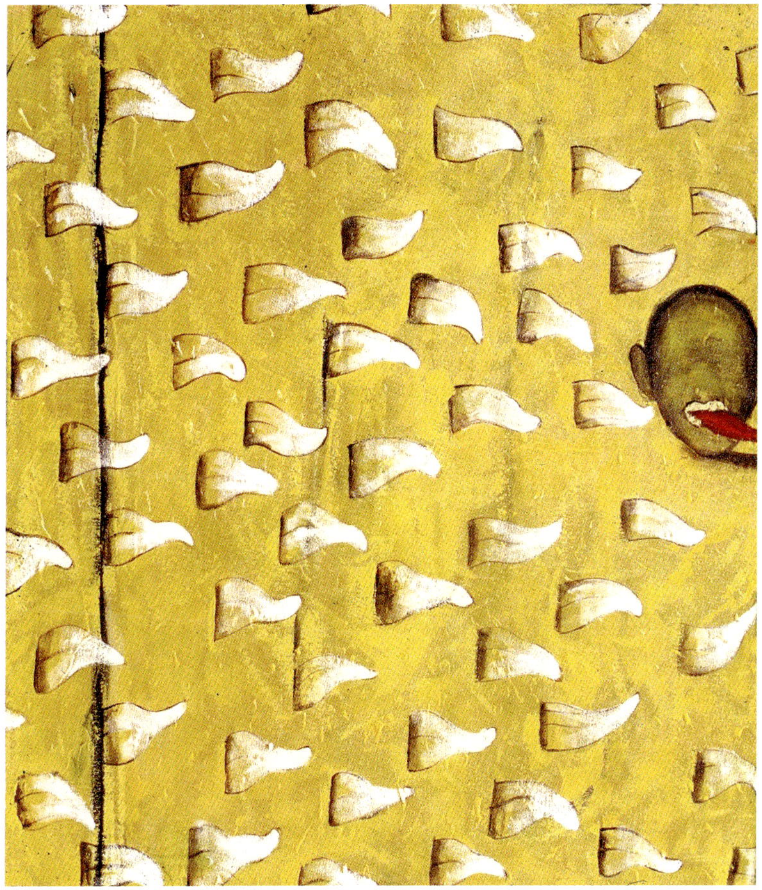

Untitled, oil on canvas, 40x48", 1996

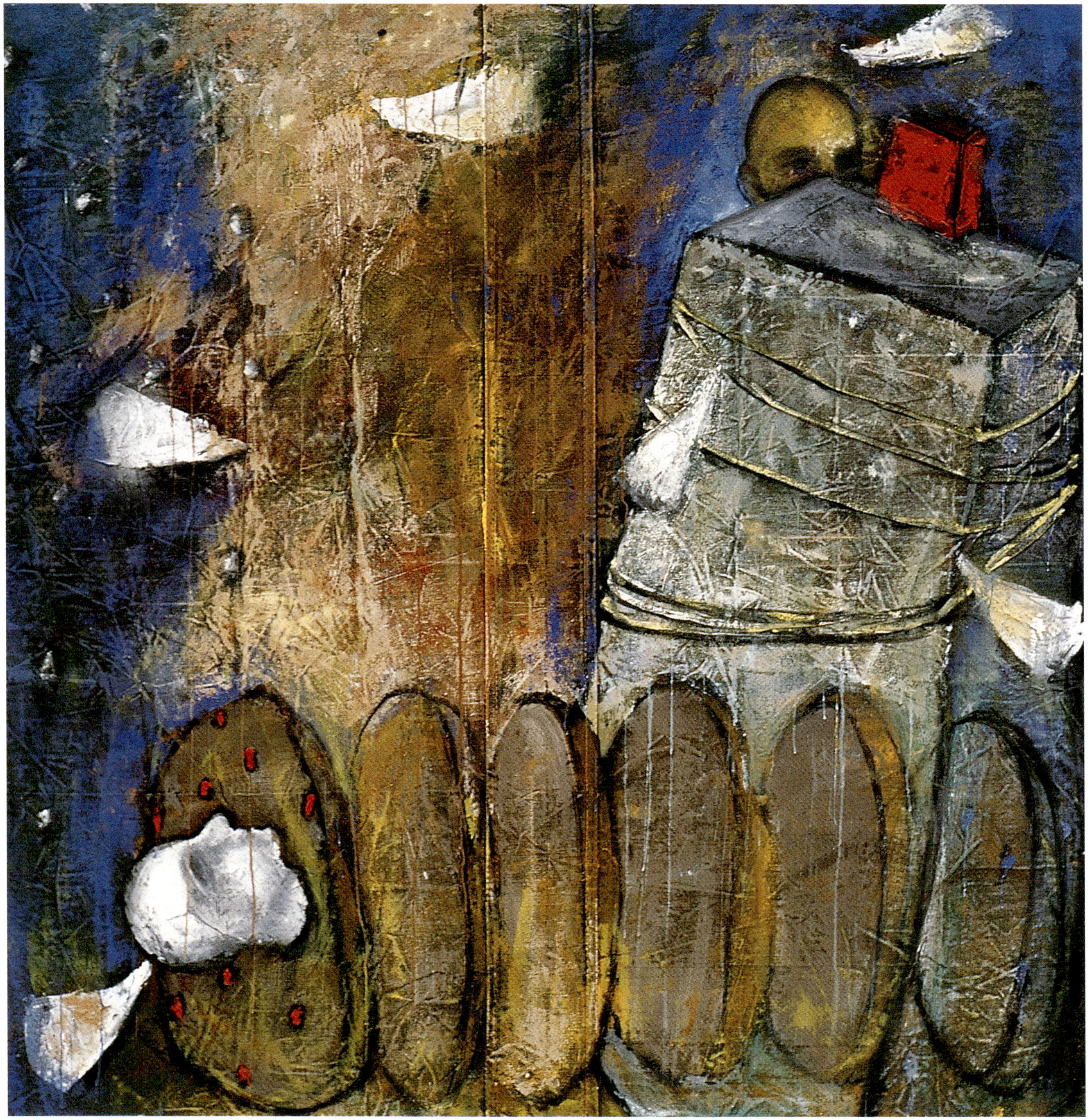

Untitled, acrylic on tarpaulin, 72x72", 1995

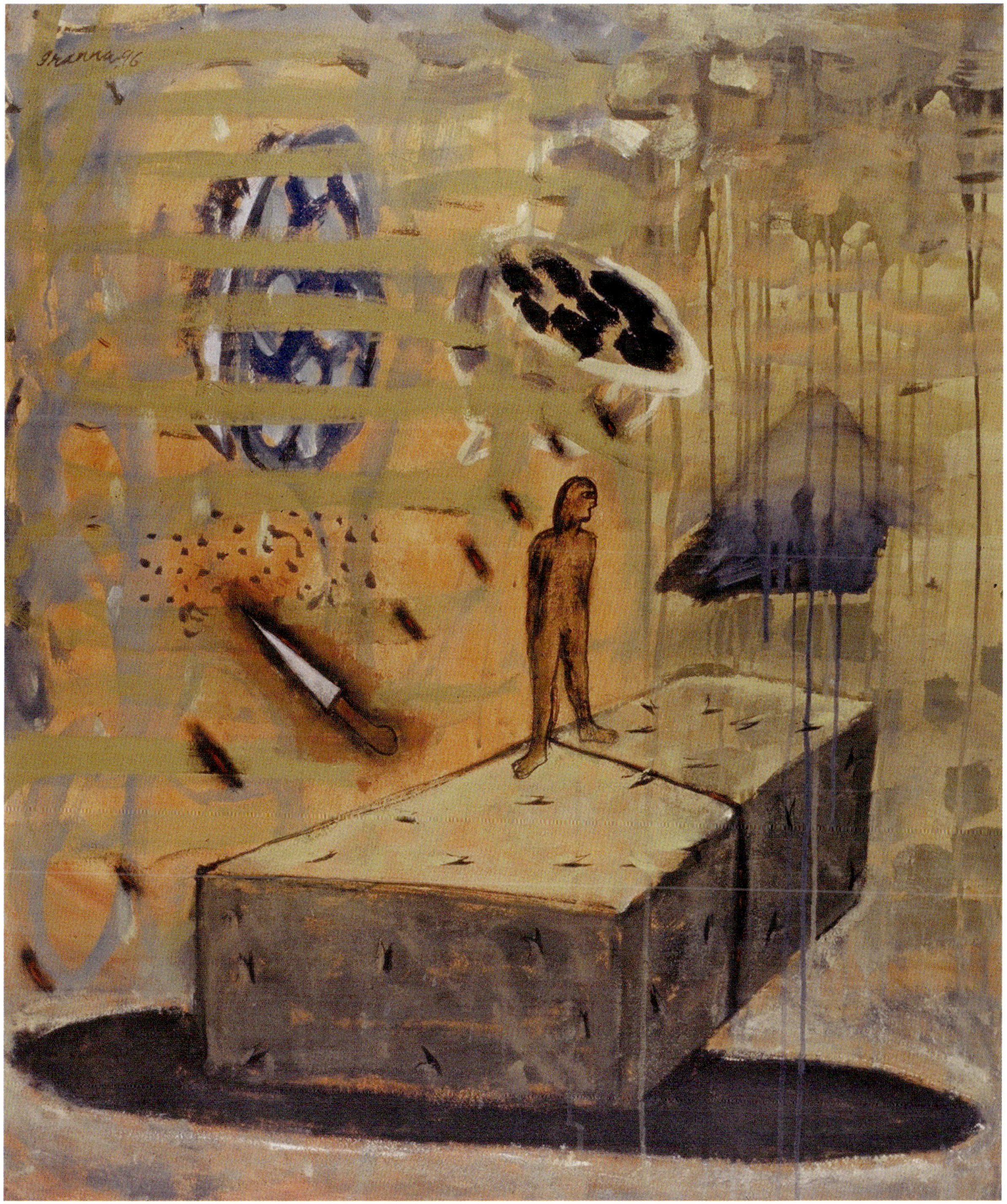

Untitled, acrylic on canvas, 42x48", 1996

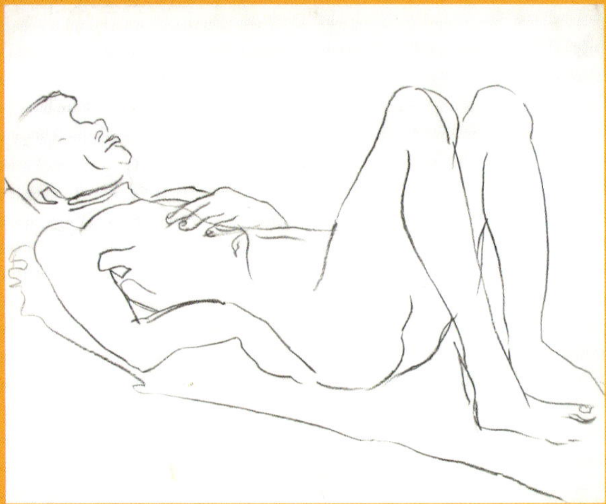

Charcoal on paper, 46x30", 1993

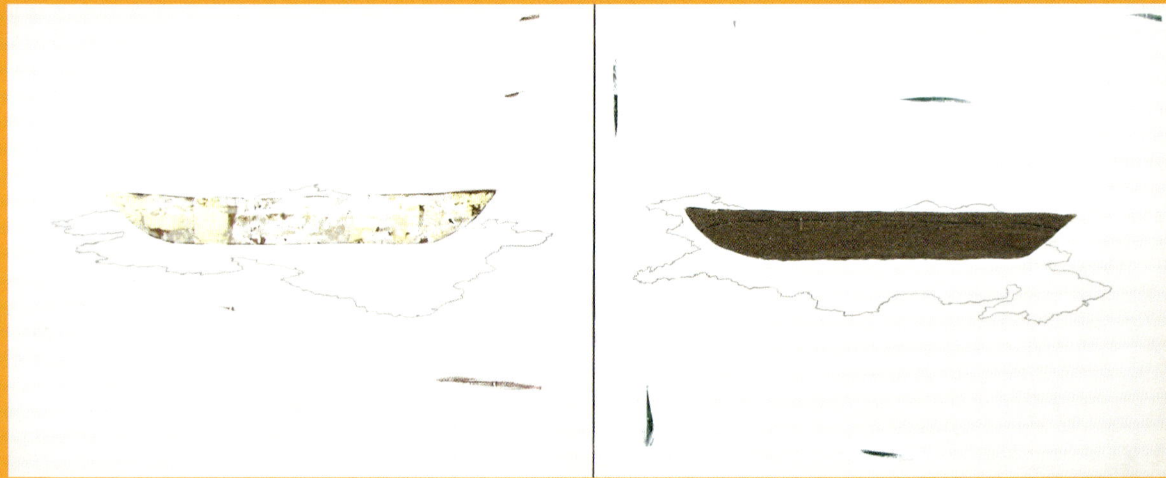

Acrylic and sand on canvas, 80x38", 2005

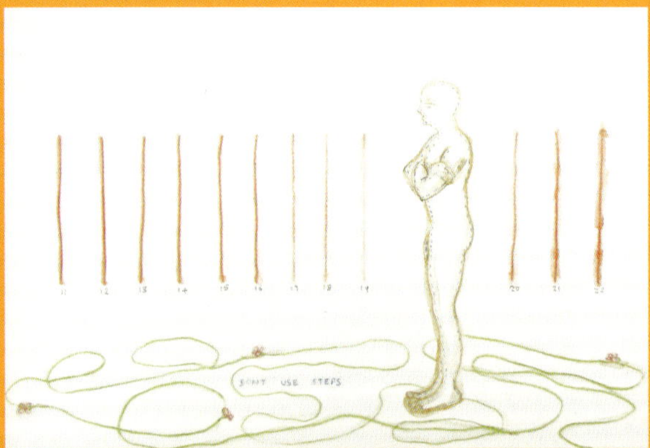

Watercolour, 18x11", 2004

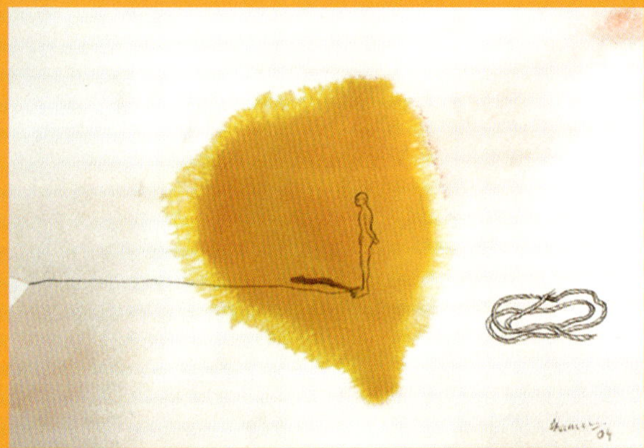

Watercolour, 18x11", 2004

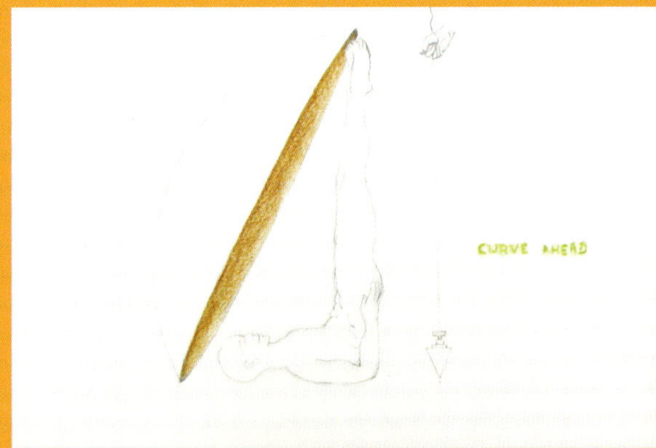

Watercolour, 18x11", 2004

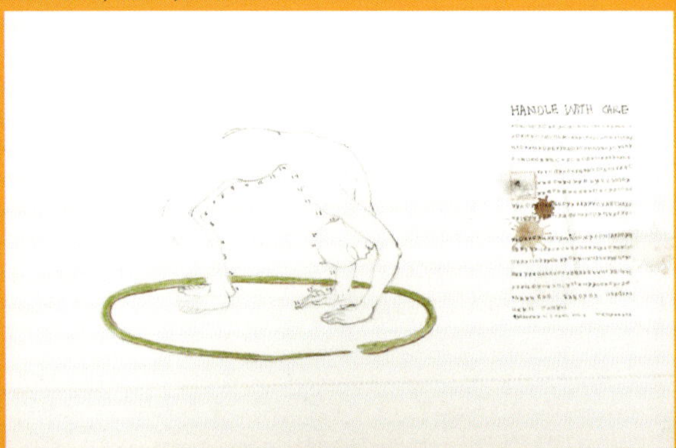

Watercolour, 18x11", 2004

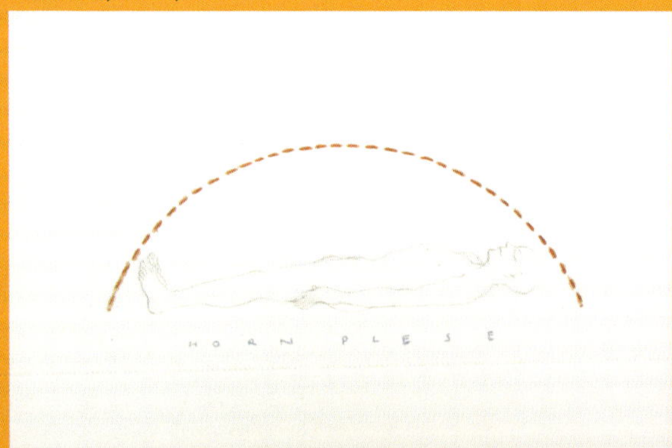

Watercolour, 18x11", 2004

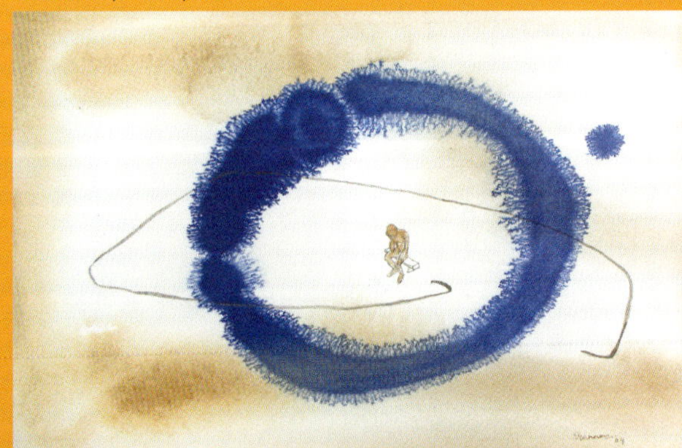

Watercolour, 18x11", 2004

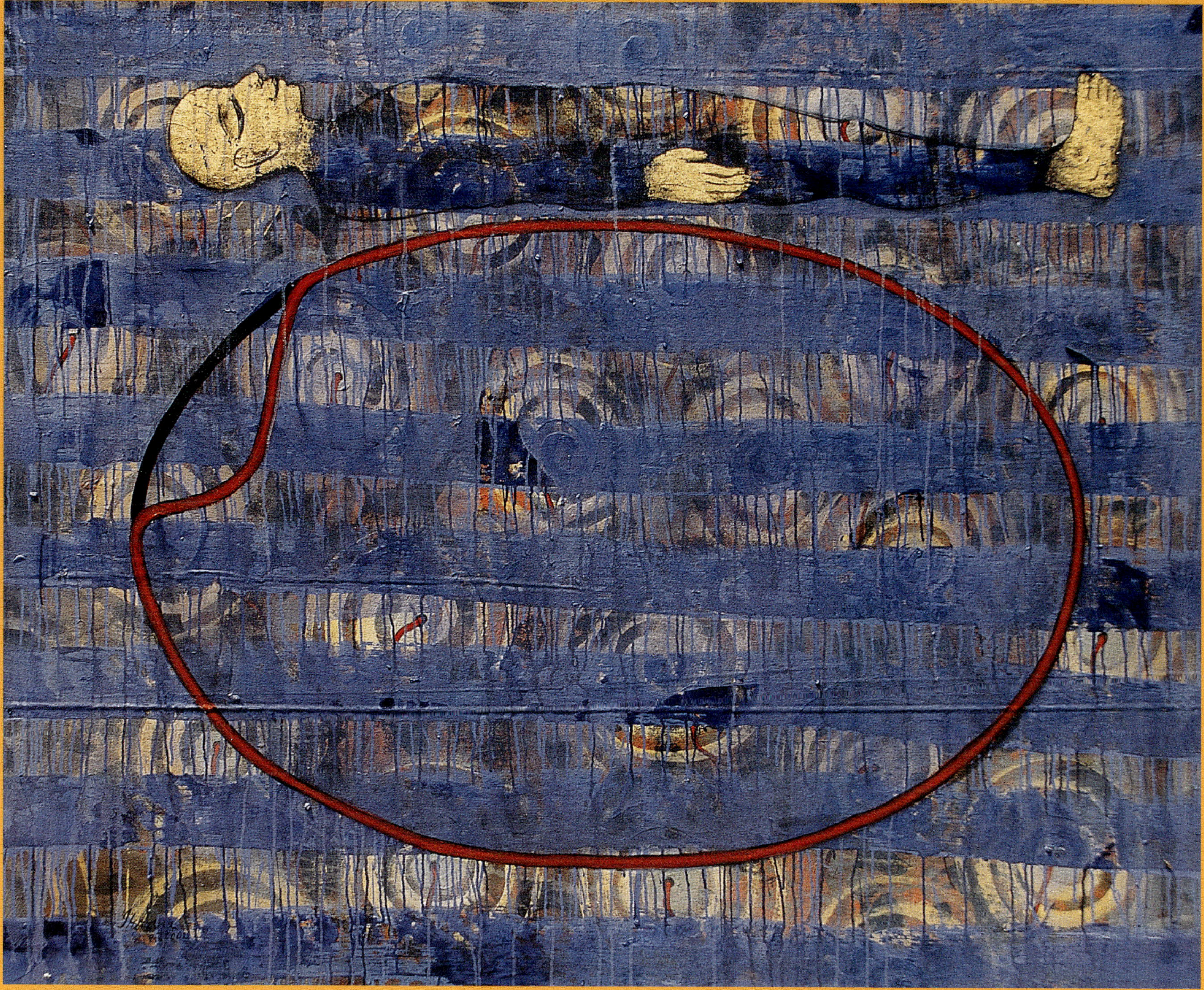

Untitled, acrylic on canvas, 66x52", 1998

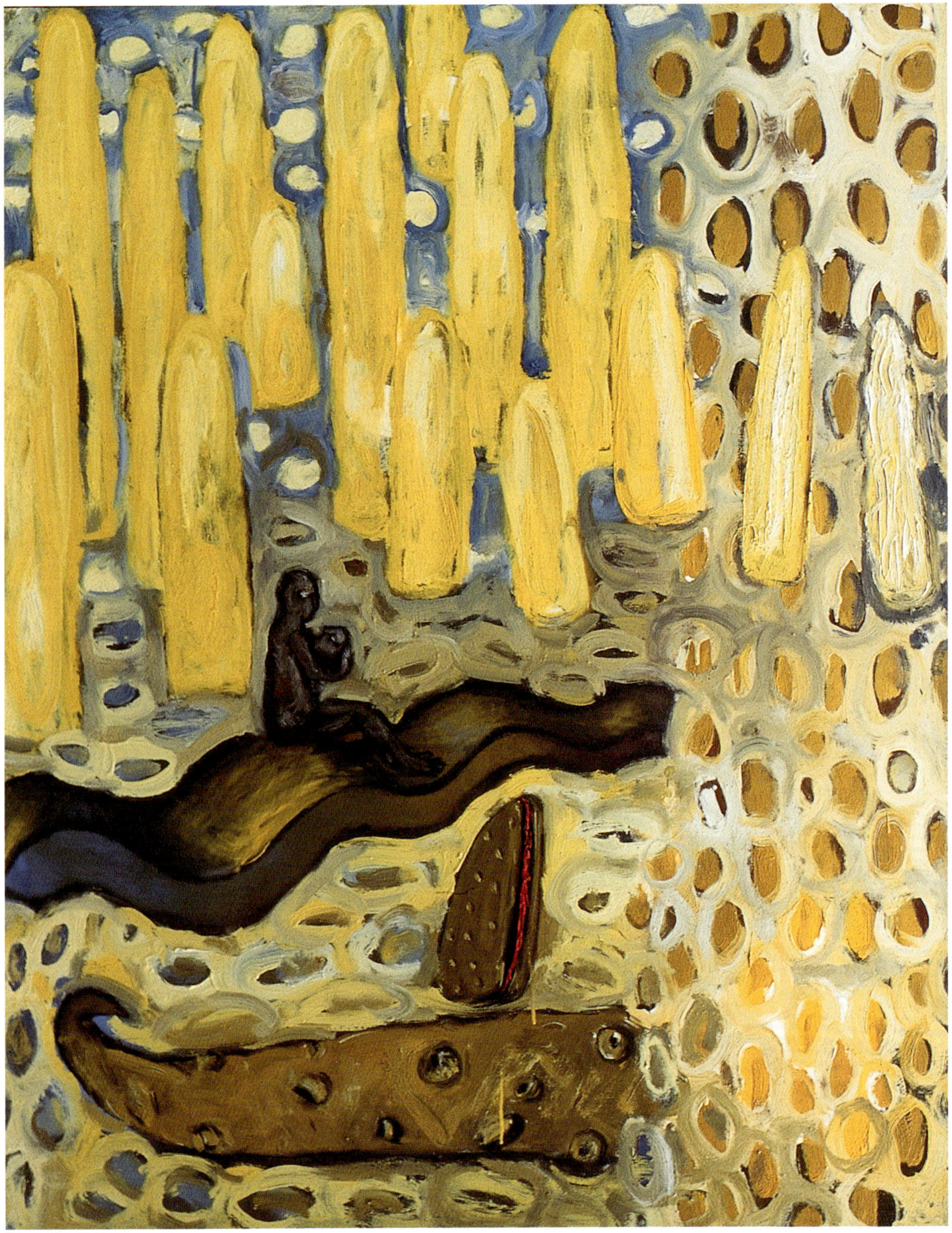

Untitled, oil on canvas, 48x60", 1996

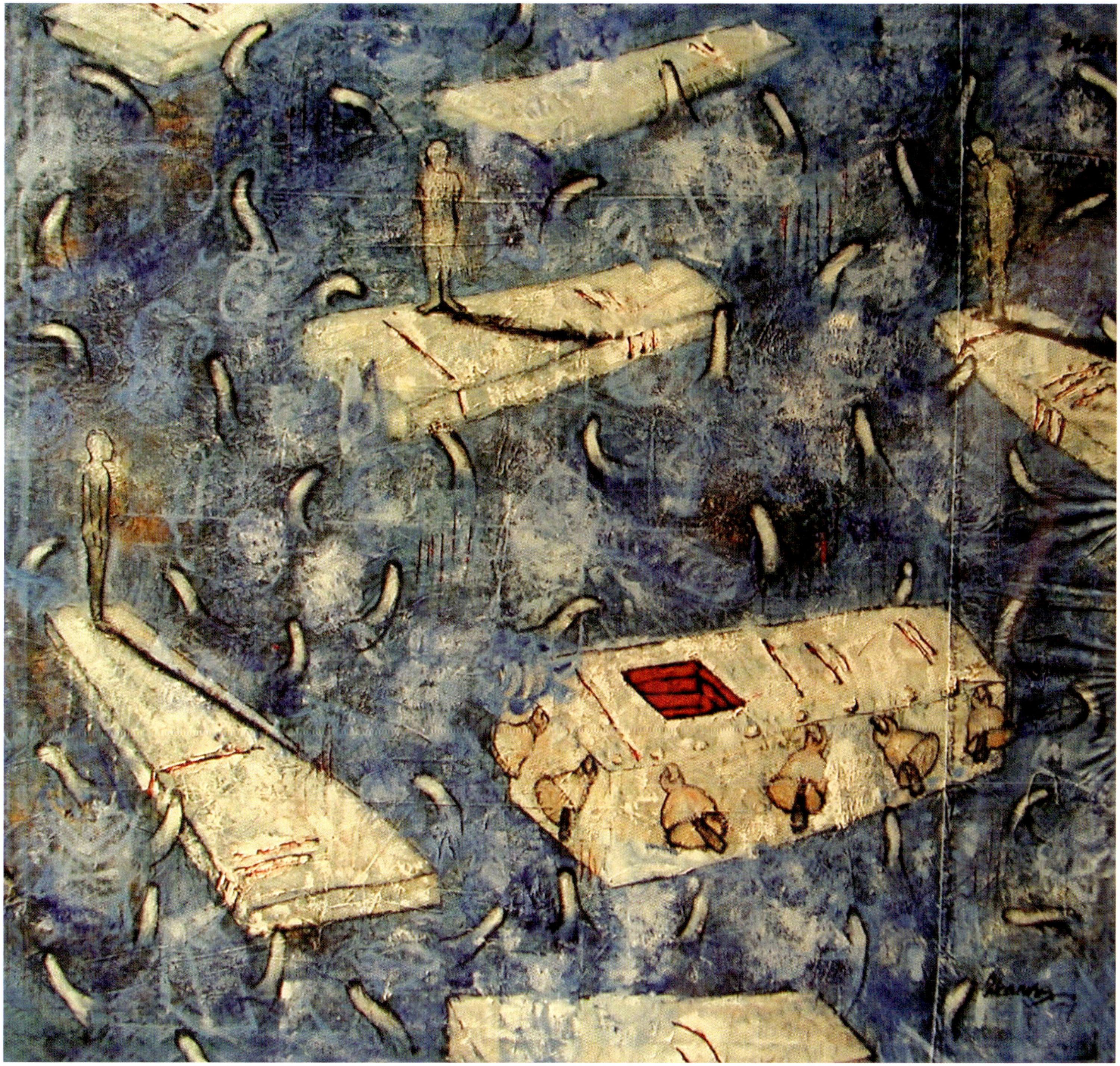

Untitled, acrylic and oil on tarpaulin, 66x66", 1997

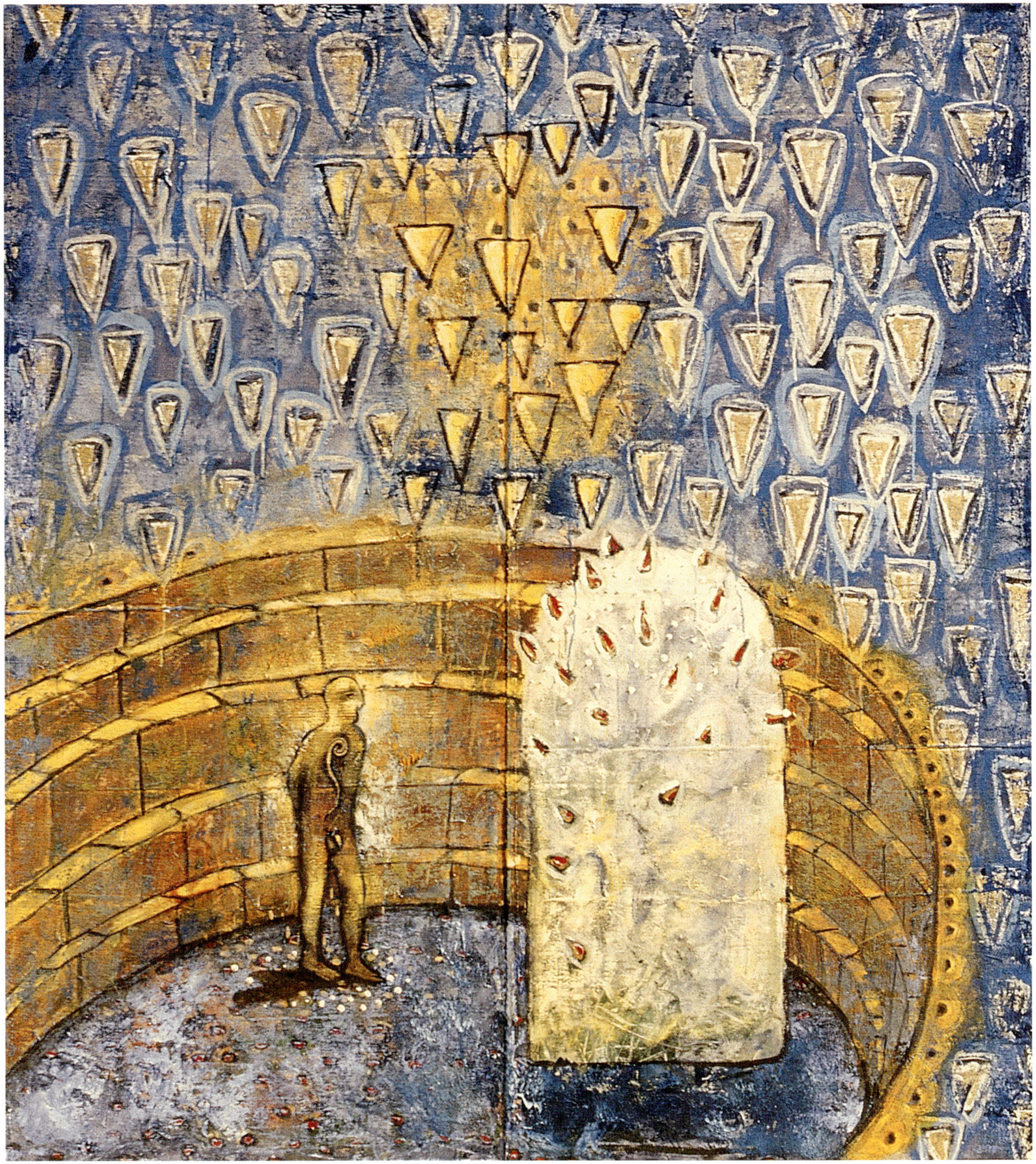

Untitled, oil on tarpaulin, 70x70", 1997

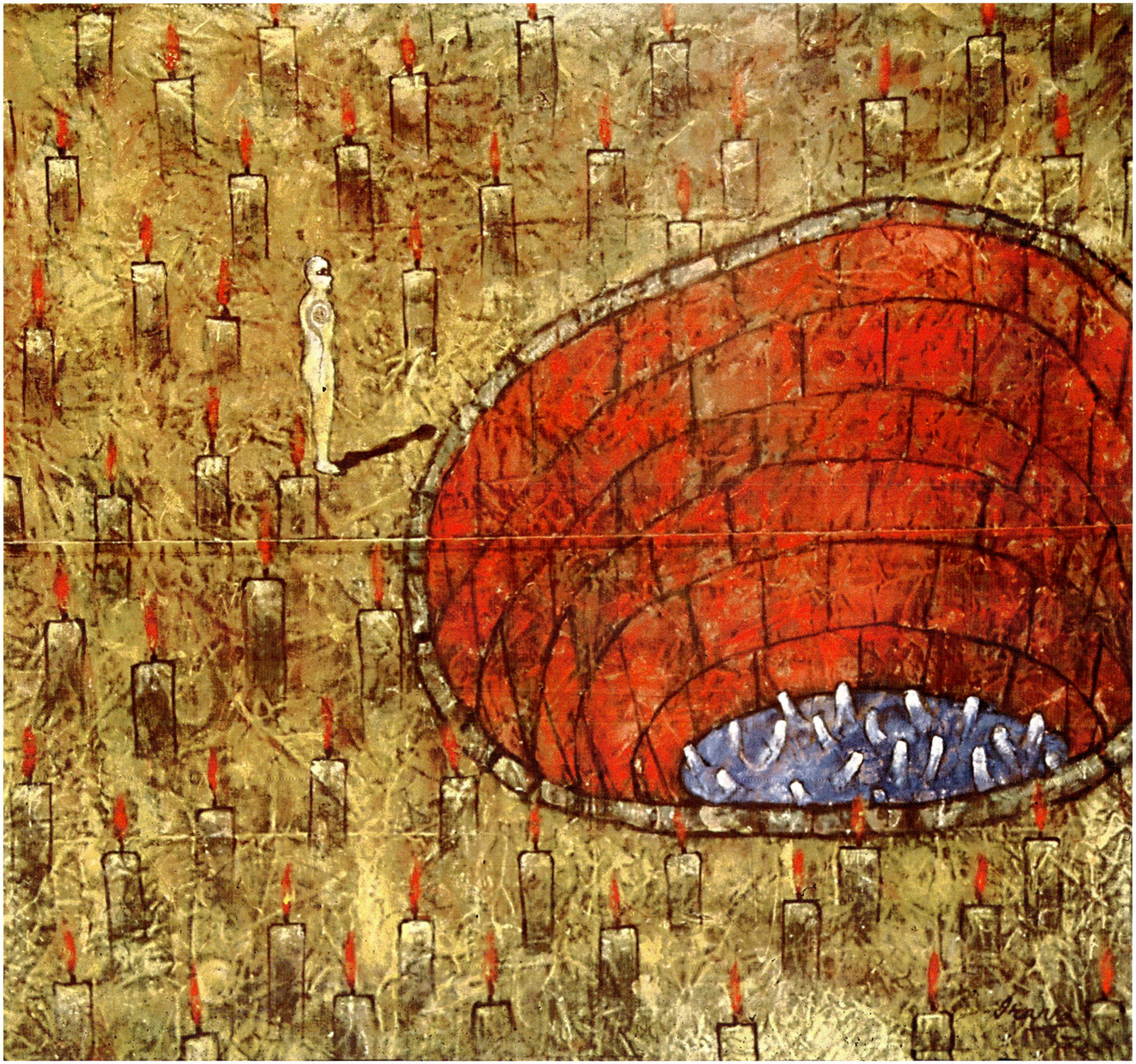

The Well, acrylic on tarpaulin, 66x66", 1997

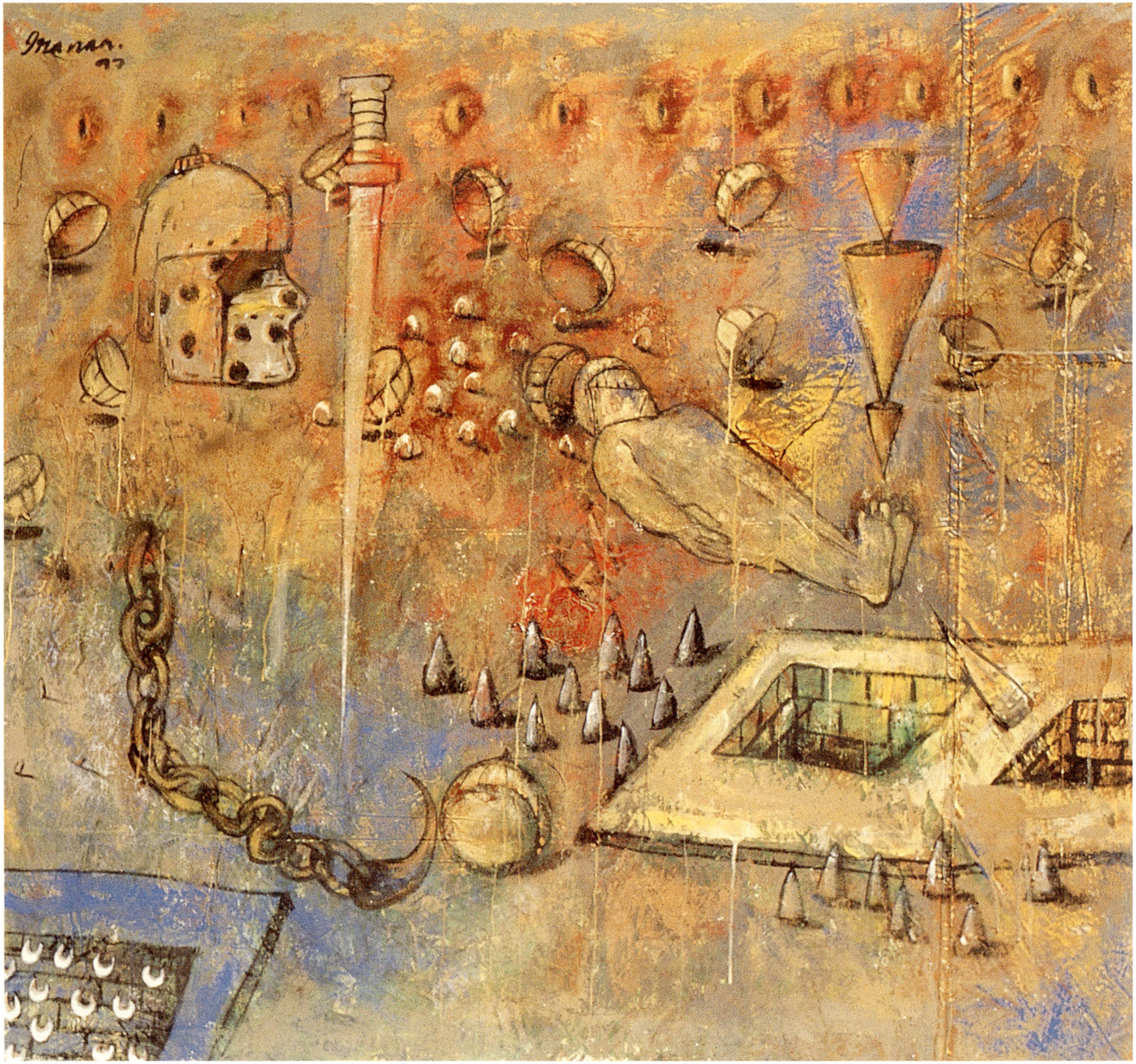

After War, acrylic on tarpaulin, 70x66", 1997

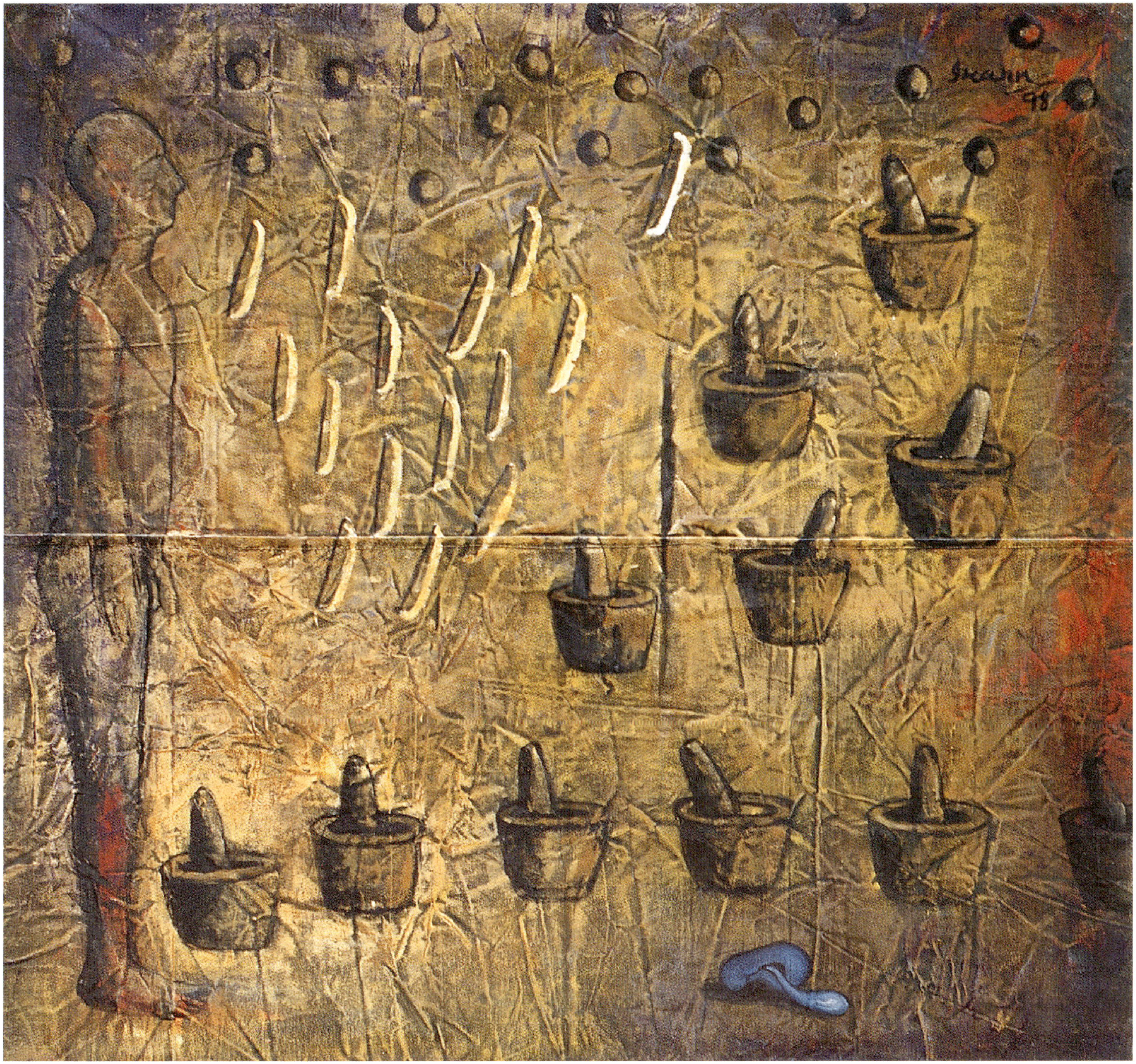

Untitled, acrylic on tarpaulin, 66x66", 1997

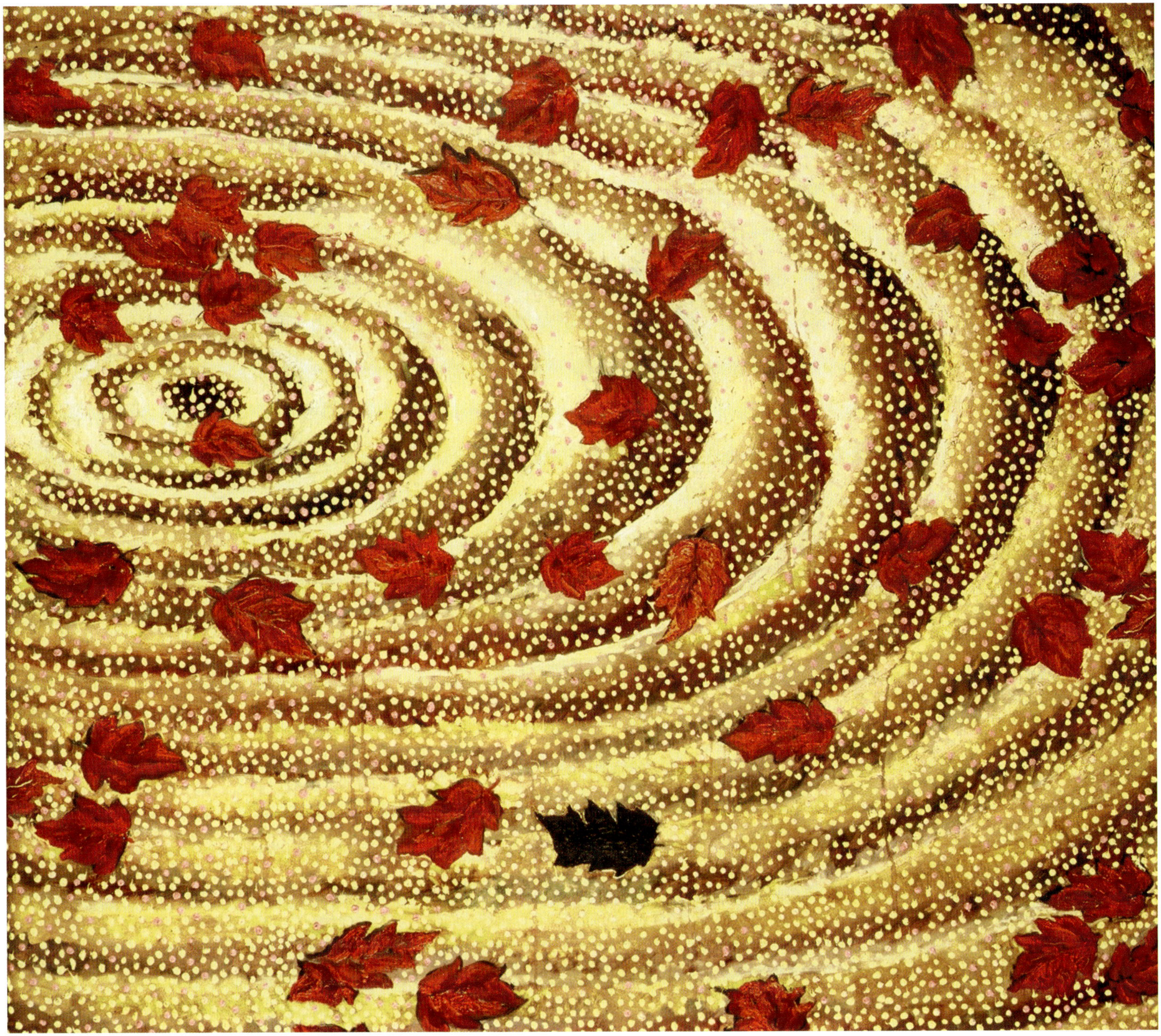

Autumn, acrylic on tarpaulin, 66x52", 1999

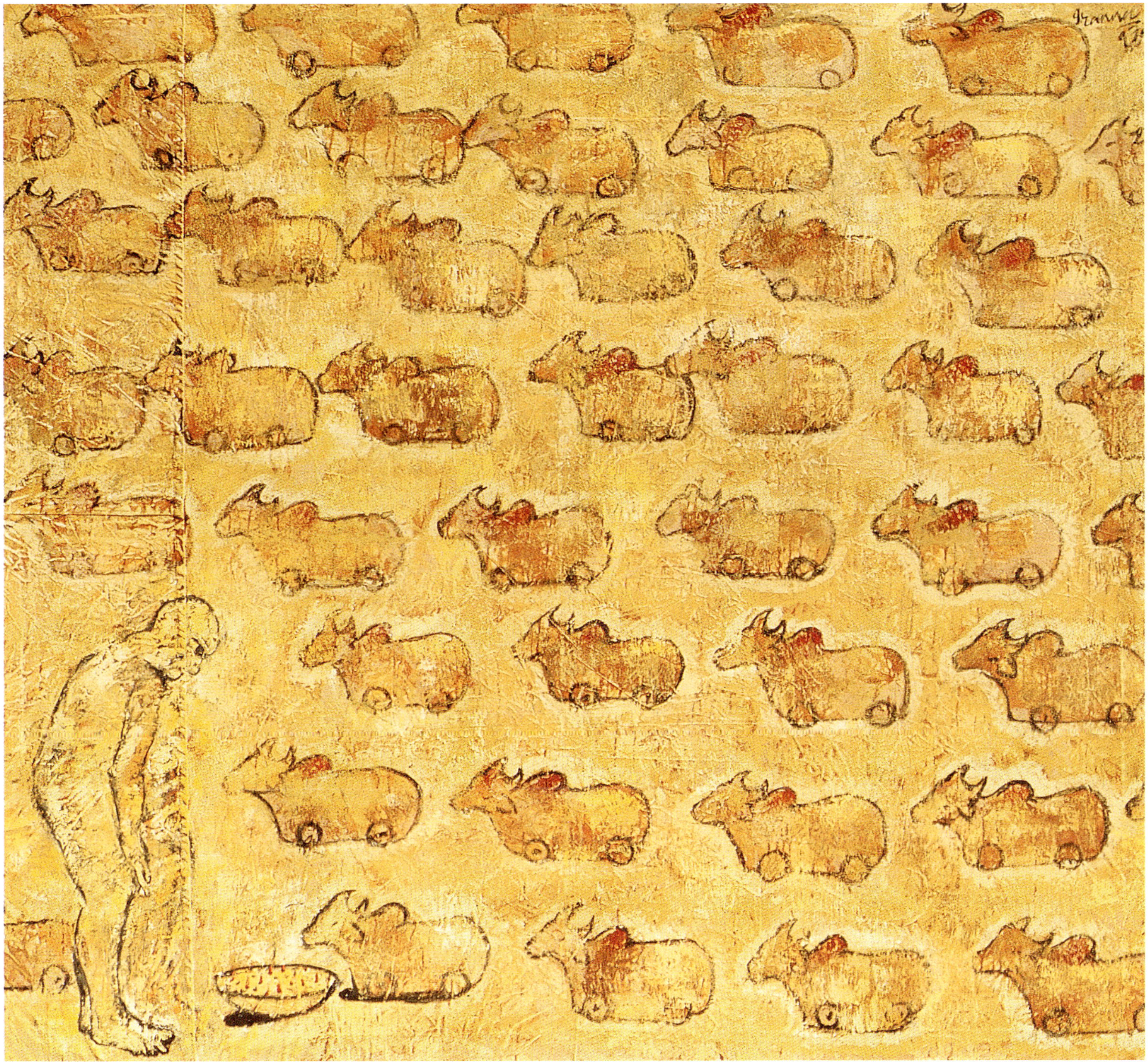

Nandi, acrylic on canvas, 70x66", 1997

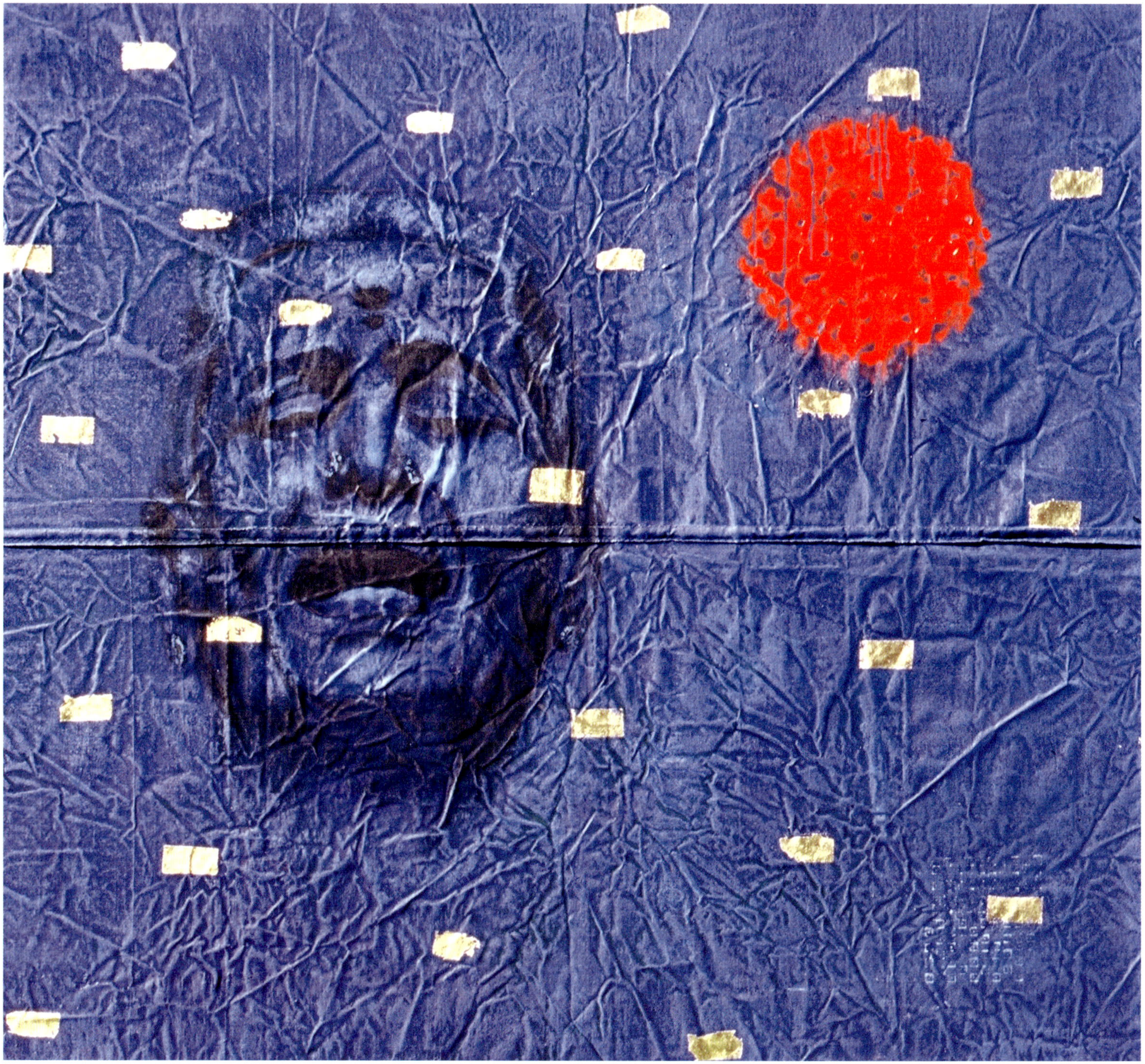

The Sound Silence, acrylic on tarpaulin, 70x66", 1998

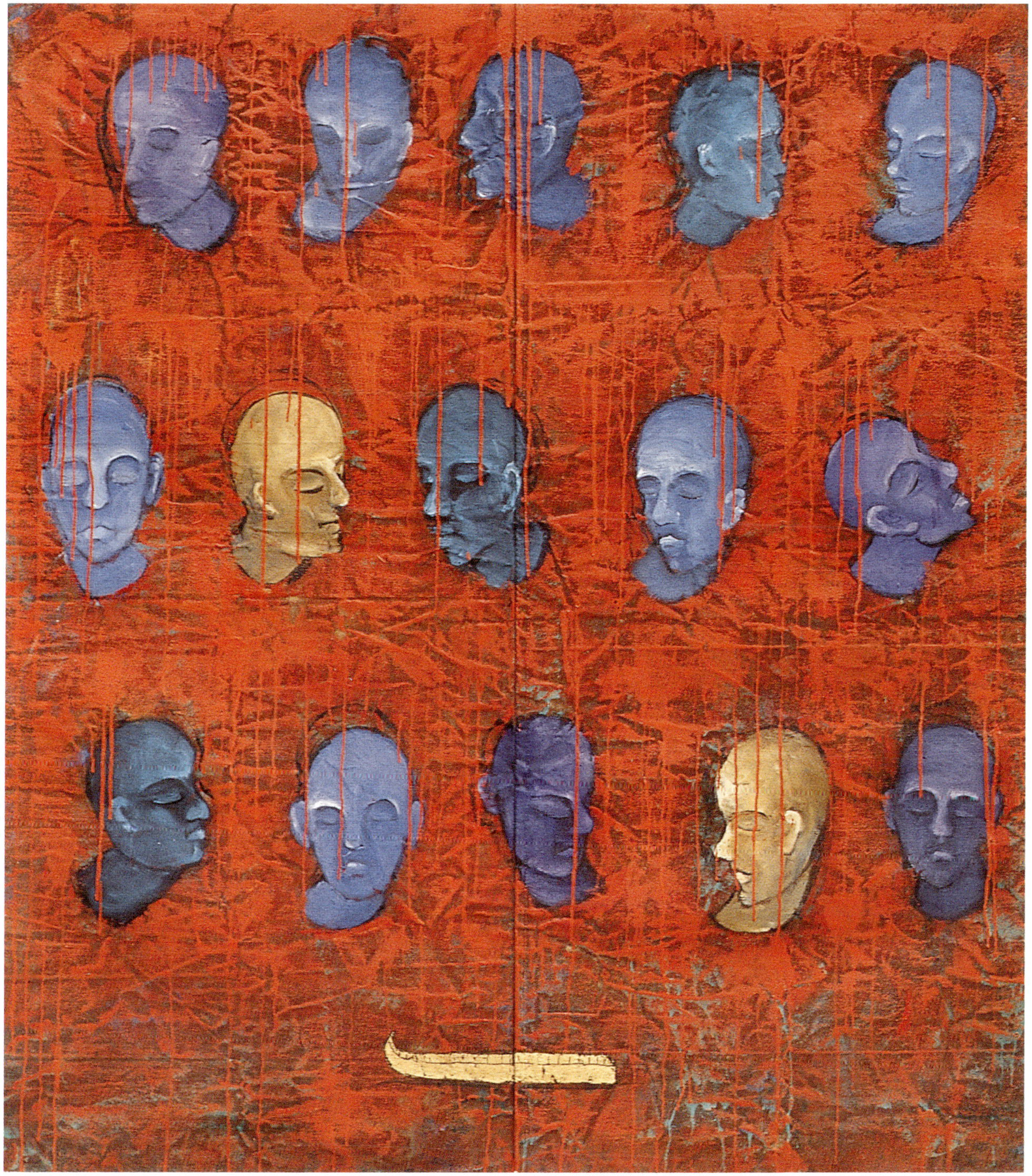

Untitled, acrylic and gold foil on tarpaulin, 66x66", 1998

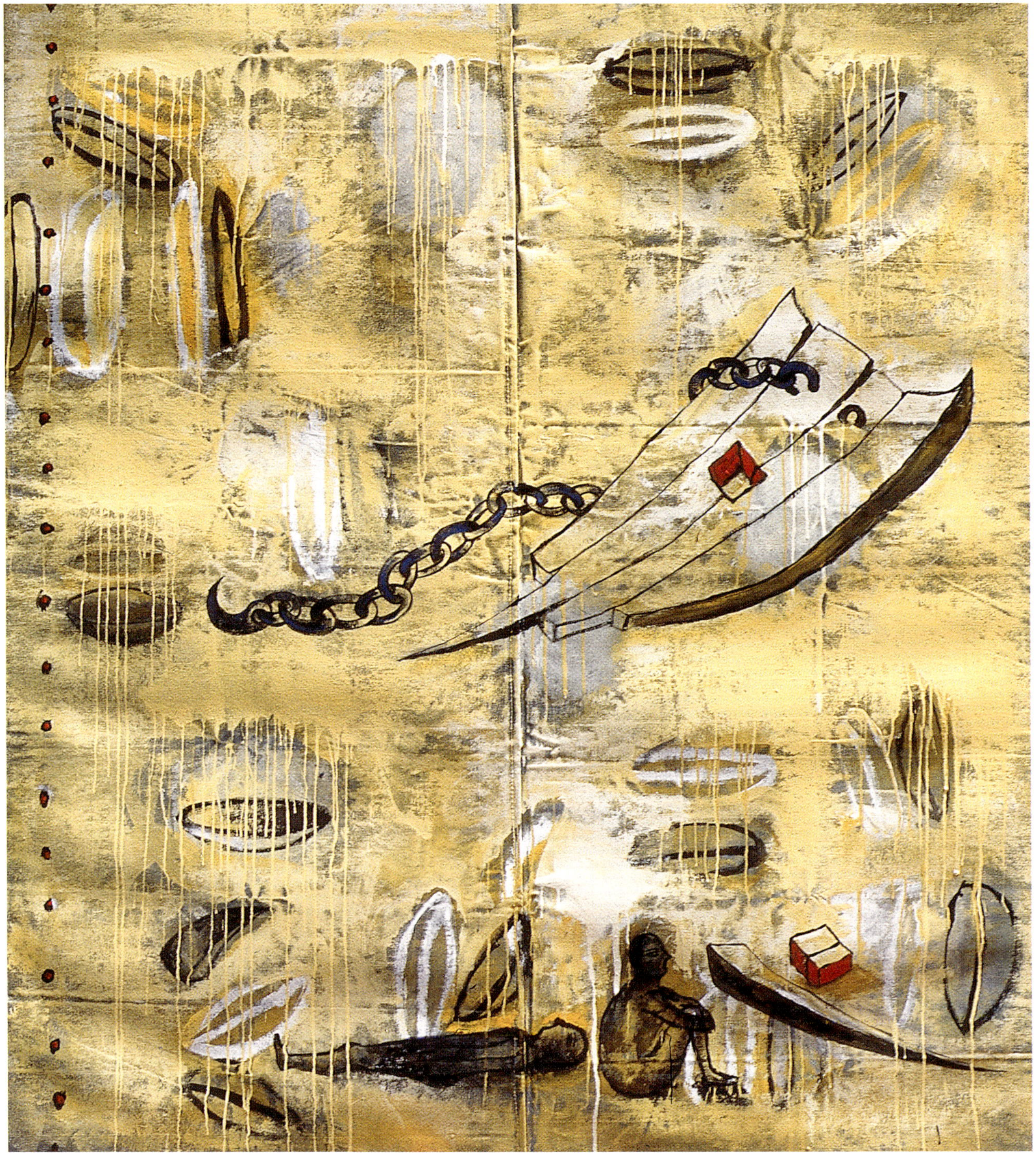

Untitled, acrylic on tarpaulin, 66x72", 1998

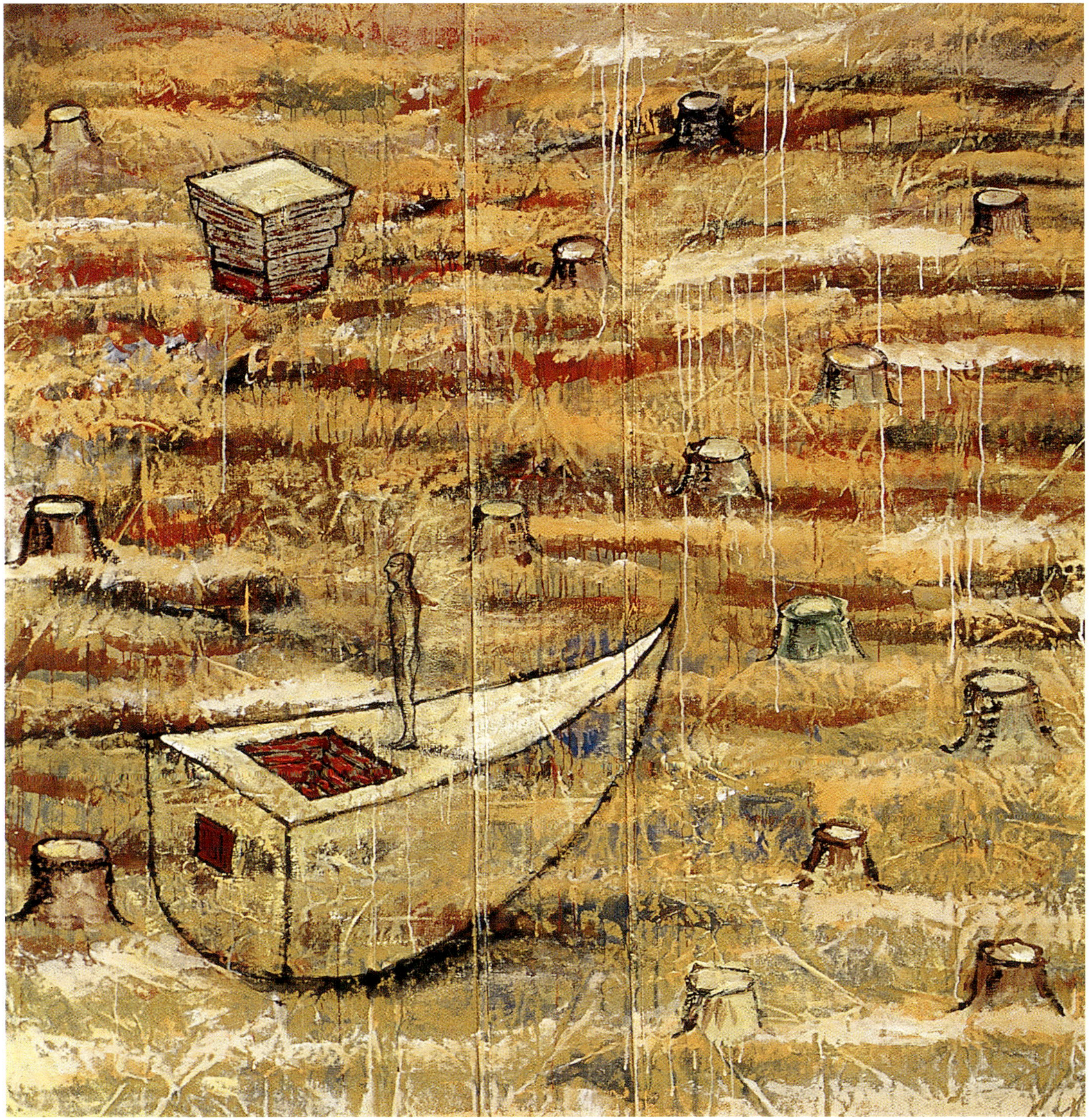

The Field, acrylic on tarpaulin, 72x72”, 1998

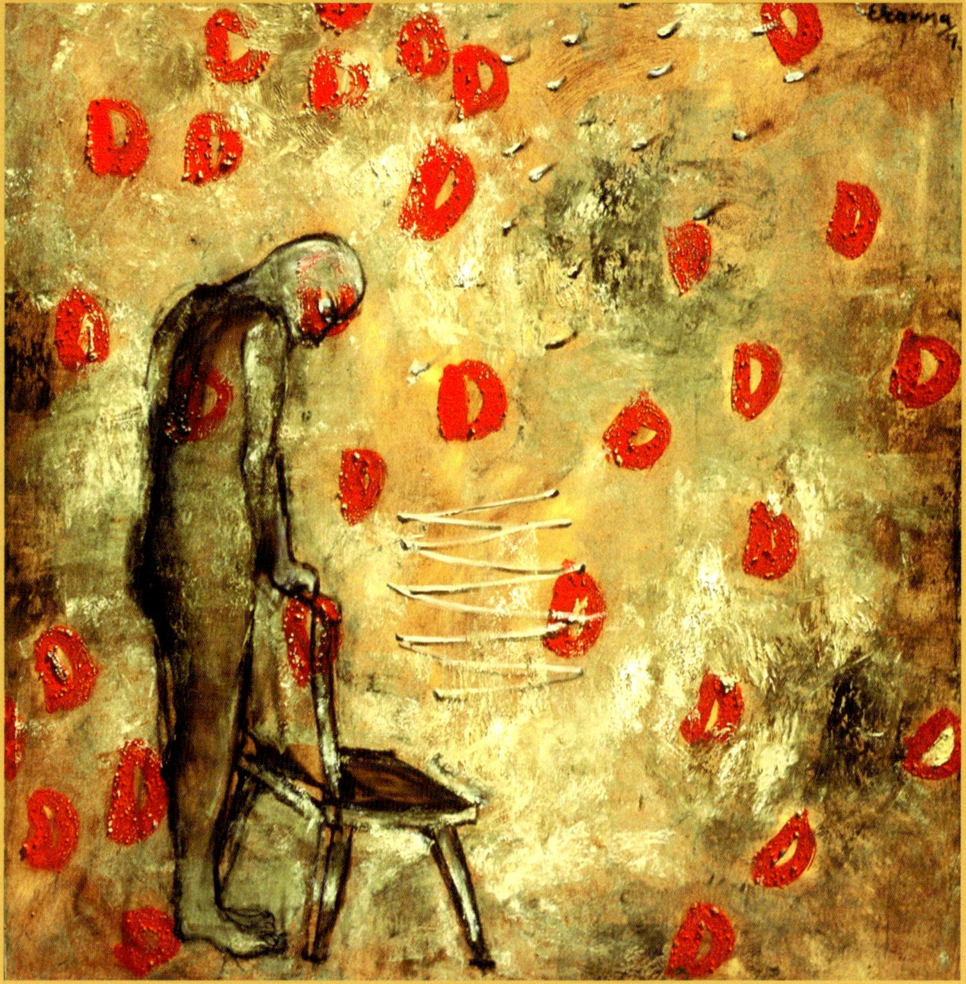

Untitled, oil on canvas, 48x48", 1997

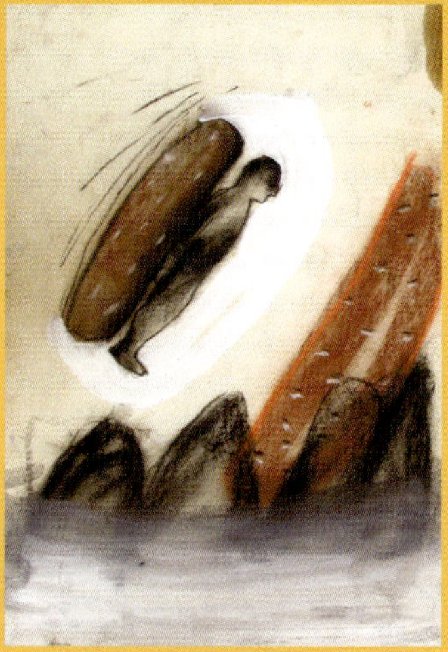

Mixed medium, 15x22", 1994

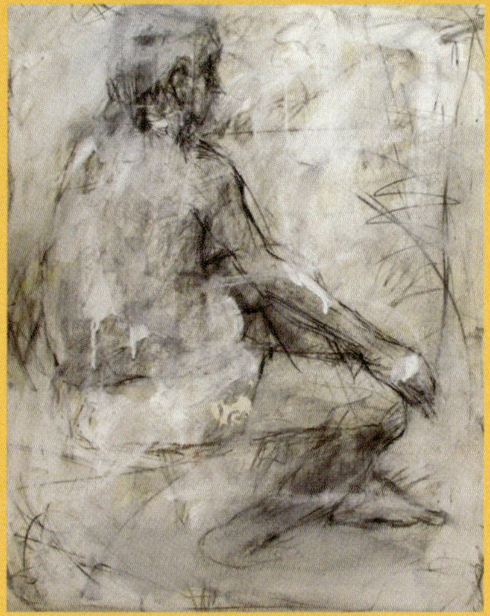

Mixed medium on paper, 30x46", 1994

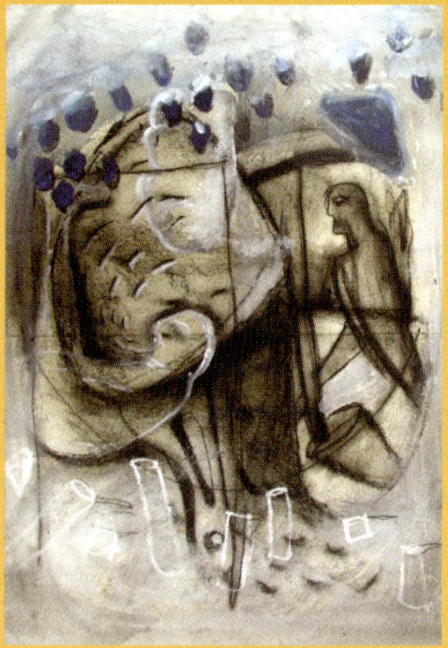

Mixed medium, 15x22", 1994

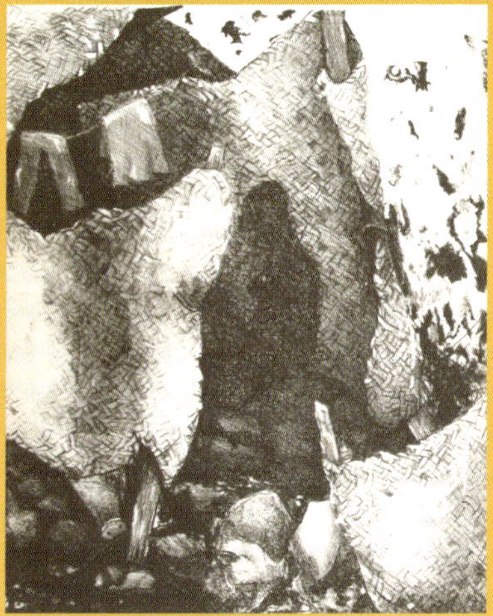

Lithograph, 11x18", 1990

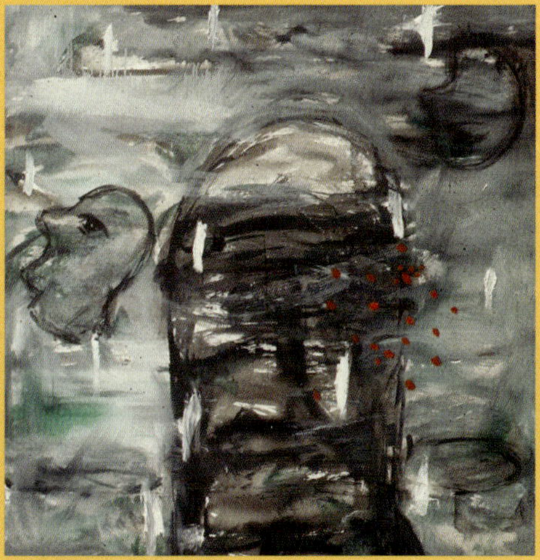

Acrylic on canvas, 48x48", 1995

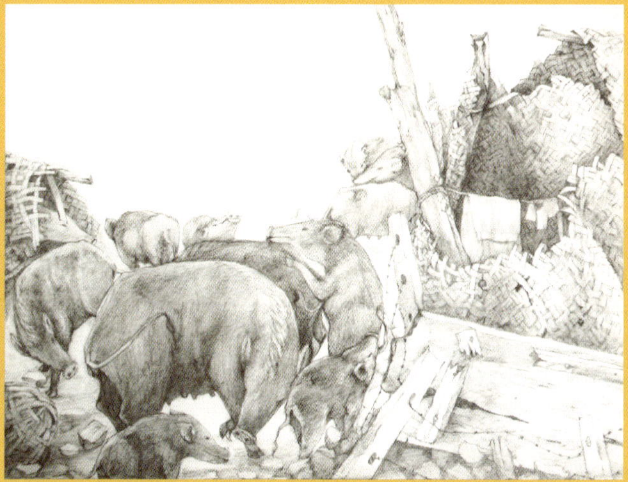

Pencil on paper, 18x12", 1989

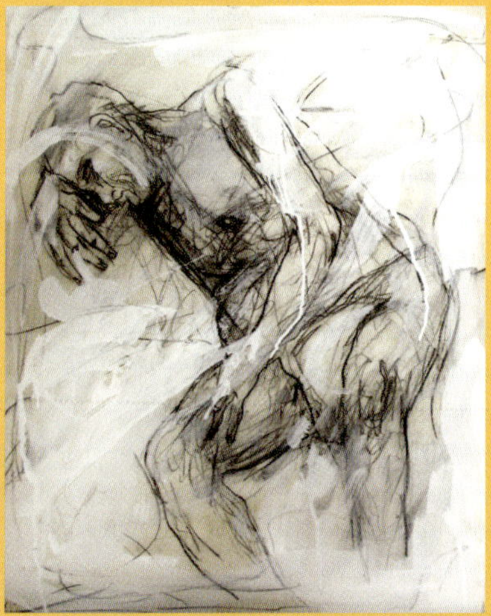

Mixed medium on paper, 30x48", 1993

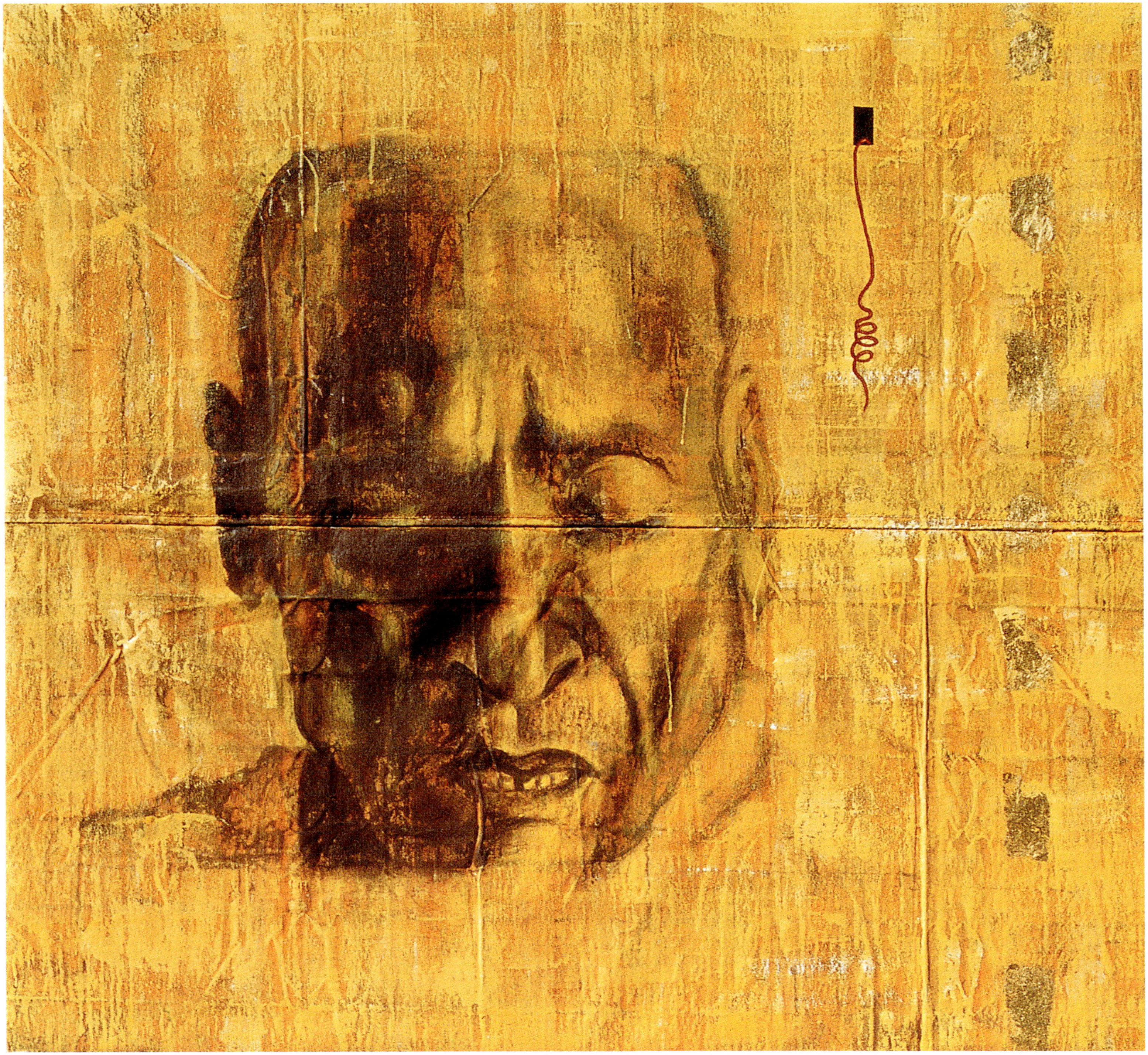

Homage to Monsoon, acrylic on tarpaulin, 66x66", 1998

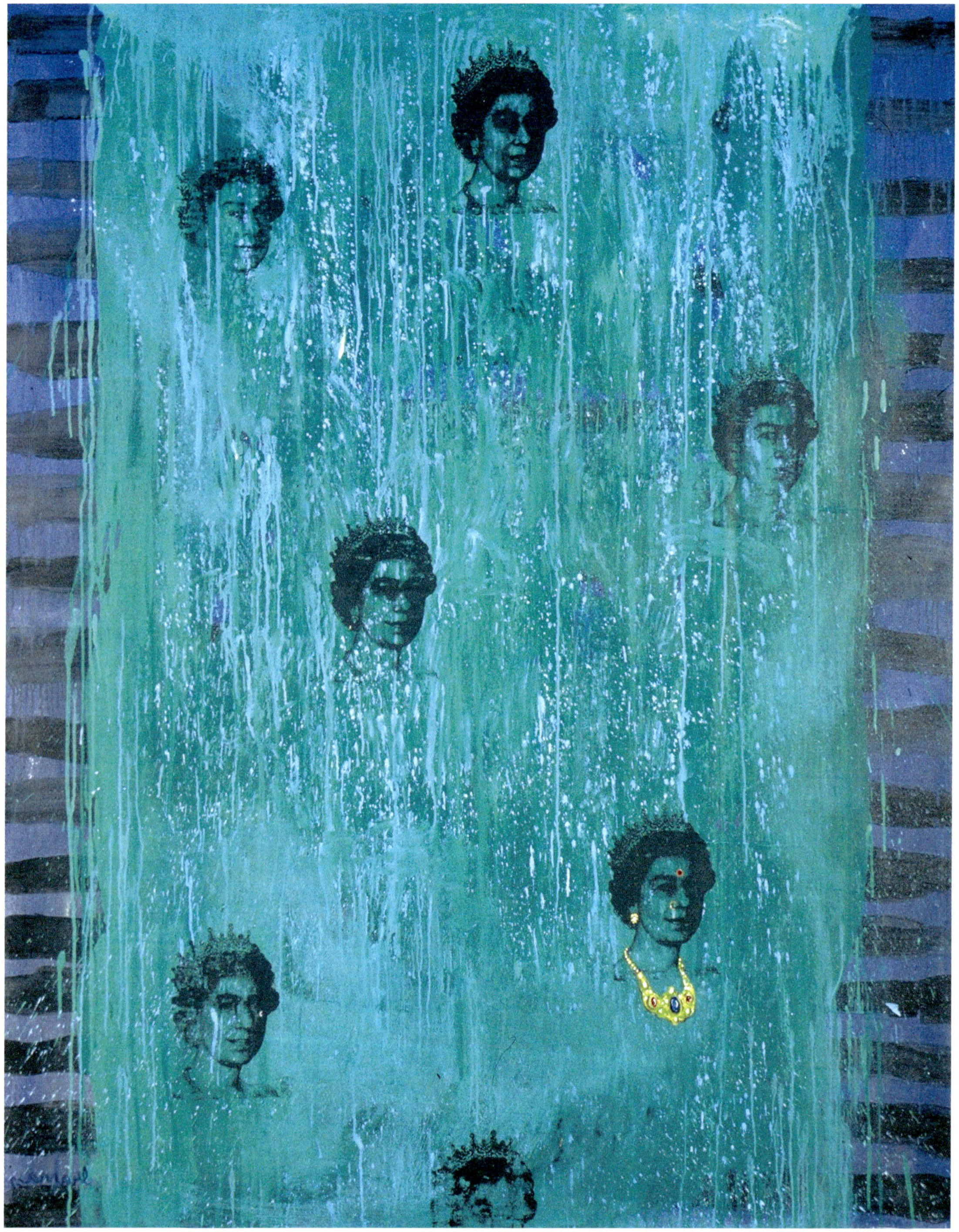

Queen Celebrating her Birthday, acrylic on canvas, 52x66", 1999

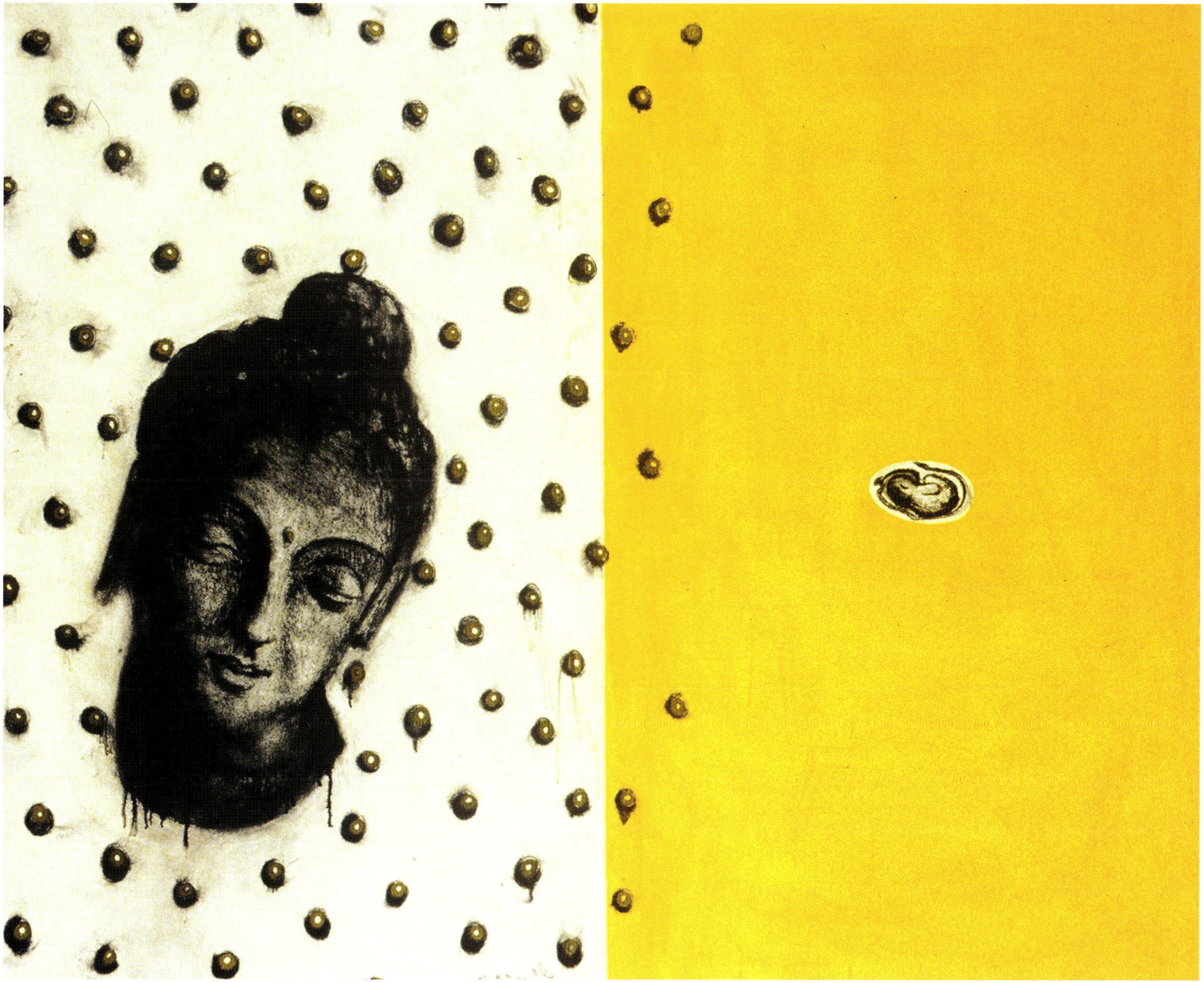

The Buddha, acrylic on canvas, 66x52", 1999

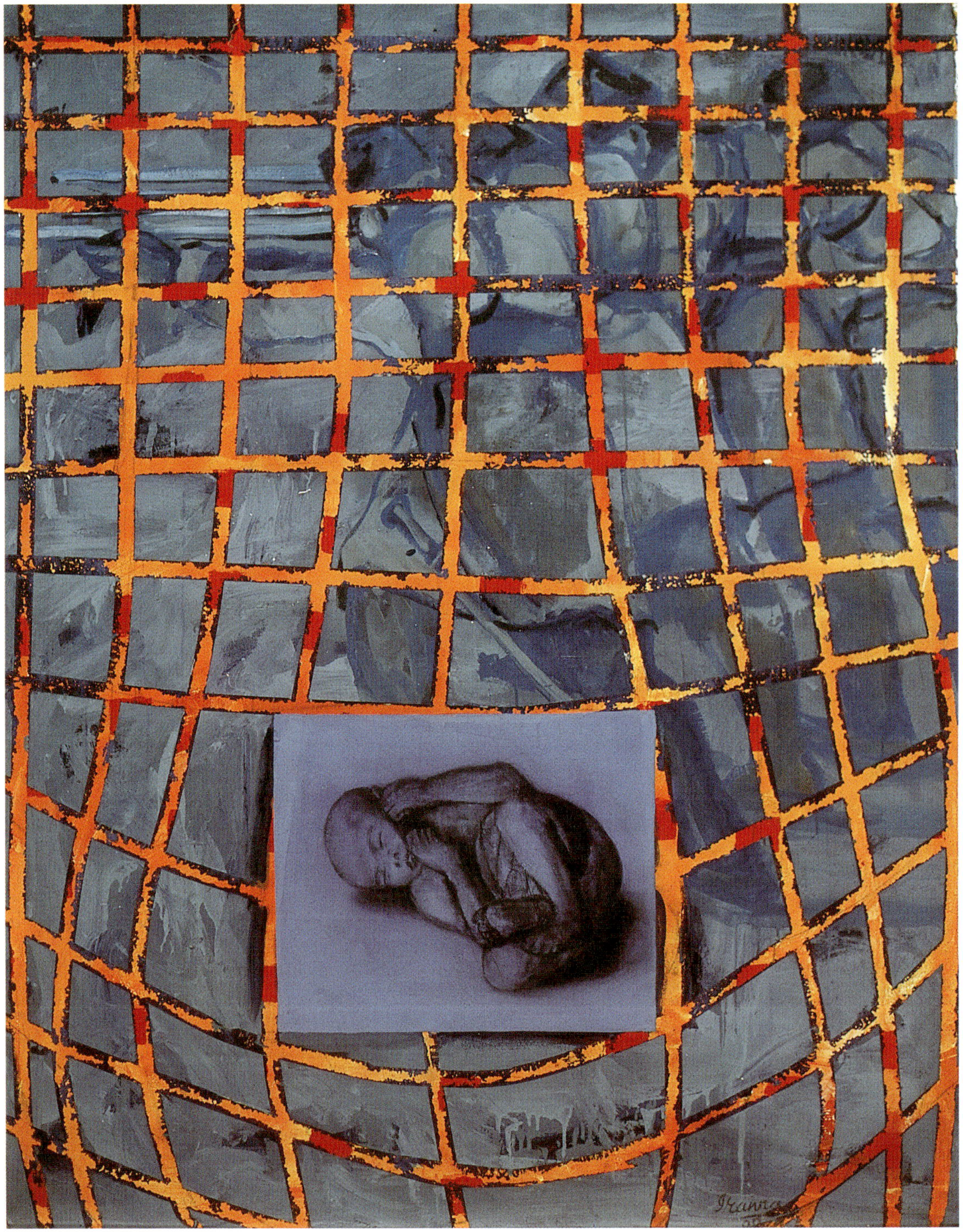

Soldier in the Womb, oil on canvas, 54x68”, 2000

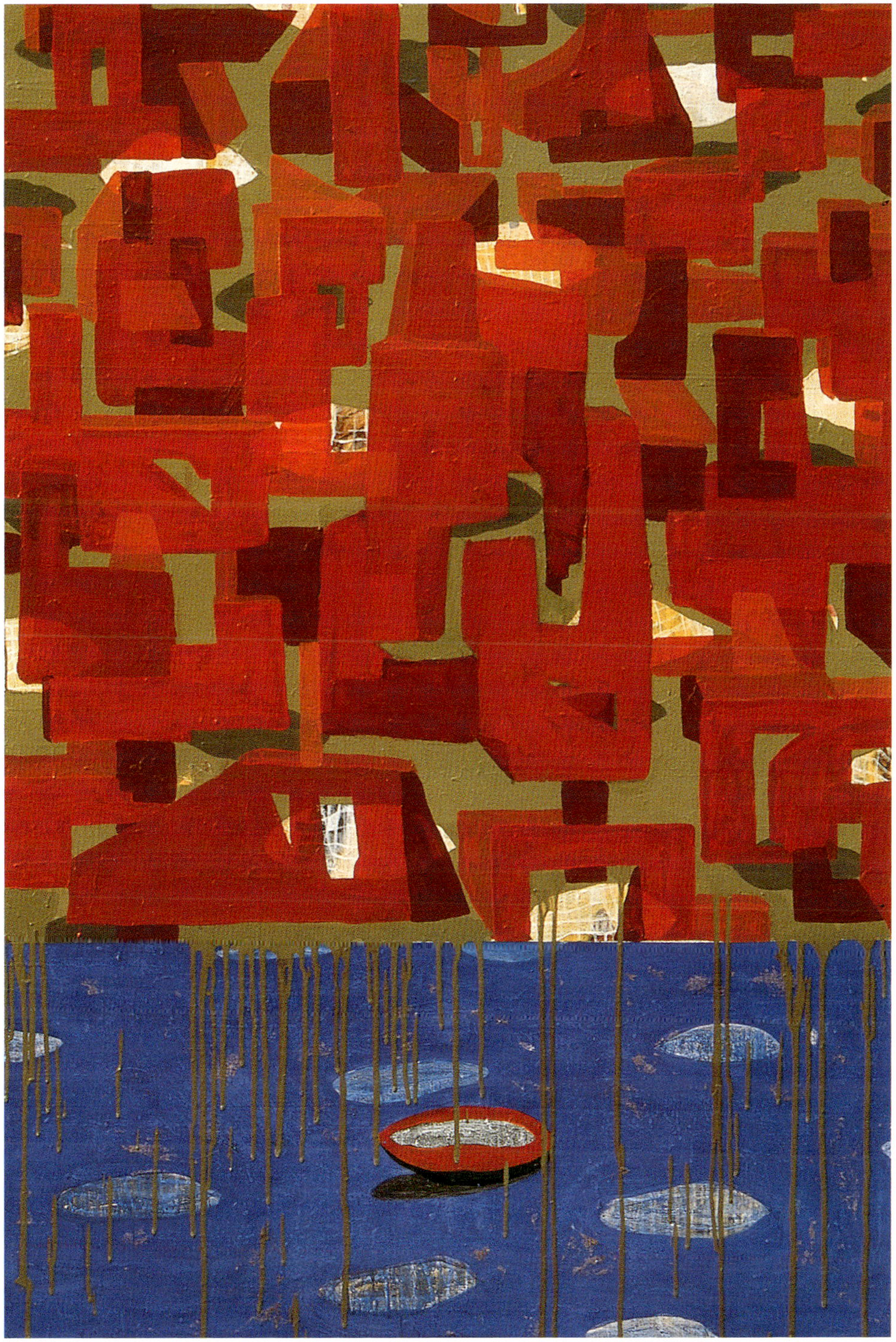

Untitled, acrylic on canvas, 48x72", 2000

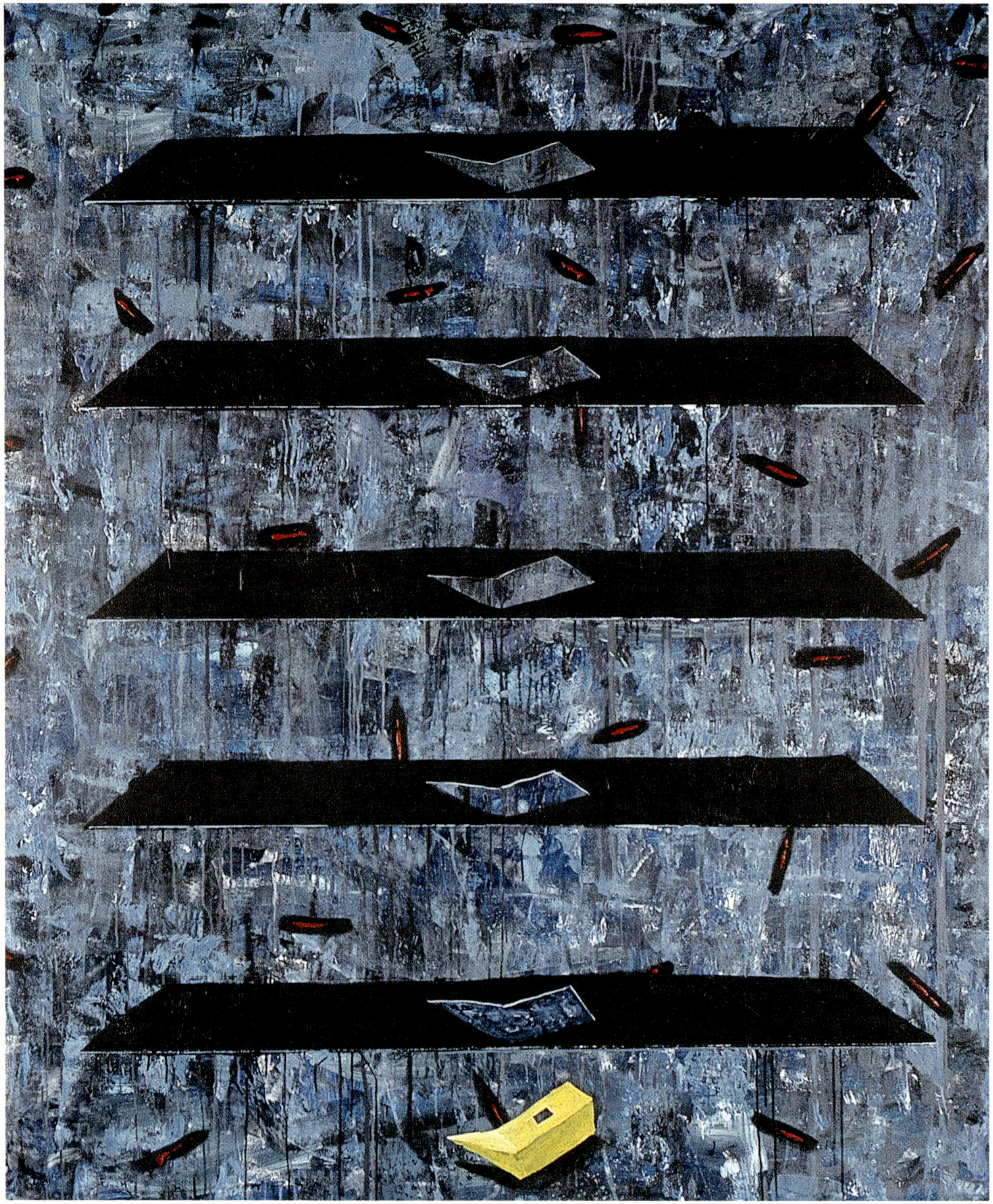

Untitled, acrylic on canvas, 63x70”, 2000

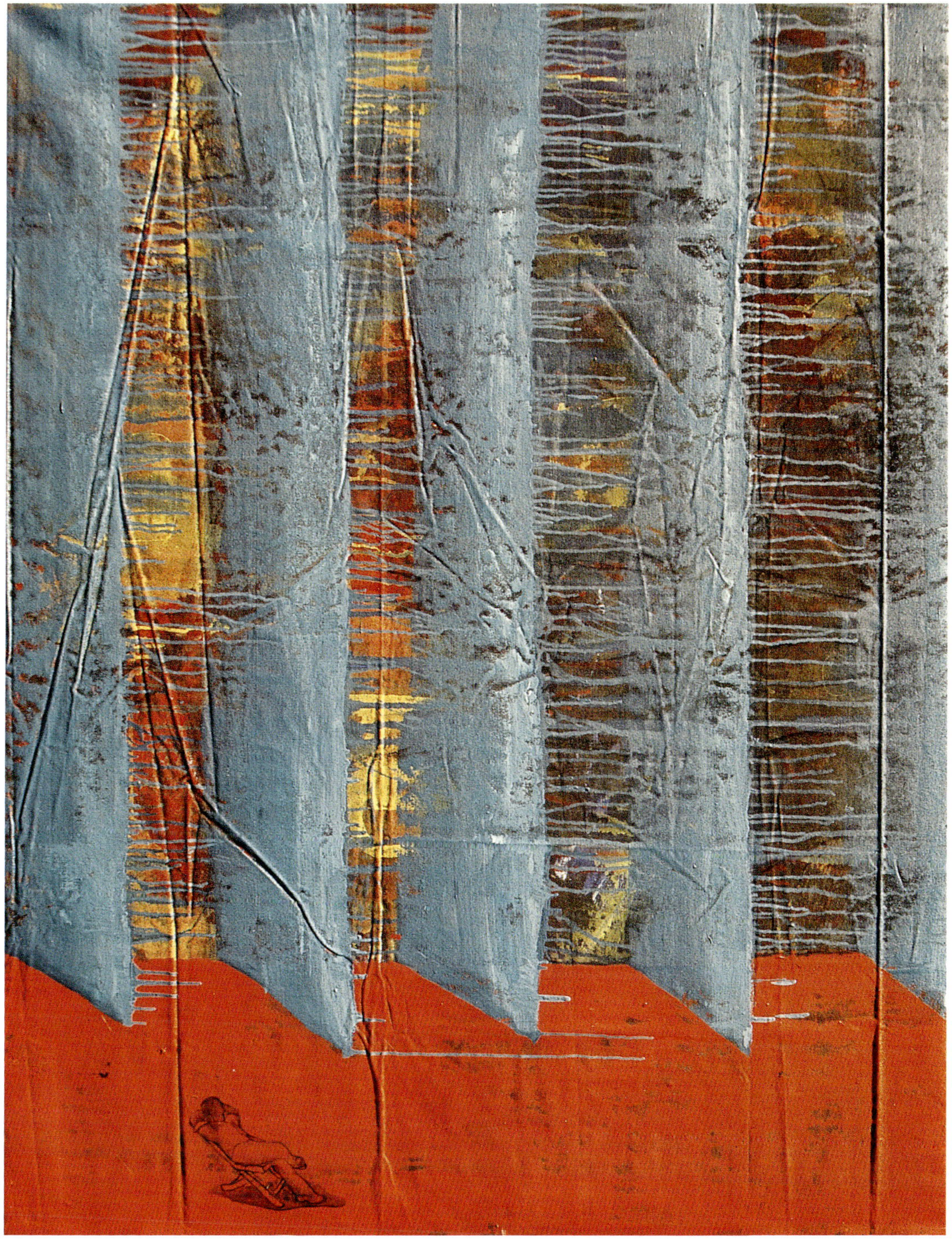

Untitled, acrylic on tarpaulin, 52x66", 2002

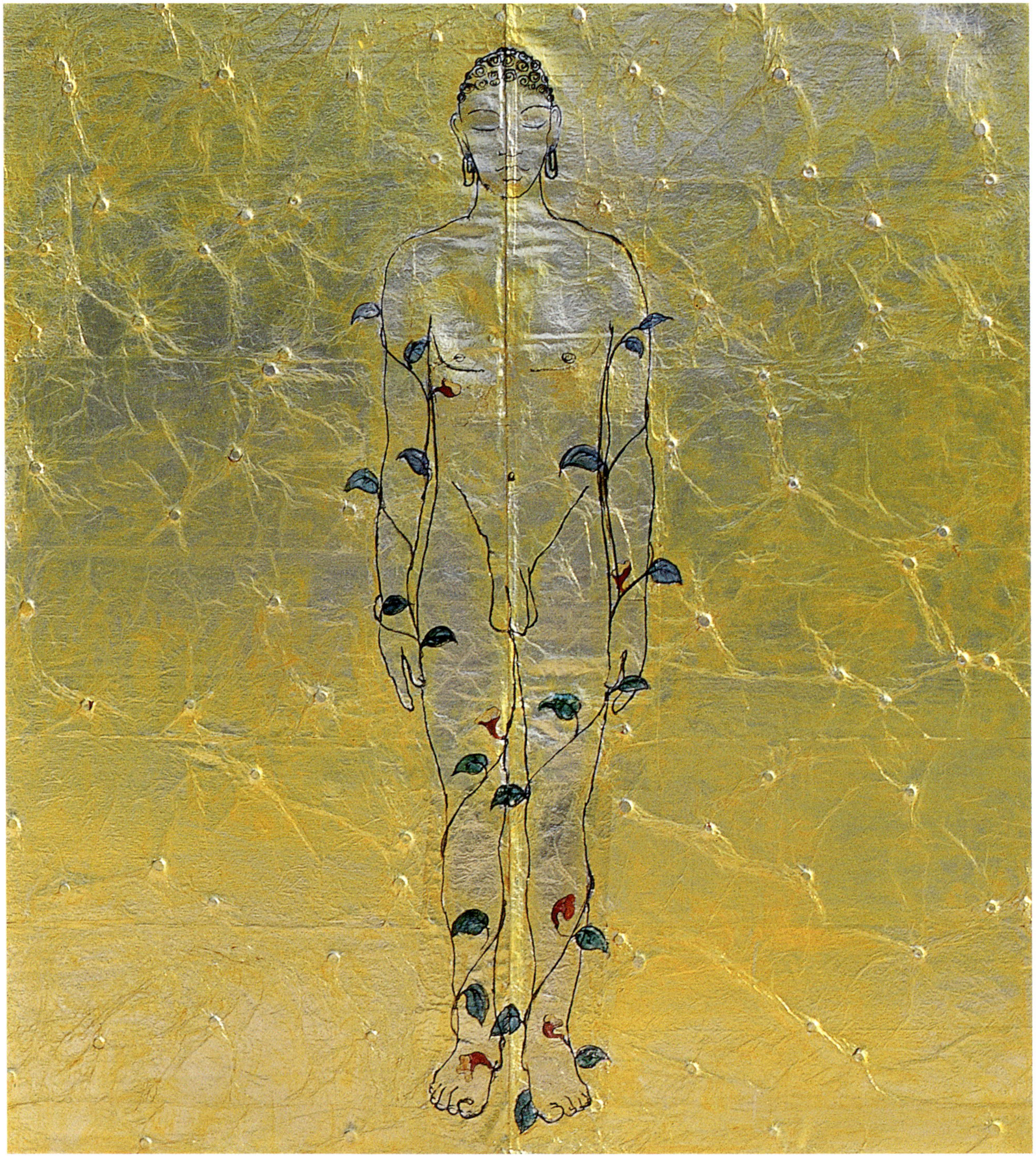

Untitled, aluminium on canvas, 70x70", 1999

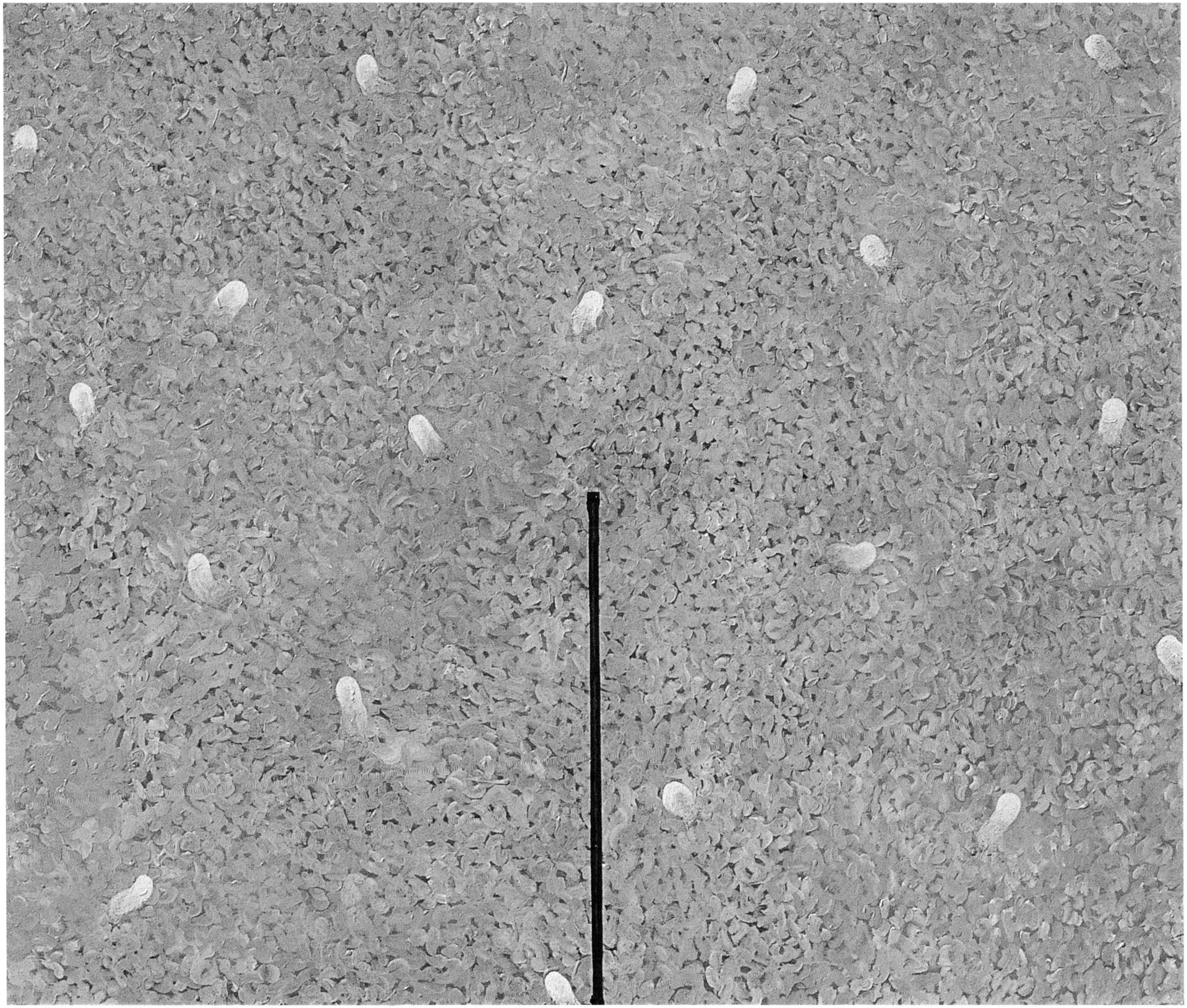

Untitled, acrylic on canvas, 66x52", 1999

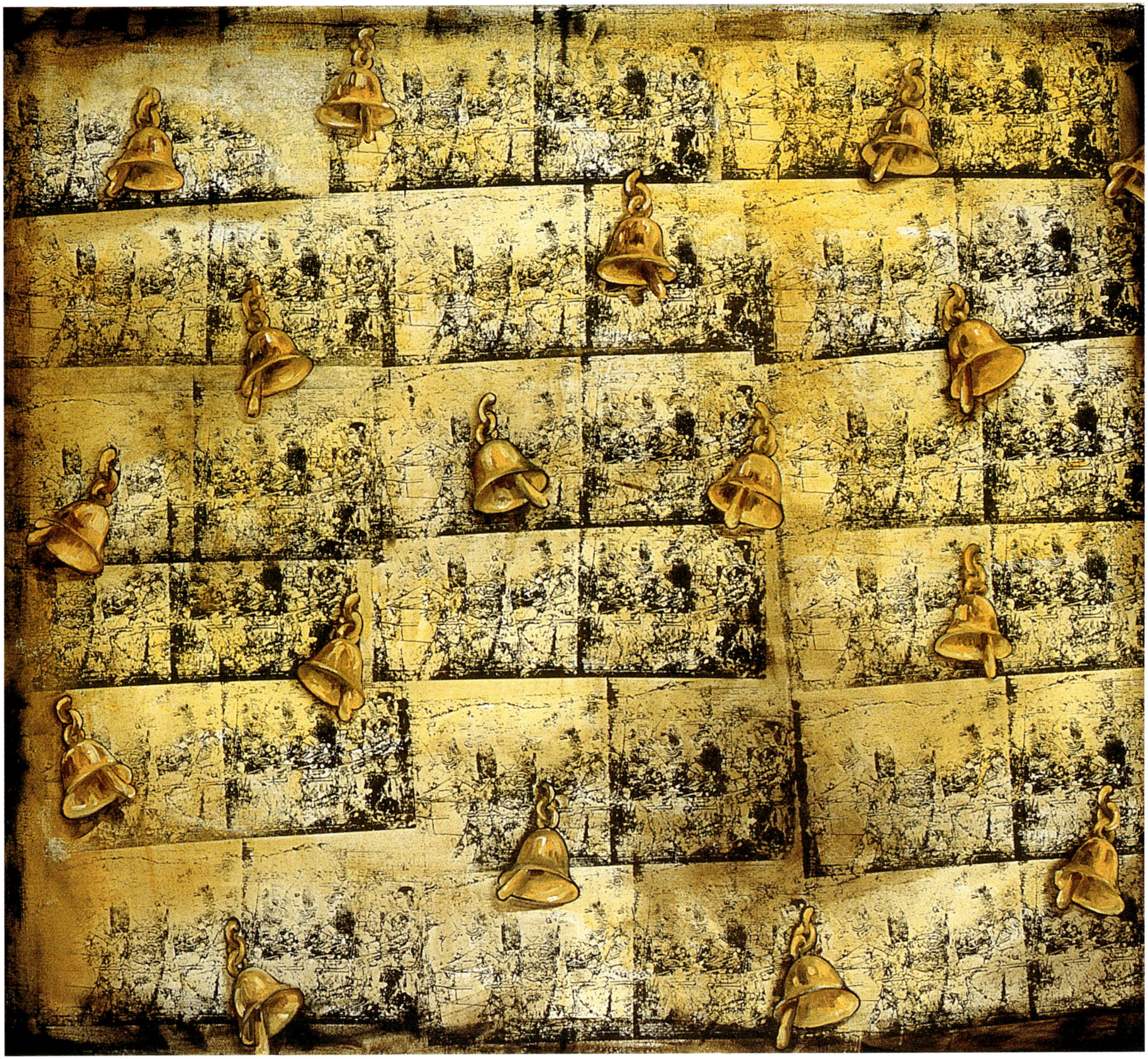

Bells, acrylic on canvas, 70x63", 2000

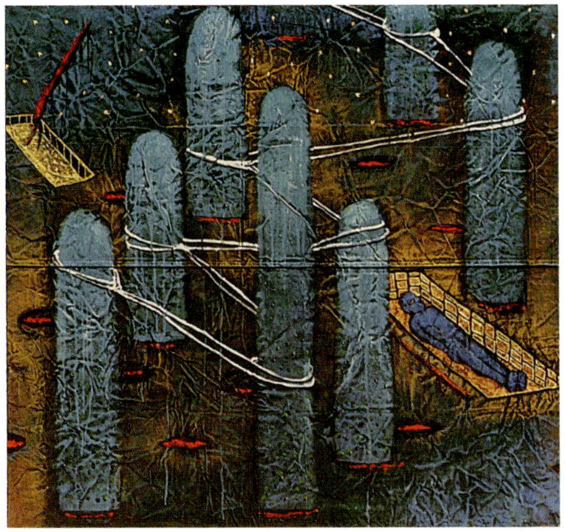
Acrylic on tarpaulin, 72x72", 1998

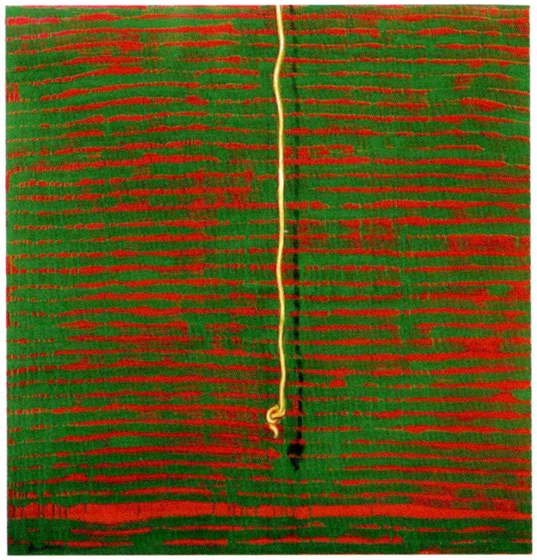
Acrylic on canvas, 48x48", 2004

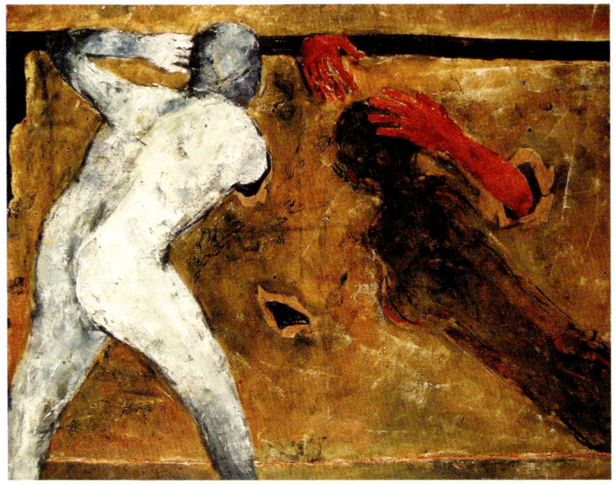
Oil on canvas, 52x42", 1995

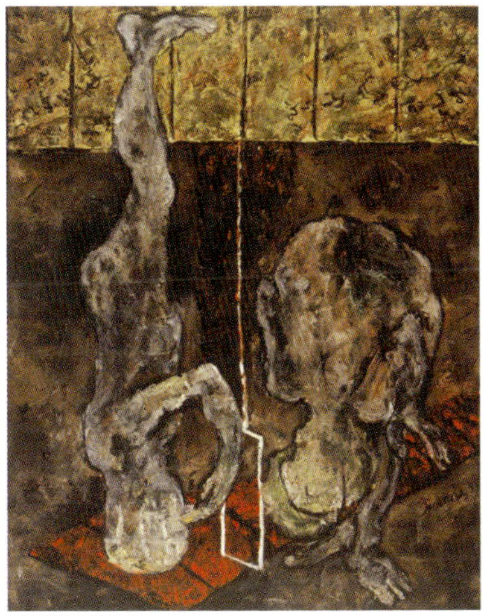
Oil on canvas, 48x60", 1994

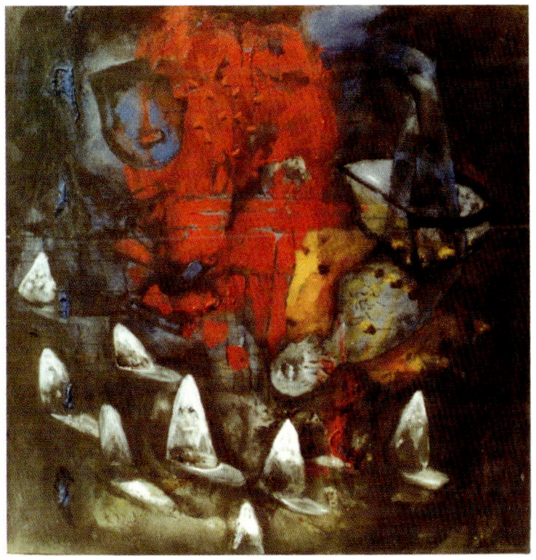
Acrylic on canvas, 48x48", 1995

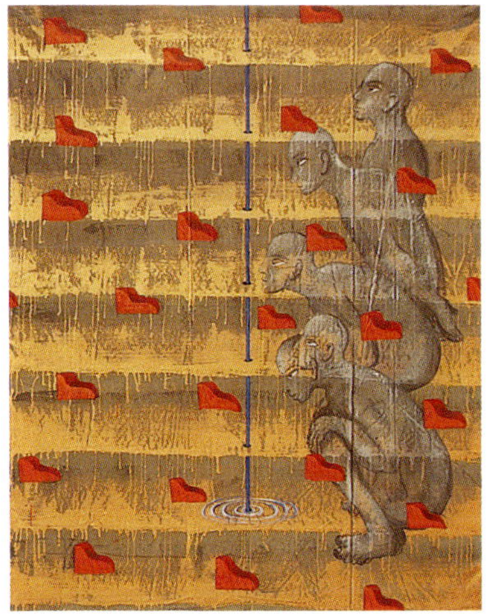
Acrylic on tarpaulin, 48x66", 1998

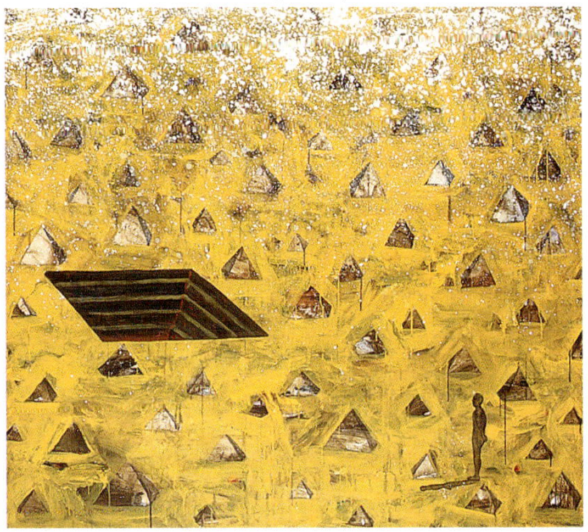
Acrylic on canvas, 66x52", 2000

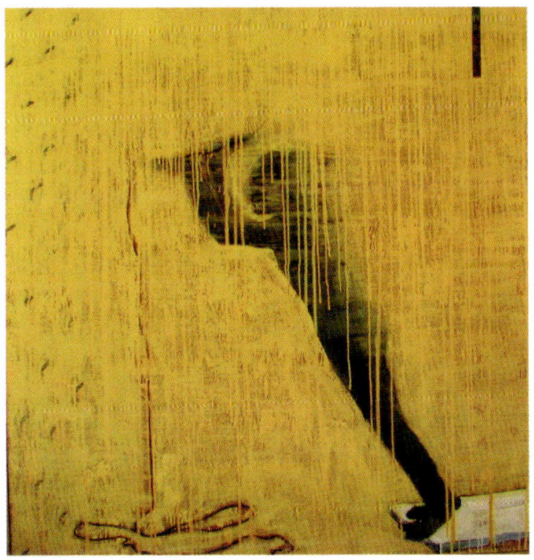
Acrylic on canvas, 60x60", 2003

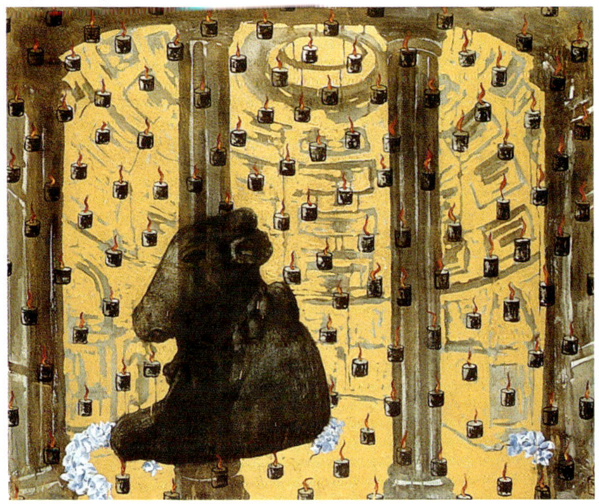
Acrylic on canvas, 66x52", 1999

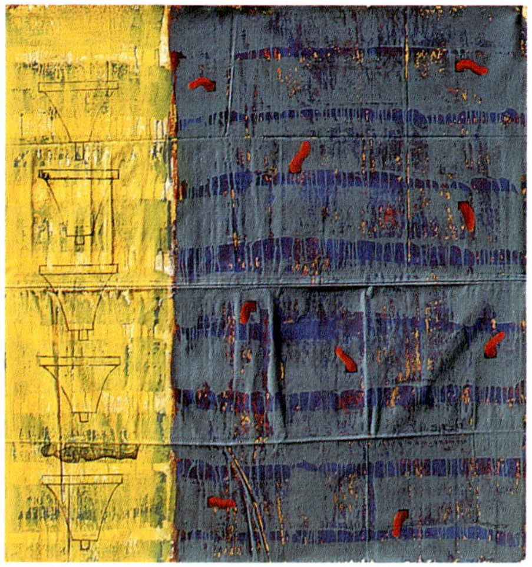
Acrylic on tarpaulin, 66x66", 2000

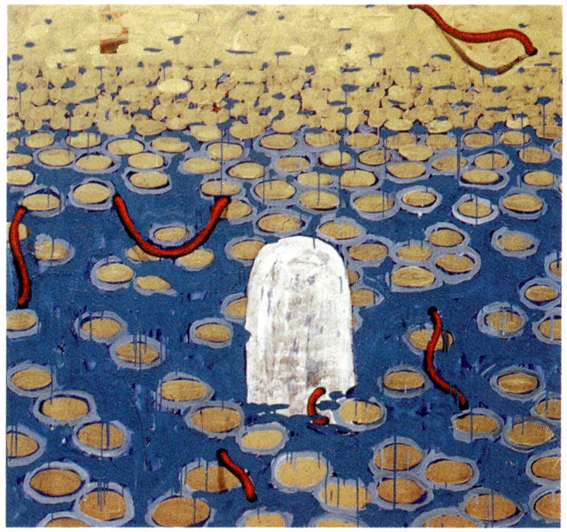
Acrylic on canvas, 66x52", 1996

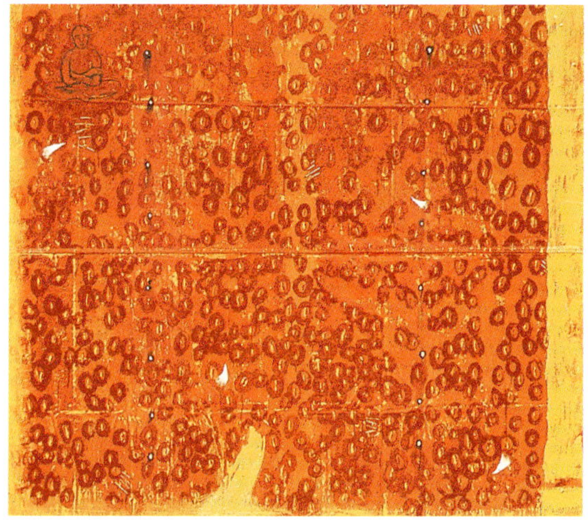
Acrylic on canvas, 66x66", 2000

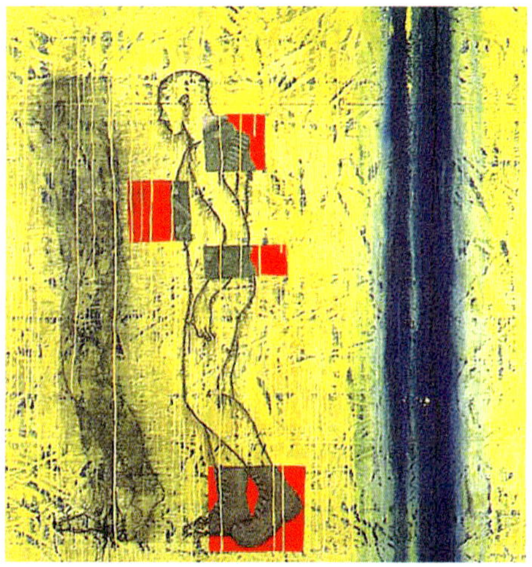
Acrylic on tarpaulin, 66x66", 2002

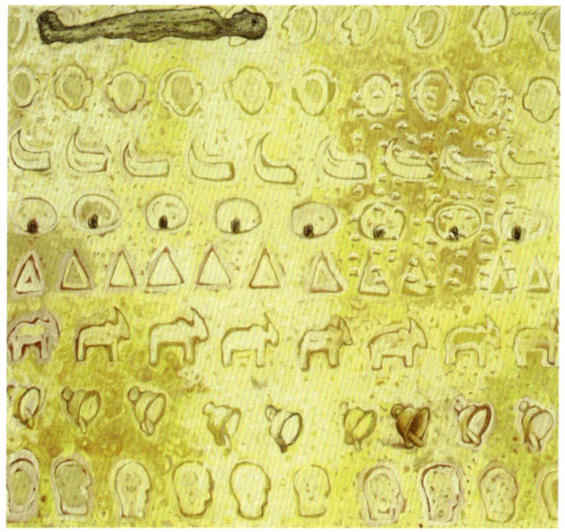
Oil on canvas, 72x72", 1997

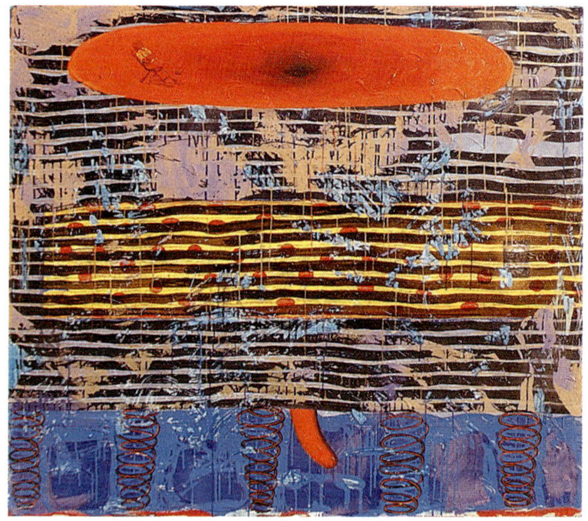
Acrylic on canvas, 72x66", 1996

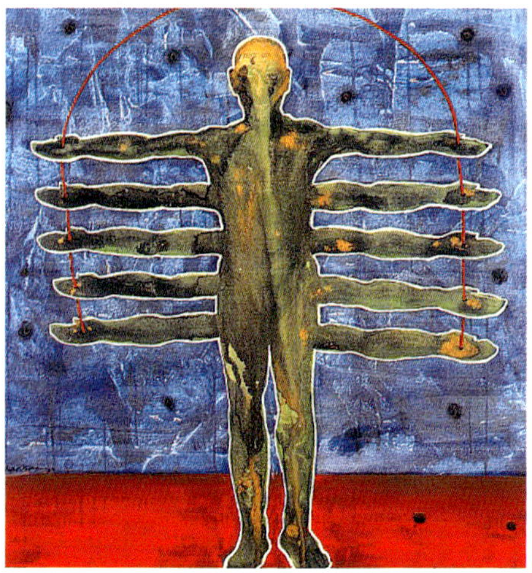
Acrylic on canvas, 30x30", 2005

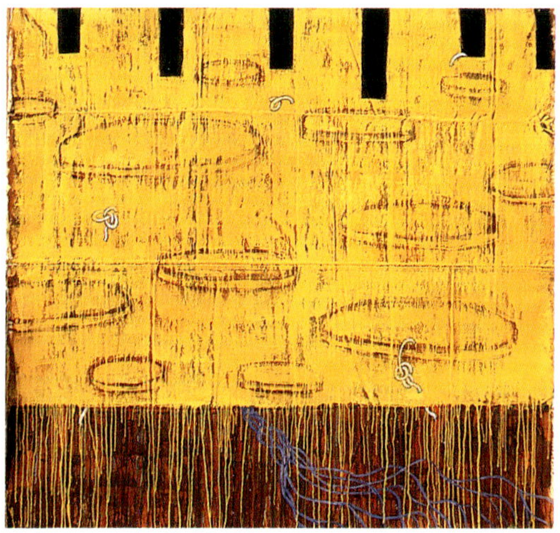
Acrylic on tarpaulin, 70x70", 2001

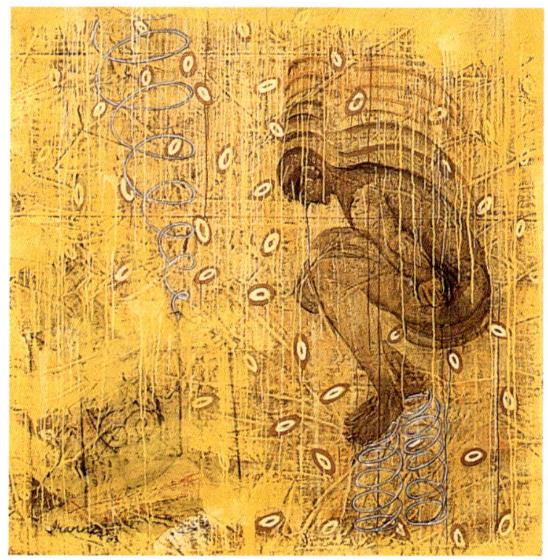
Acrylic on tarpaulin, 66x66", 2003

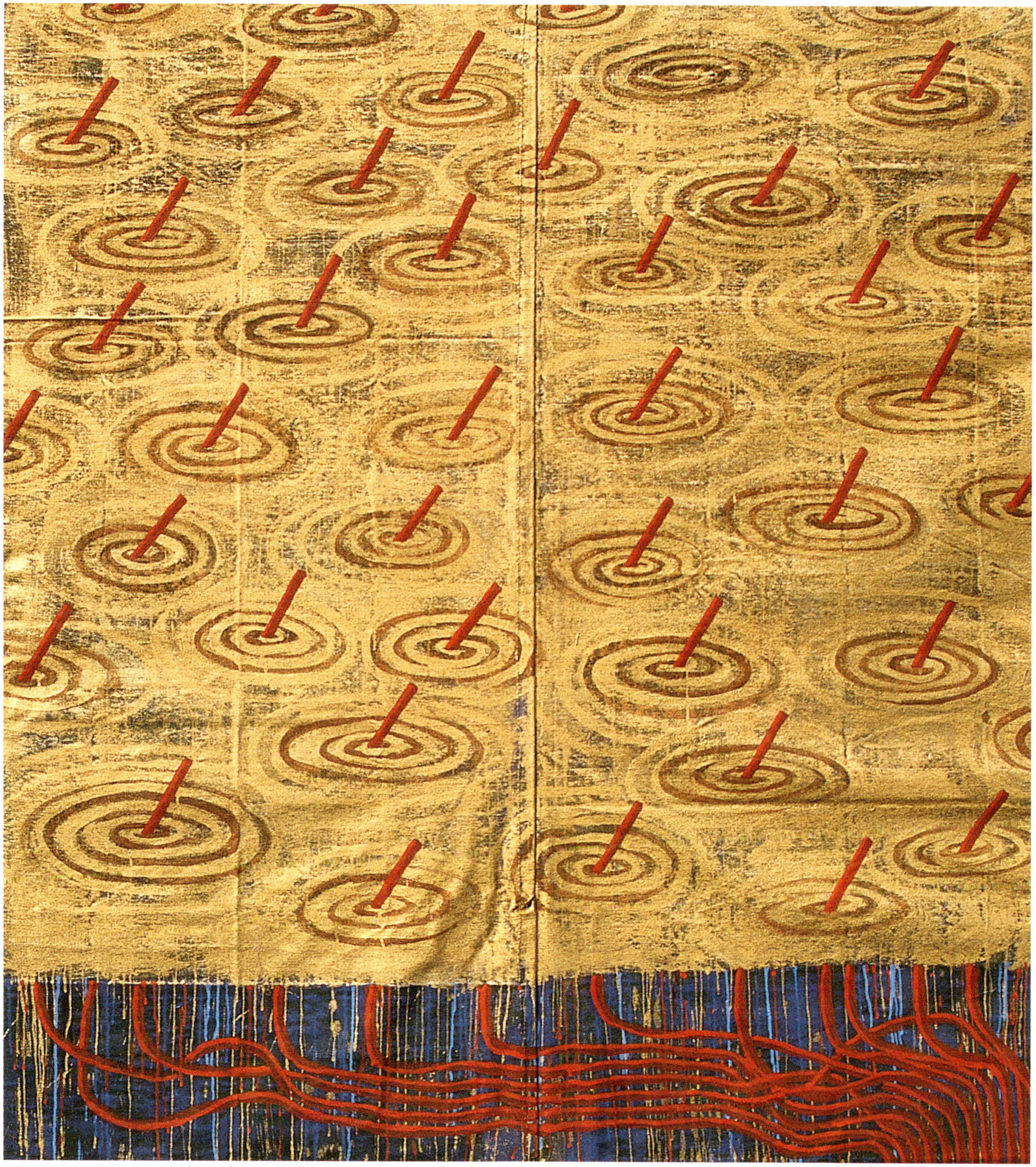

The Roots, acrylic on tarpaulin, 60x66", 2001

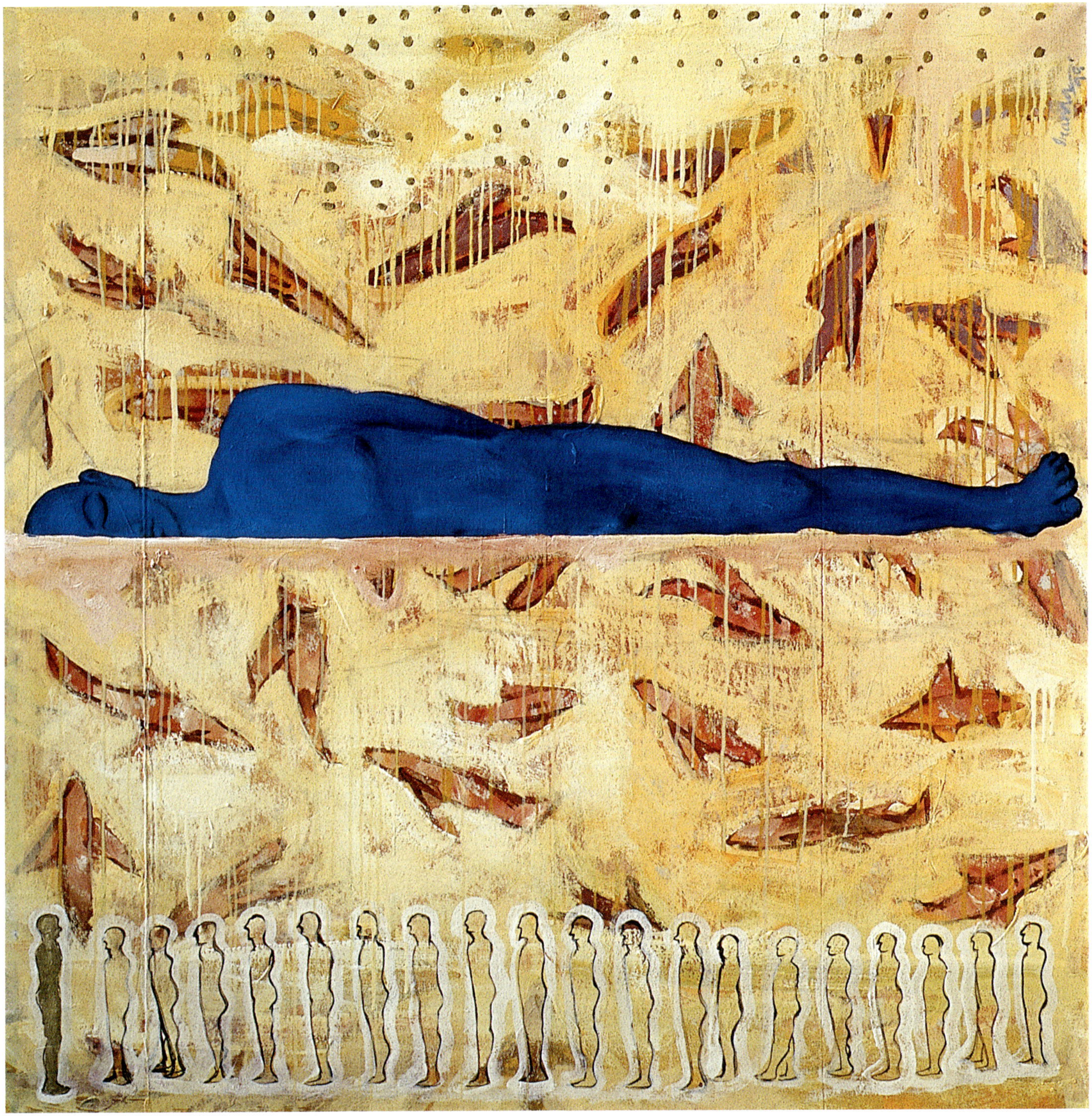

Untitled, acrylic on canvas, 66x66", 1998

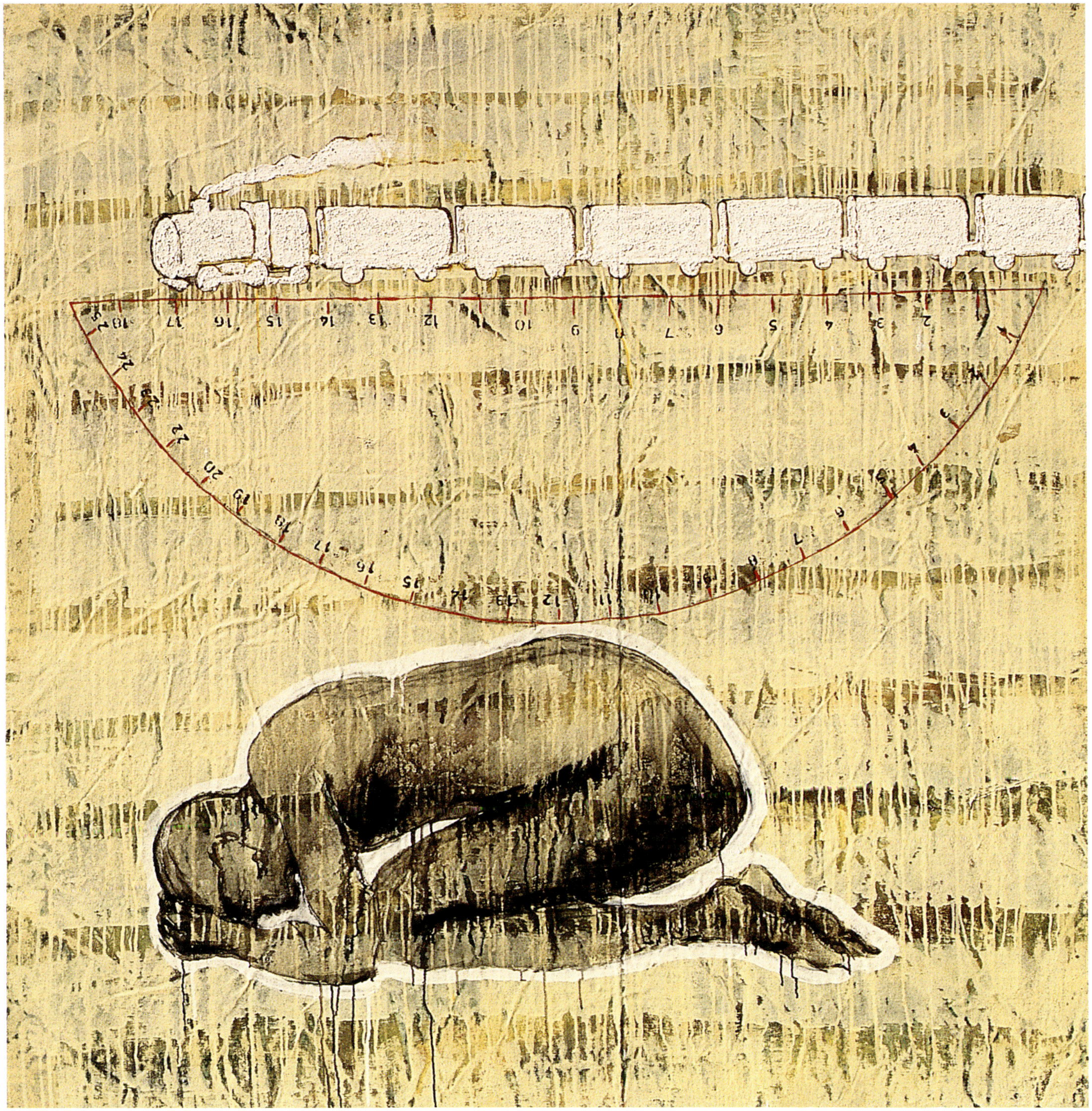

Untitled, acrylic on tarpaulin, 66x66", 2003

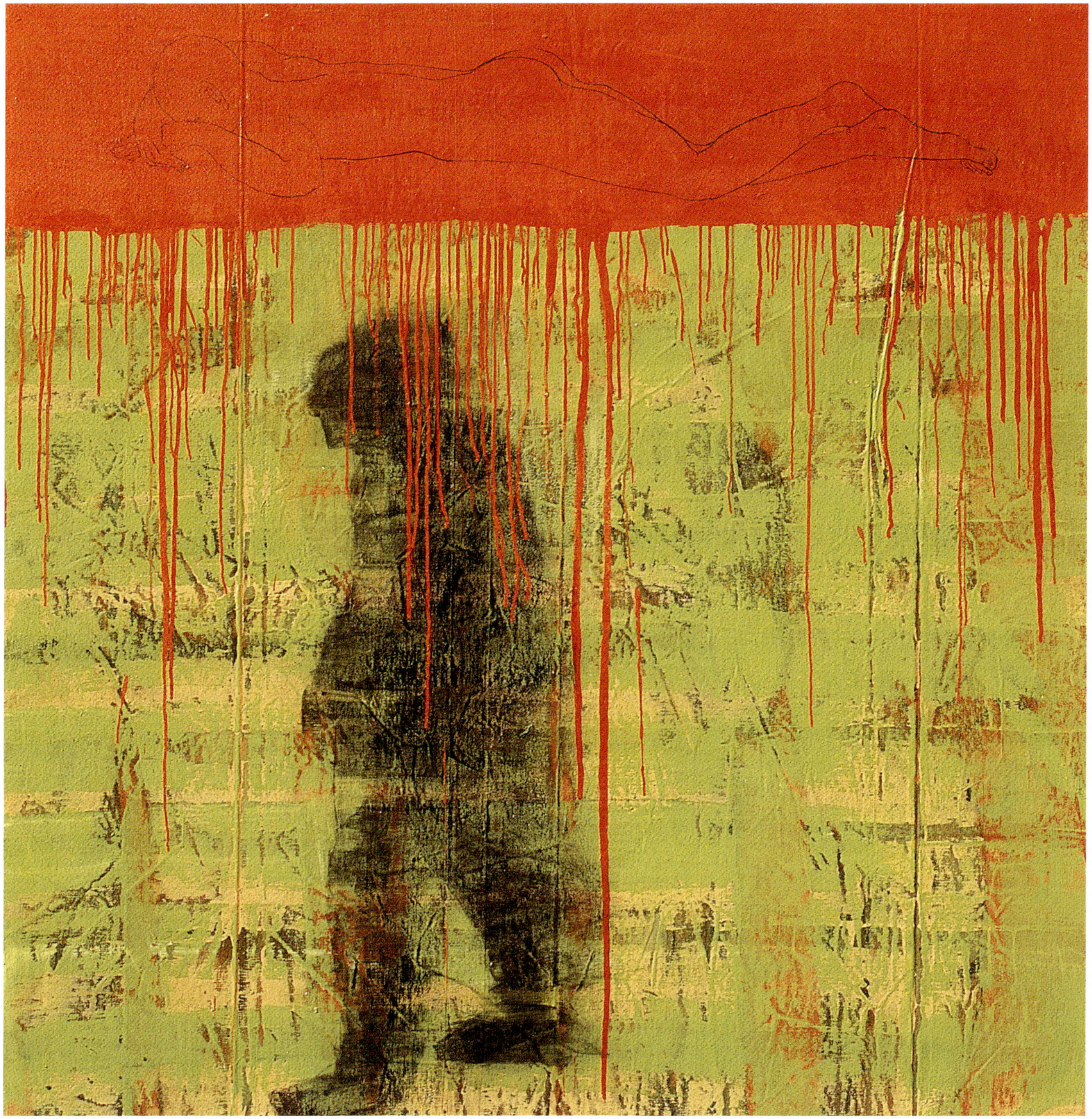

Untitled, acrylic on tarpaulin, 66x66”, 2003

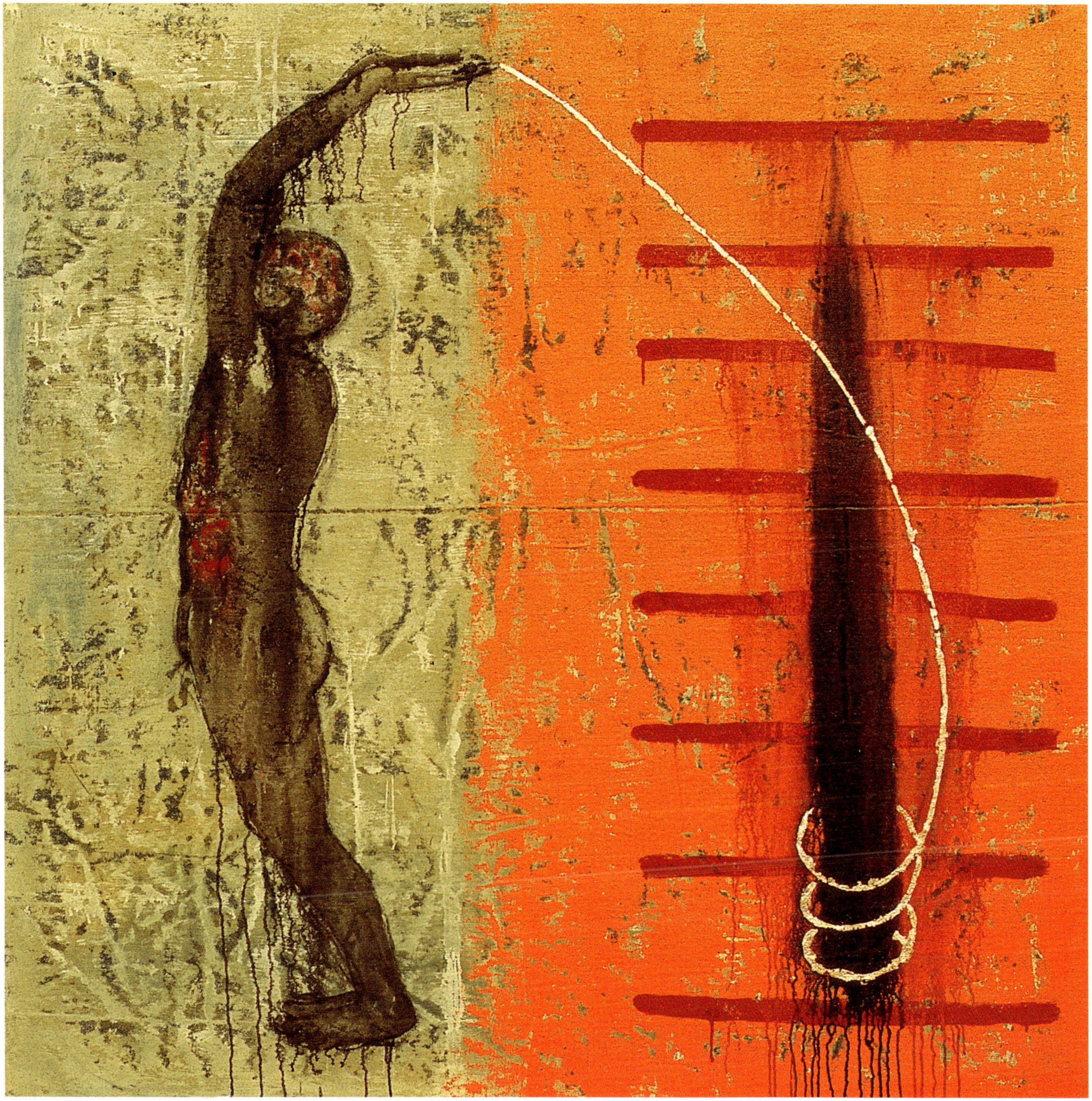

Untitled, acrylic and gold foil on tarpaulin, 66x66", 2003

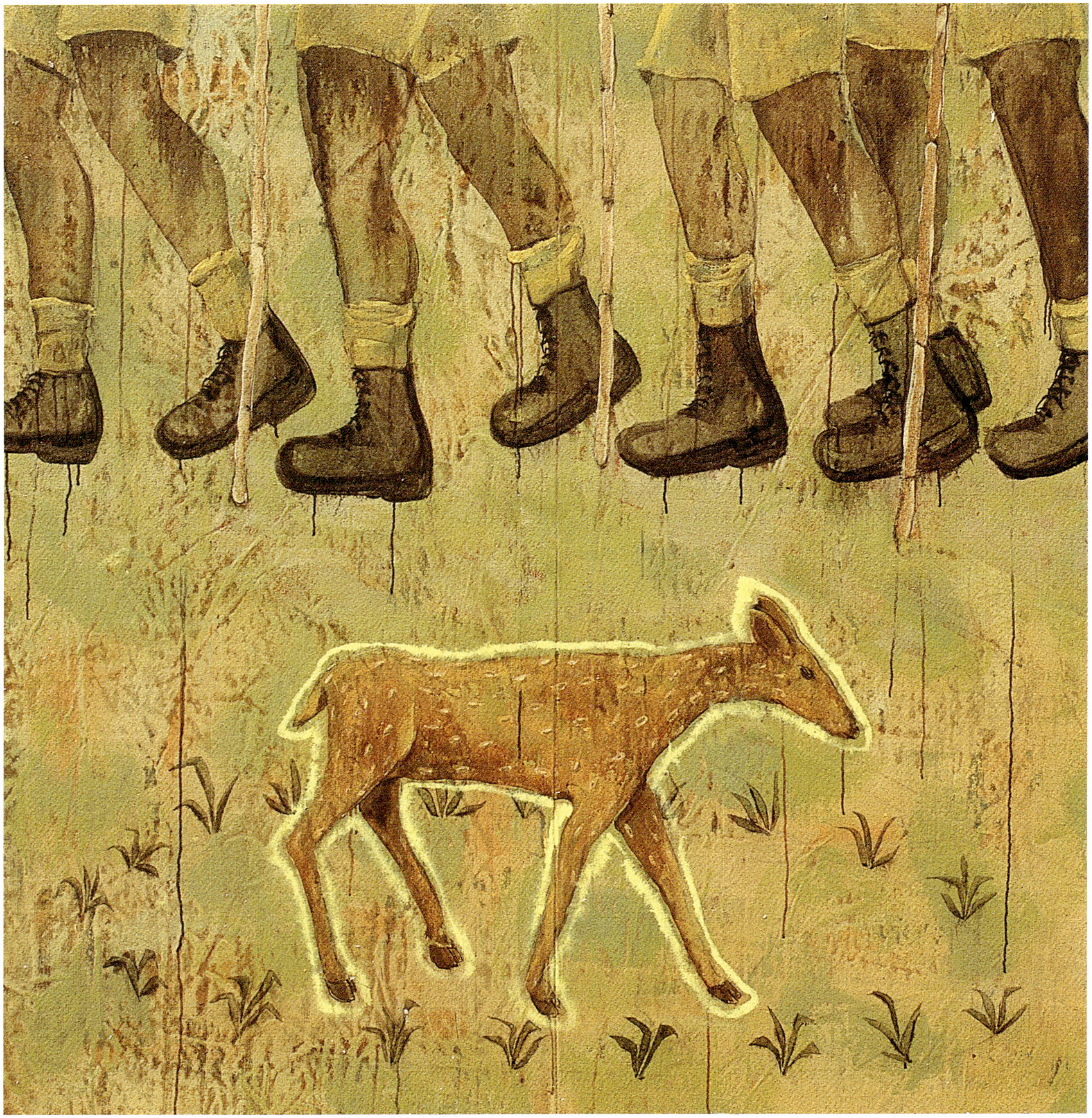

Untitled, acrylic on tarpaulin, 66x66", 2004

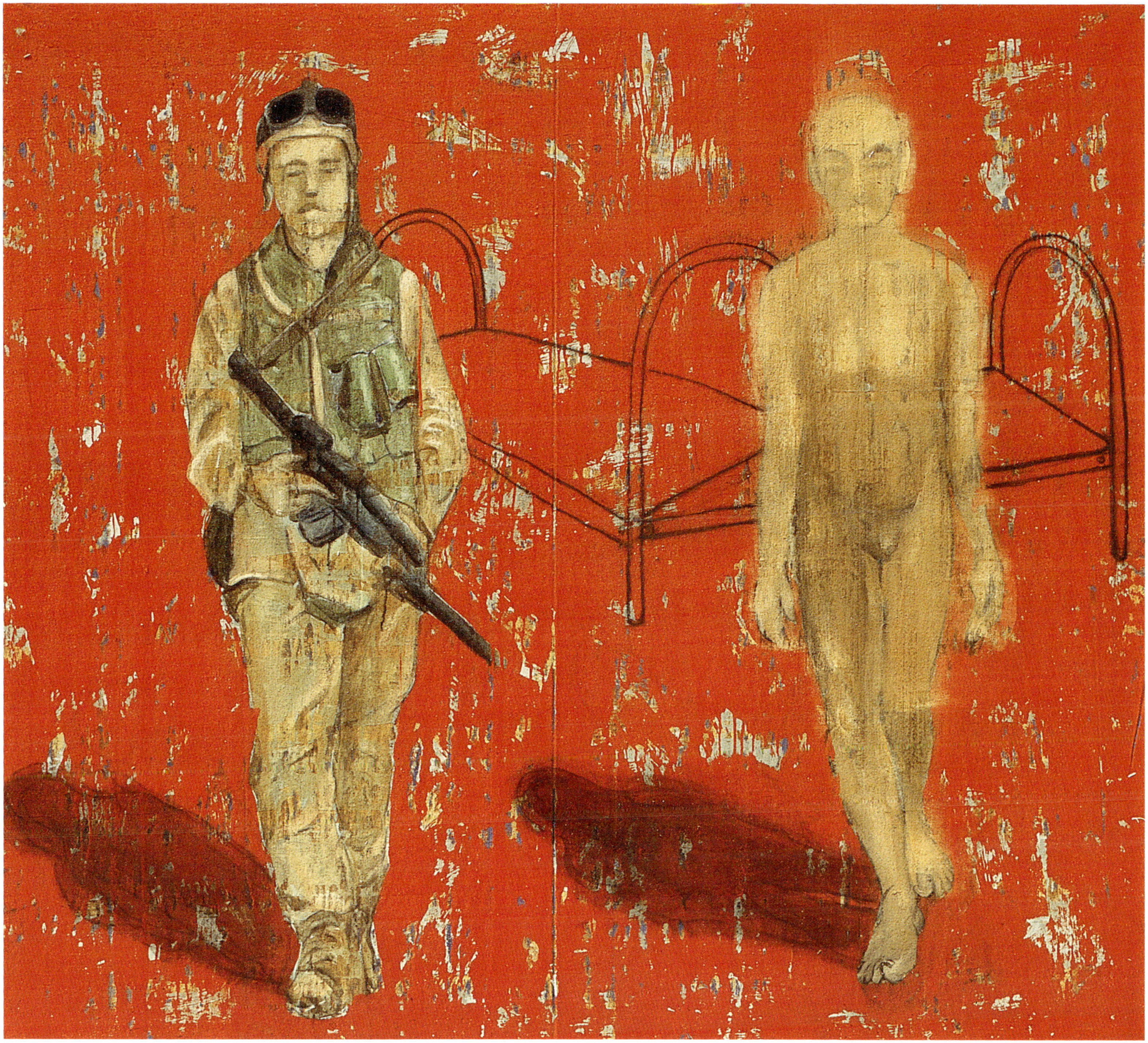

Design for Two, acrylic on tarpaulin, 80x66", 2003

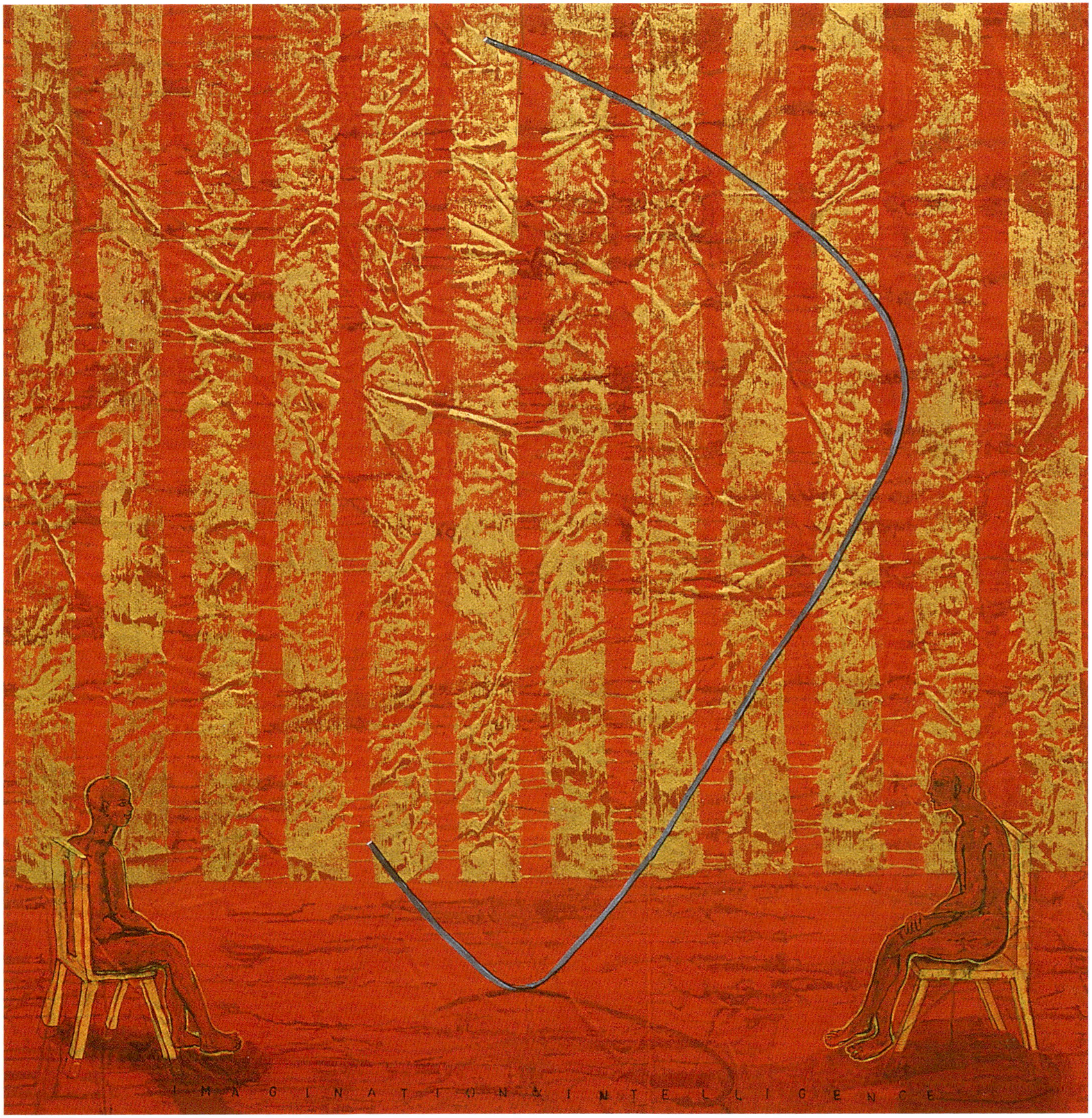

Imagination and Intelligence, acrylic on tarpaulin, 66x66", 2003

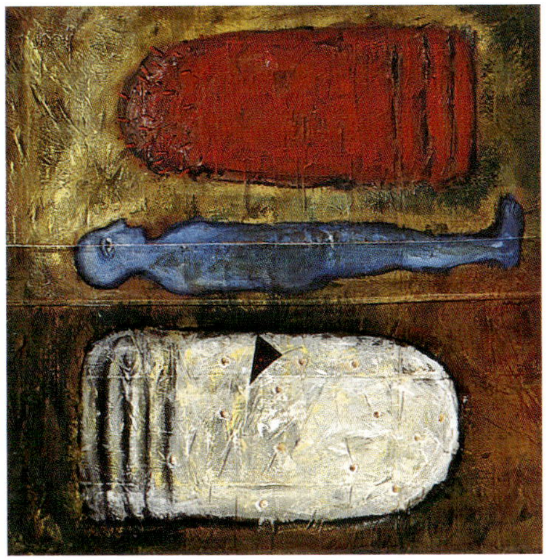
Acrylic on canvas, 72x72", 1996

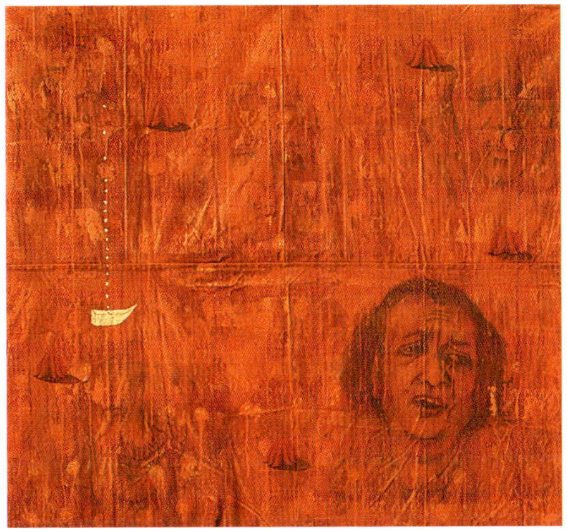
Acrylic on tarpaulin, 66x66", 1998

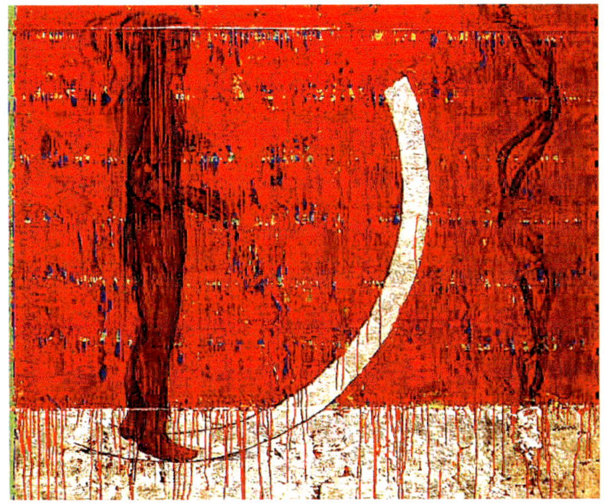
Acrylic and silver foil on tarpaulin, 66x48", 2003

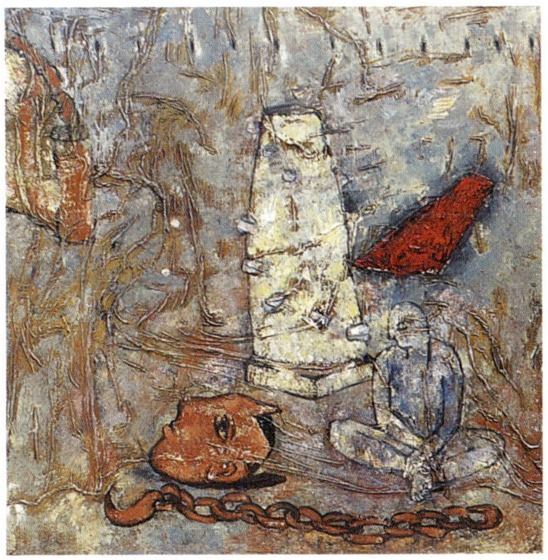
Oil on canvas, 52x52", 1997

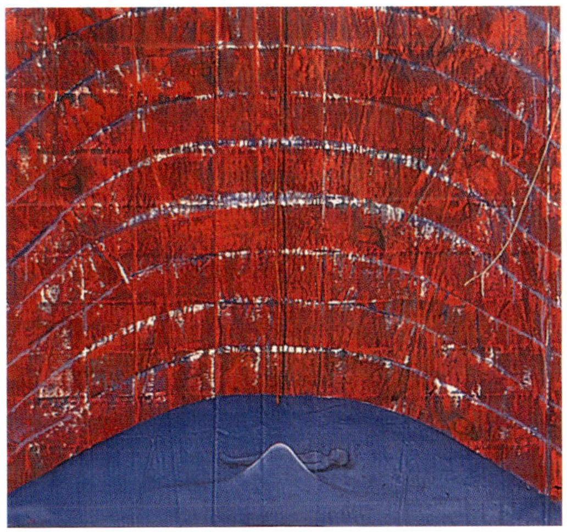
Acrylic on canvas, 48x46", 1995

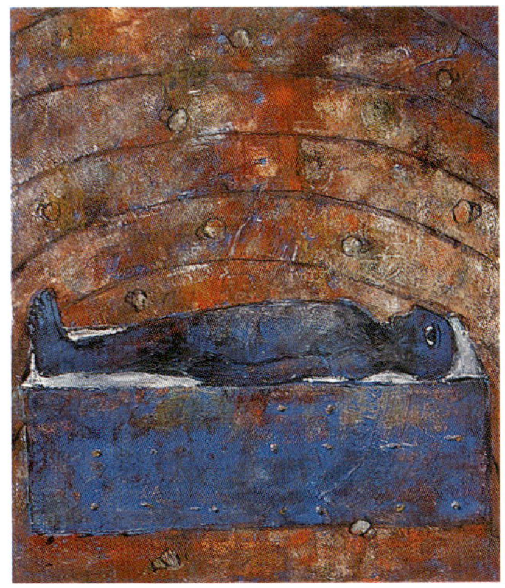
Oil on canvas, 36x48", 1994

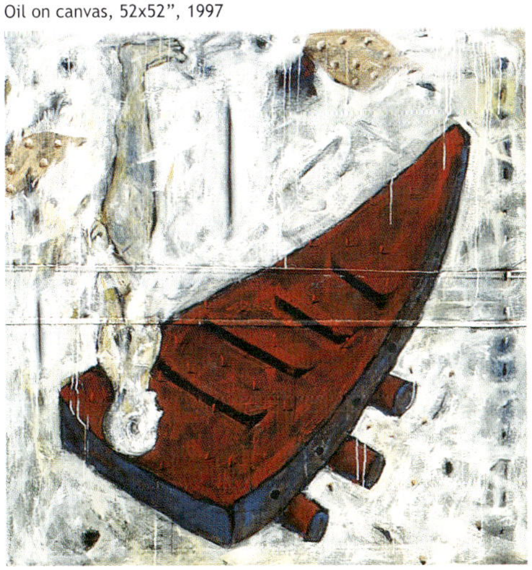
Acrylic on canvas, 72x72", 1996

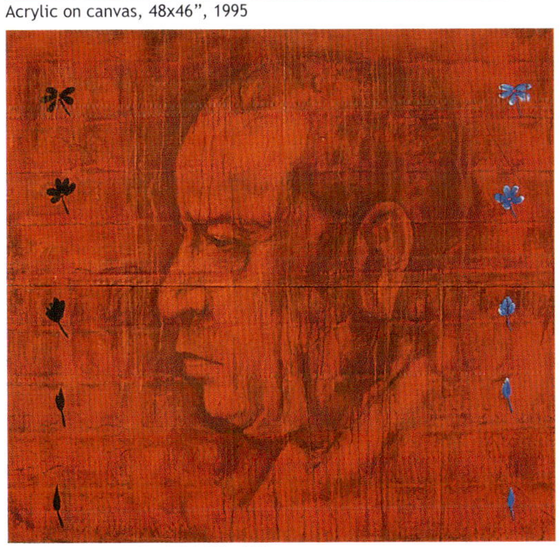
Acrylic on tarpaulin, 70x70", 1998

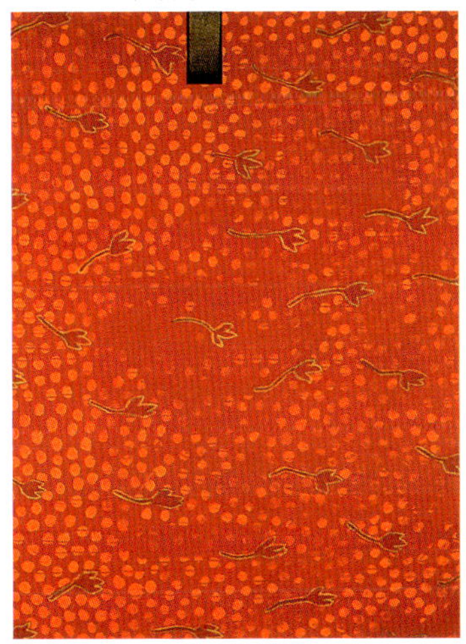
Acrylic on canvas, 52x66", 2002

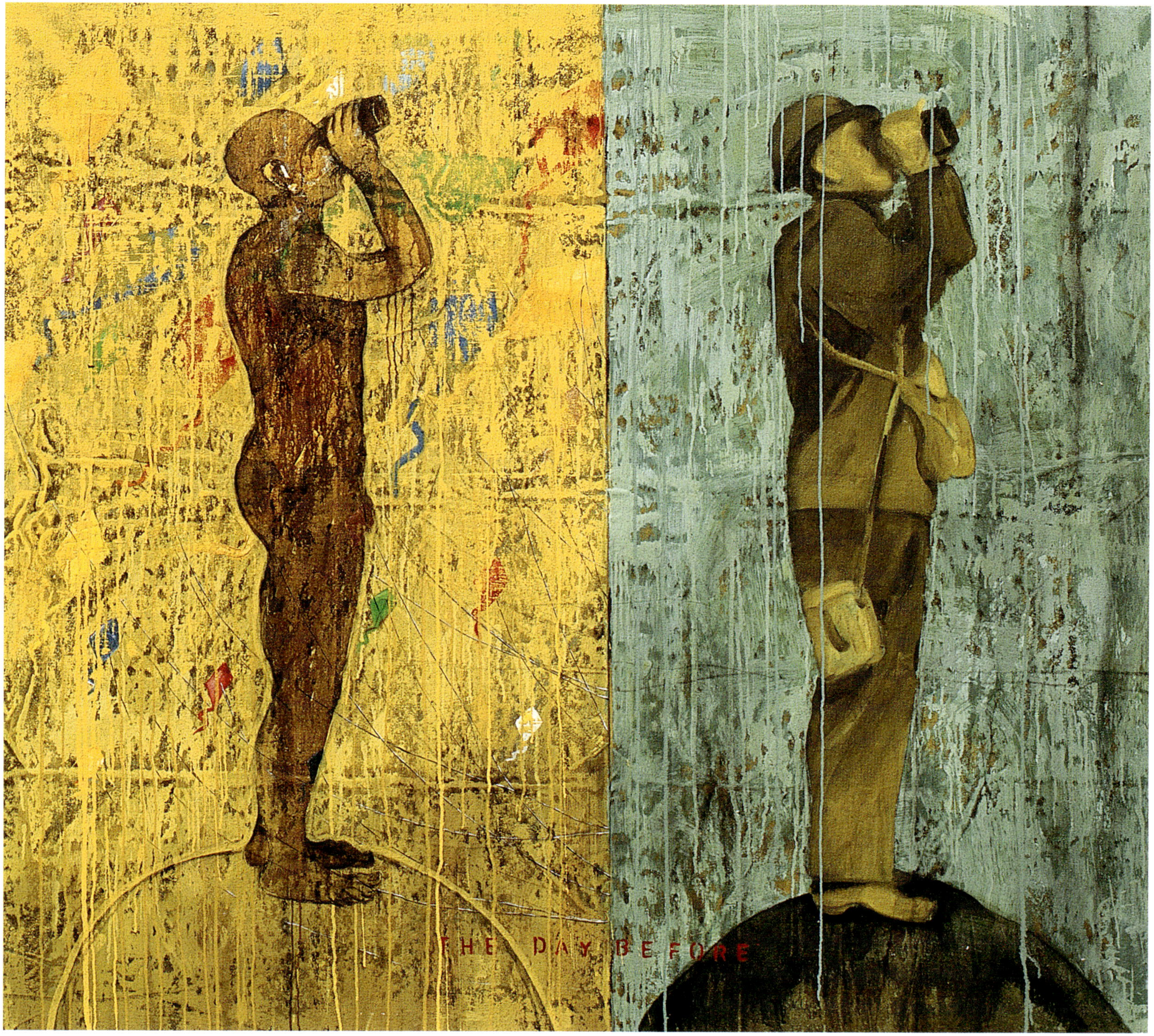

Untitled, acrylic on canvas, 80x66", 2003

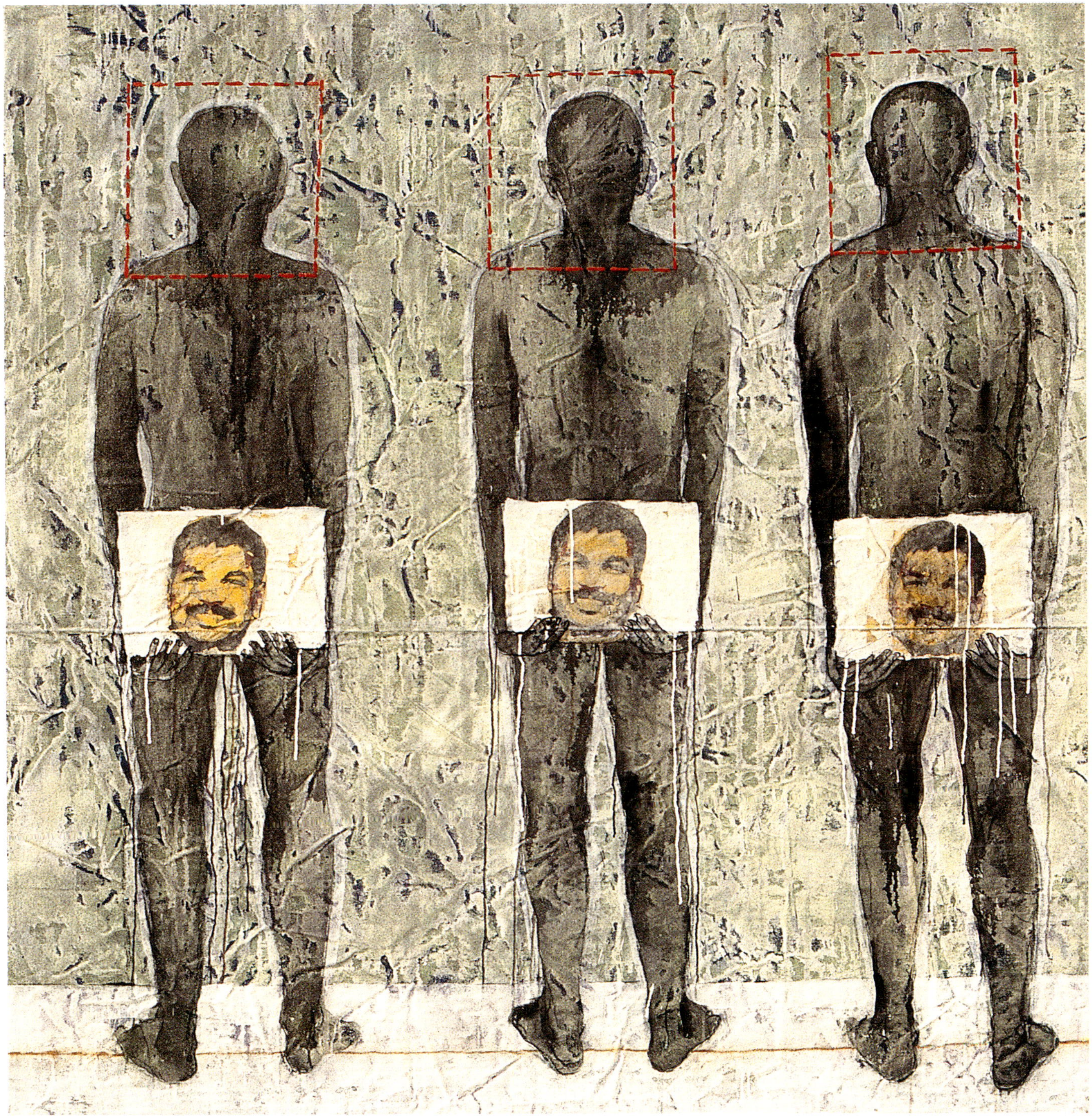

Untitled, acrylic on tarpaulin, 66x66", 2003

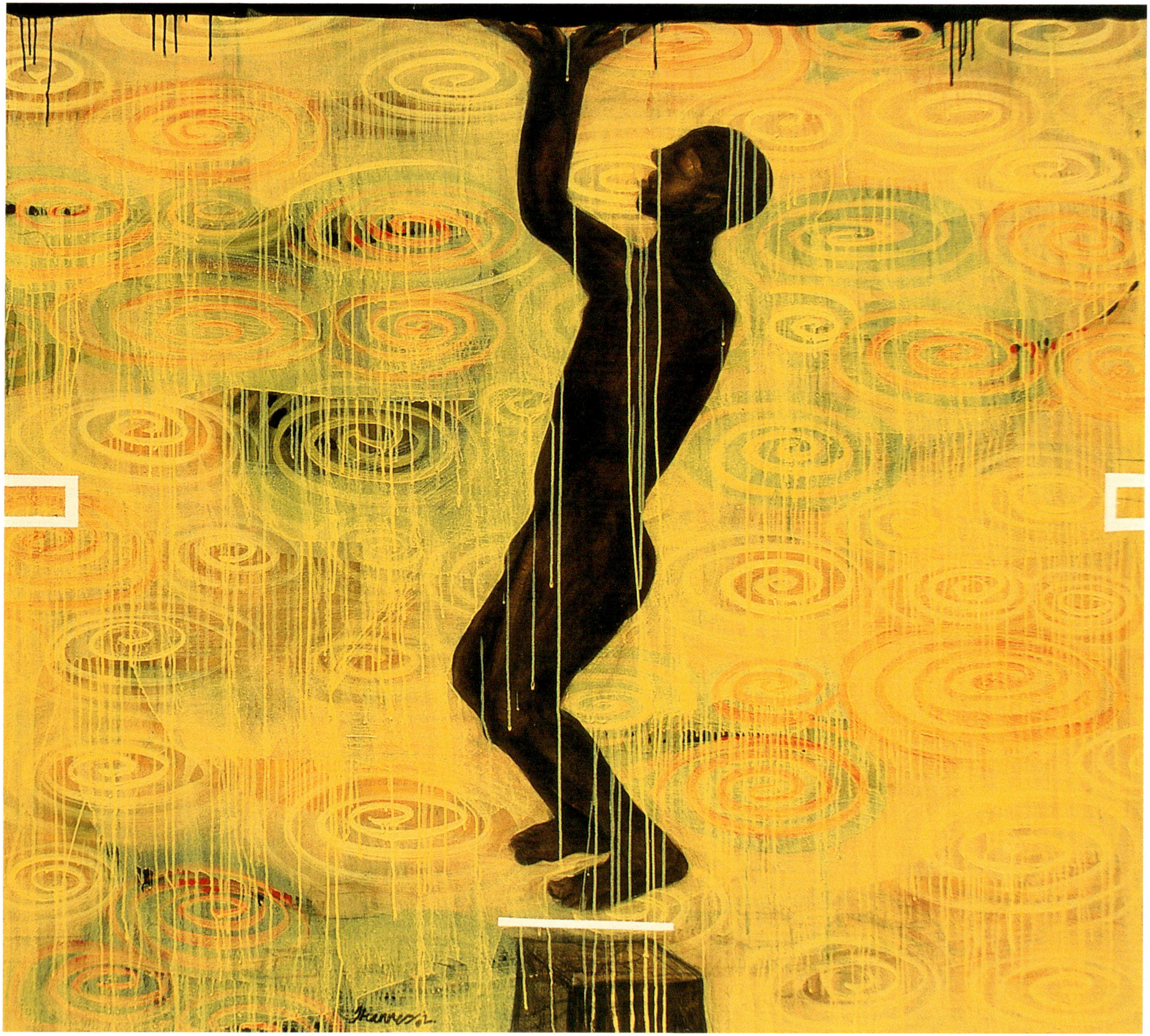

Untitled, acrylic on tarpaulin, 66x66", 2003

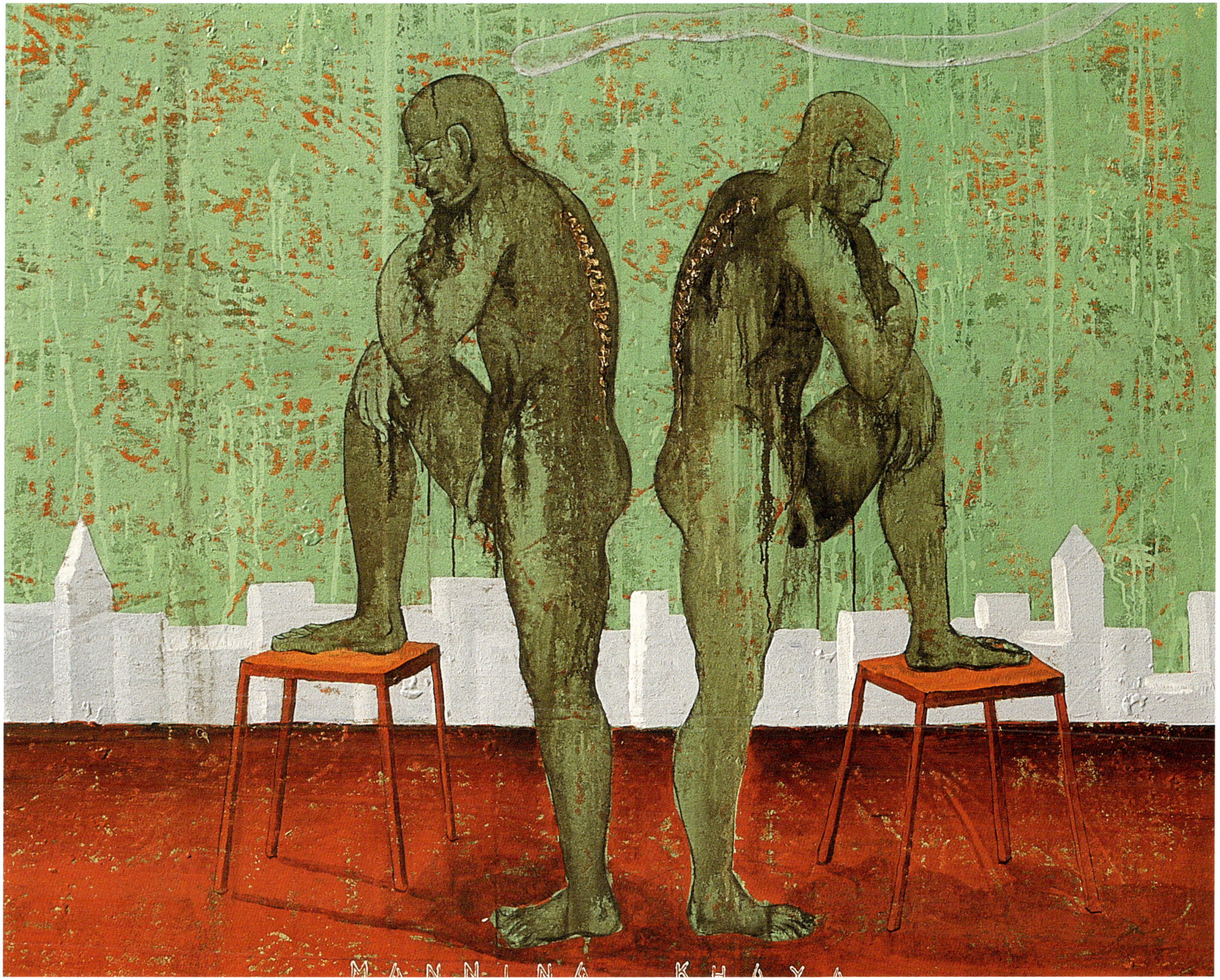

Mannina Kaya, acrylic on tarpaulin, 66x52”, 2003

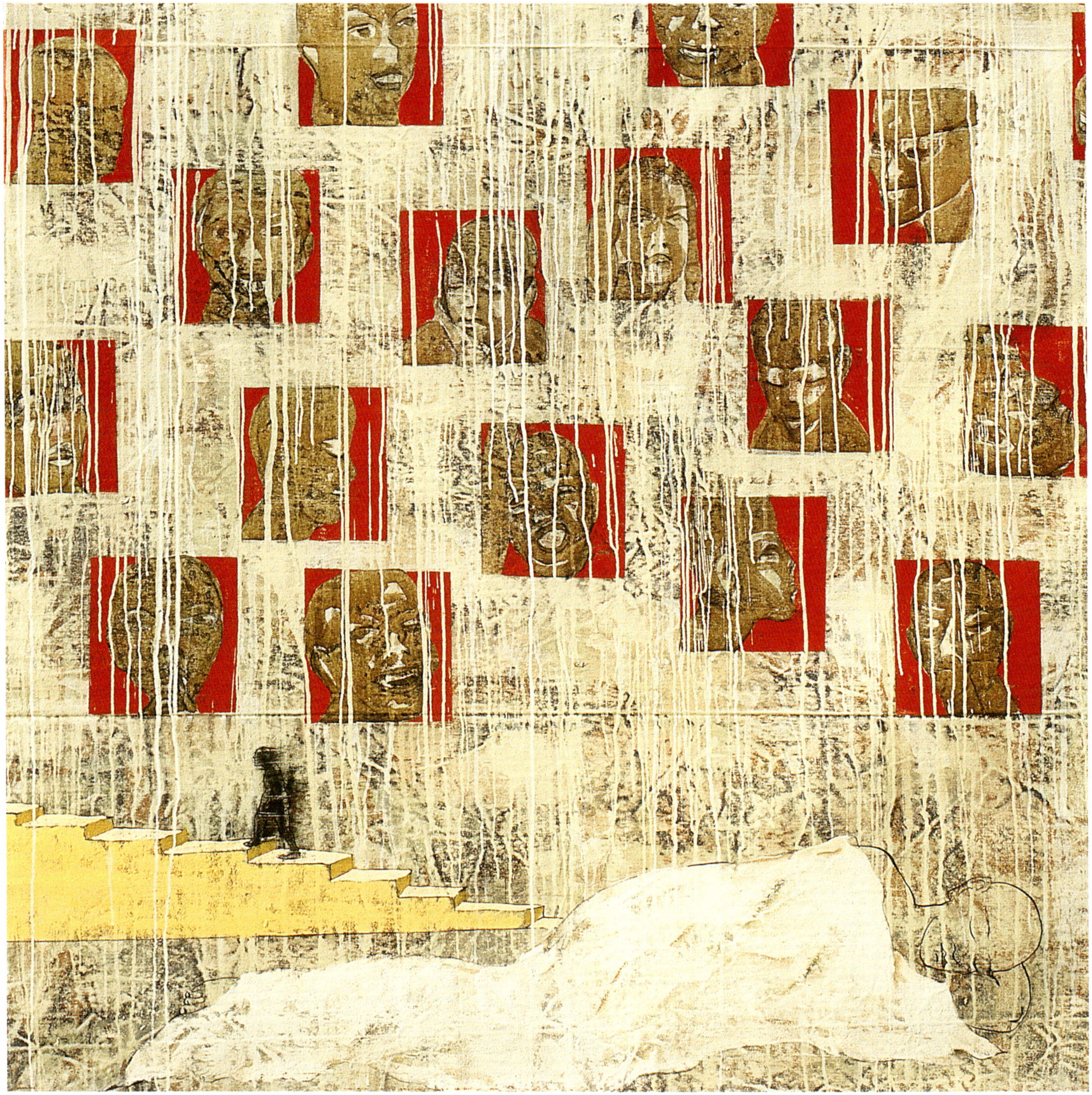

No One's Faces, acrylic on tarpaulin, 66x66", 2003

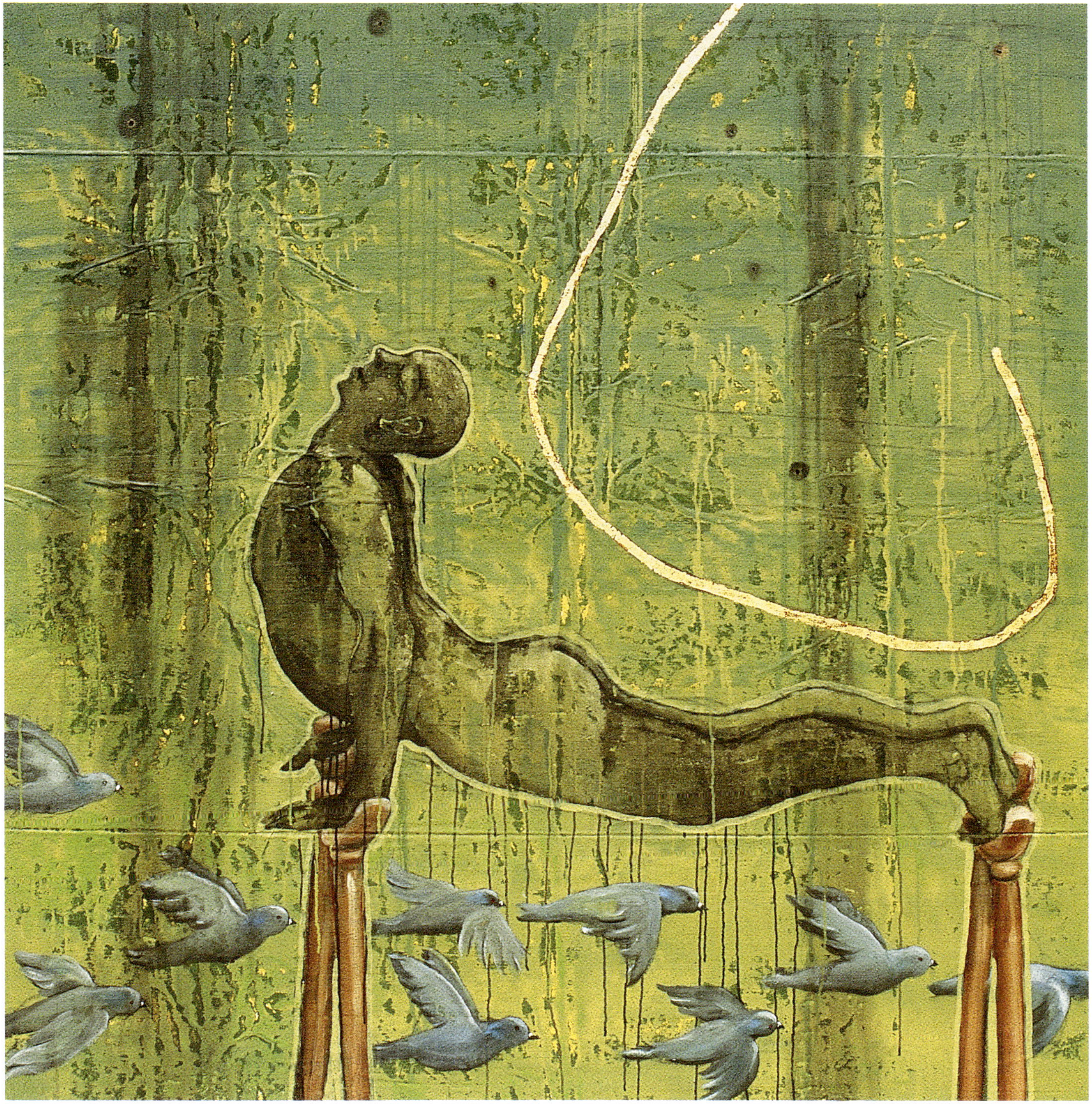

Looking for Land, acrylic on tarpaulin, 66x66", 2004

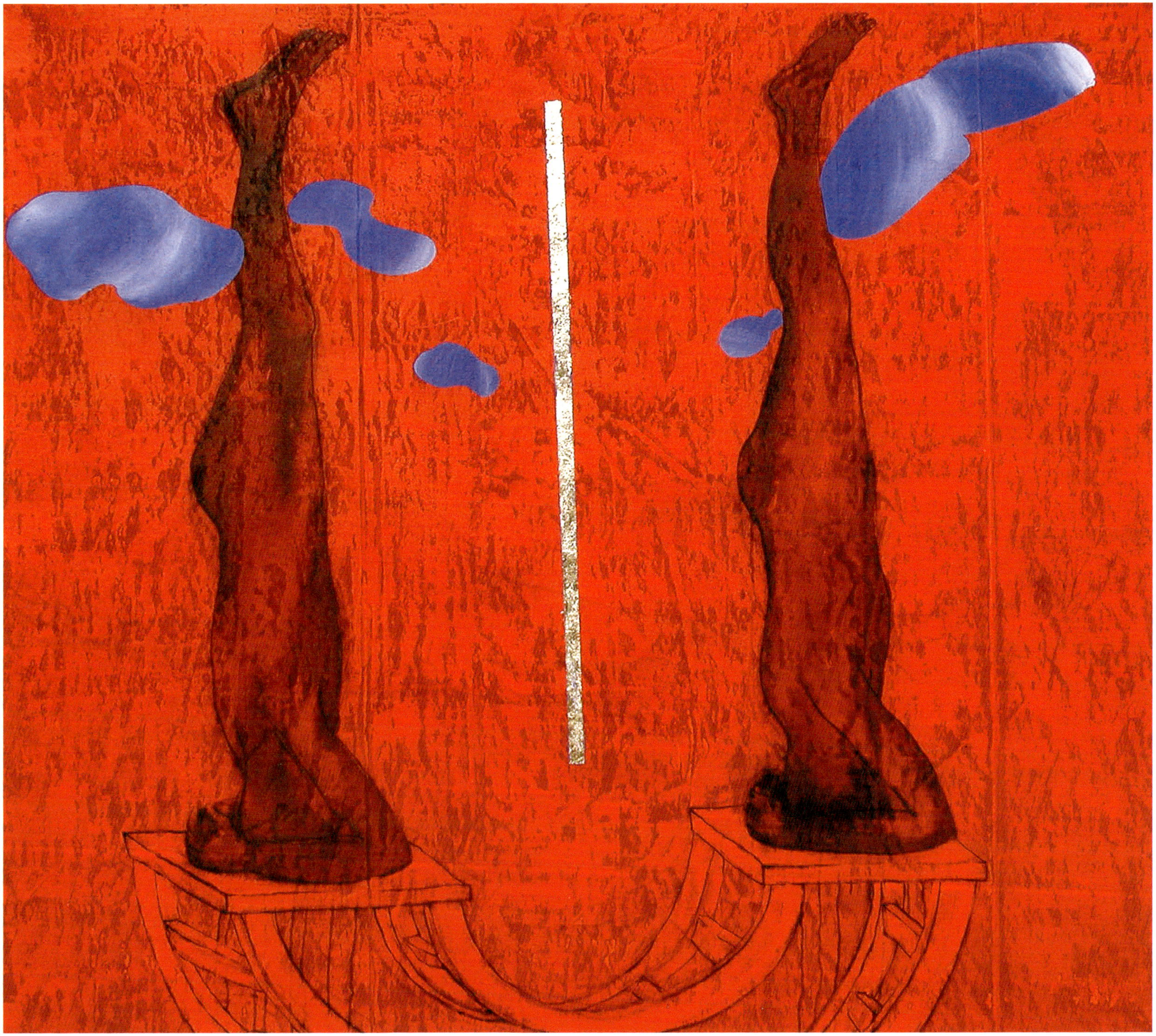

Untitled, acrylic and tarpaulin, 80x66", 2004

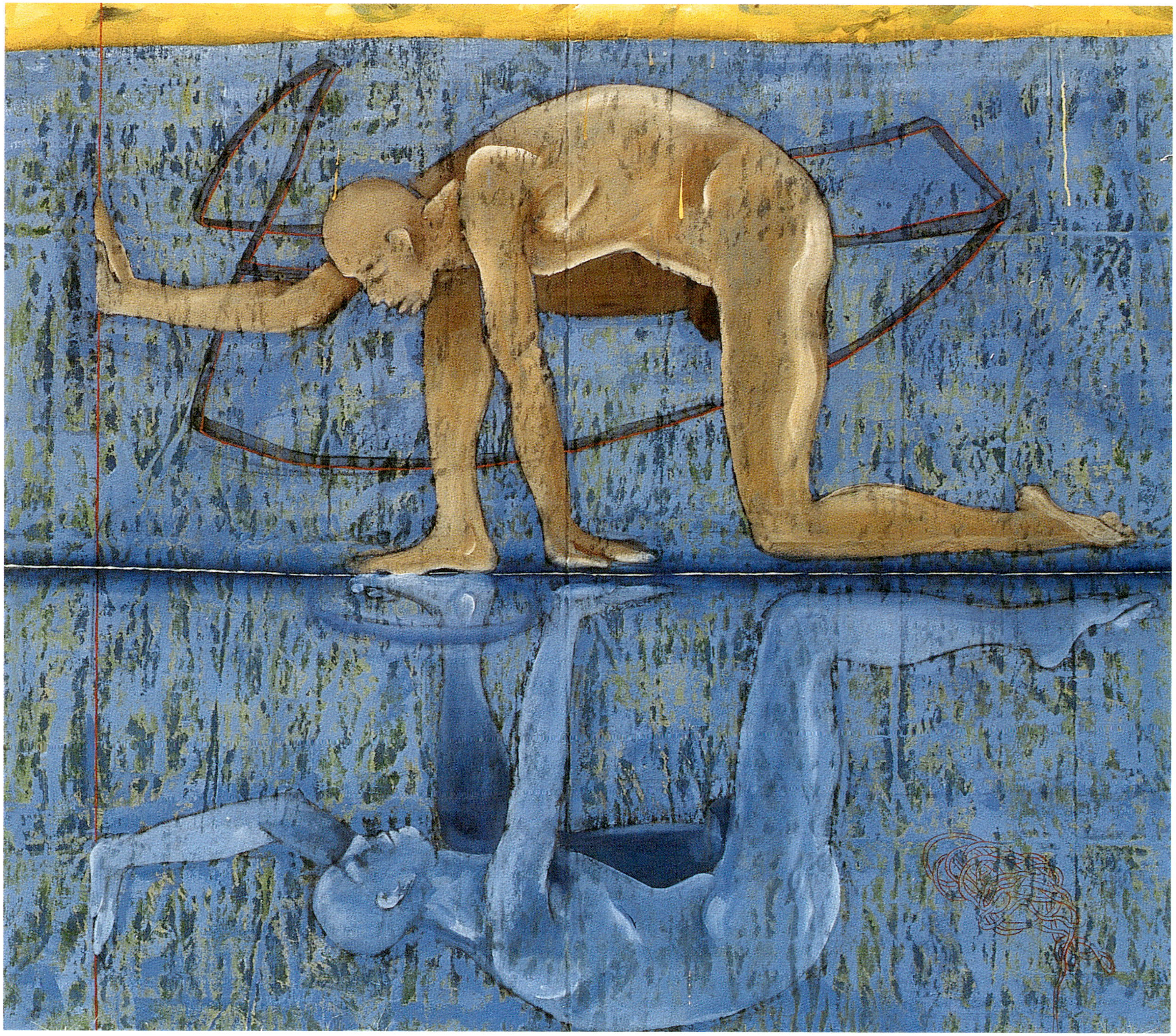

Searching Souls, acrylic on tarpaulin, 80x66", 2004

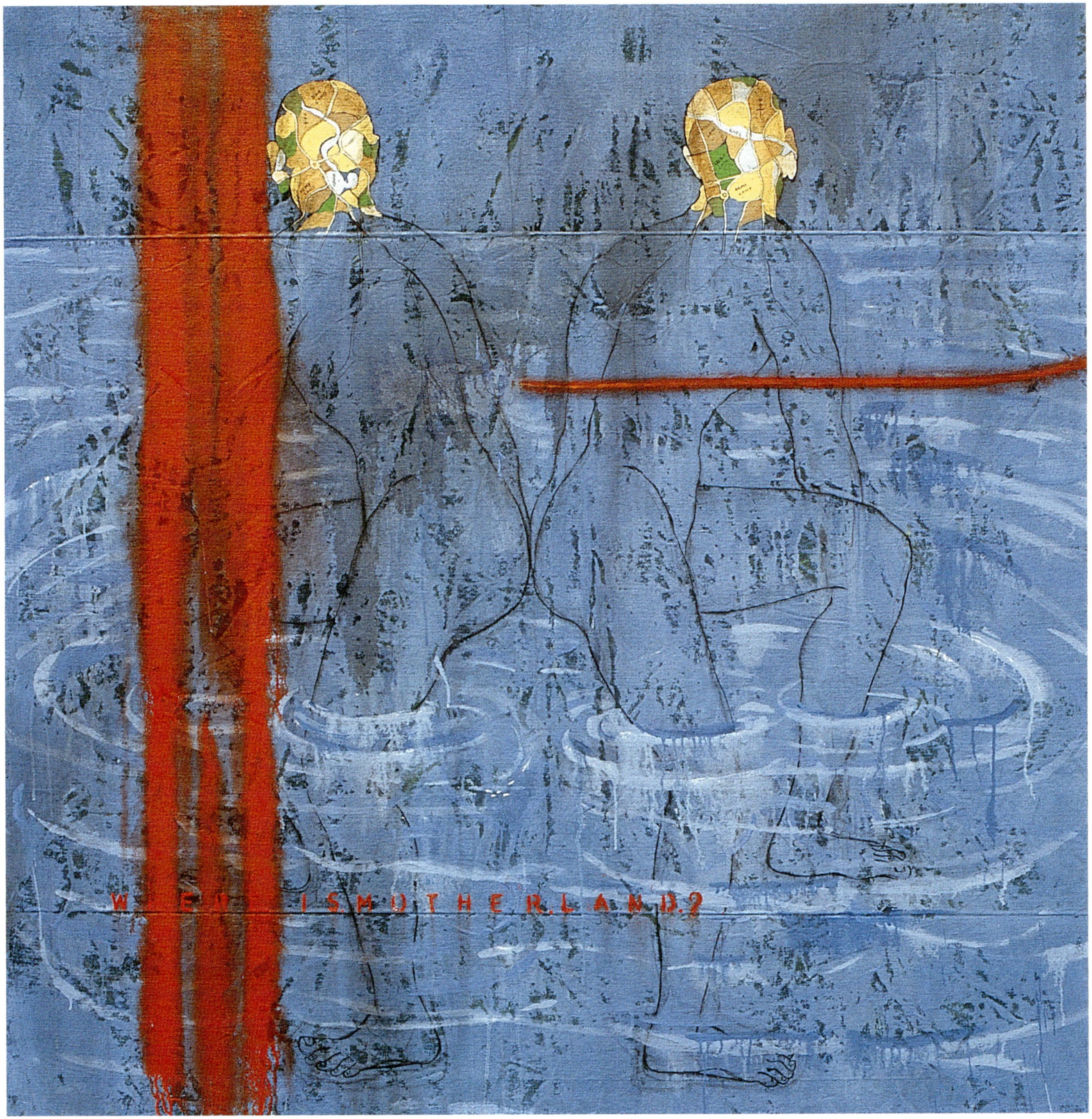

Where is Mother is Motherland, acrylic on tarpaulin, 70x66", 2004

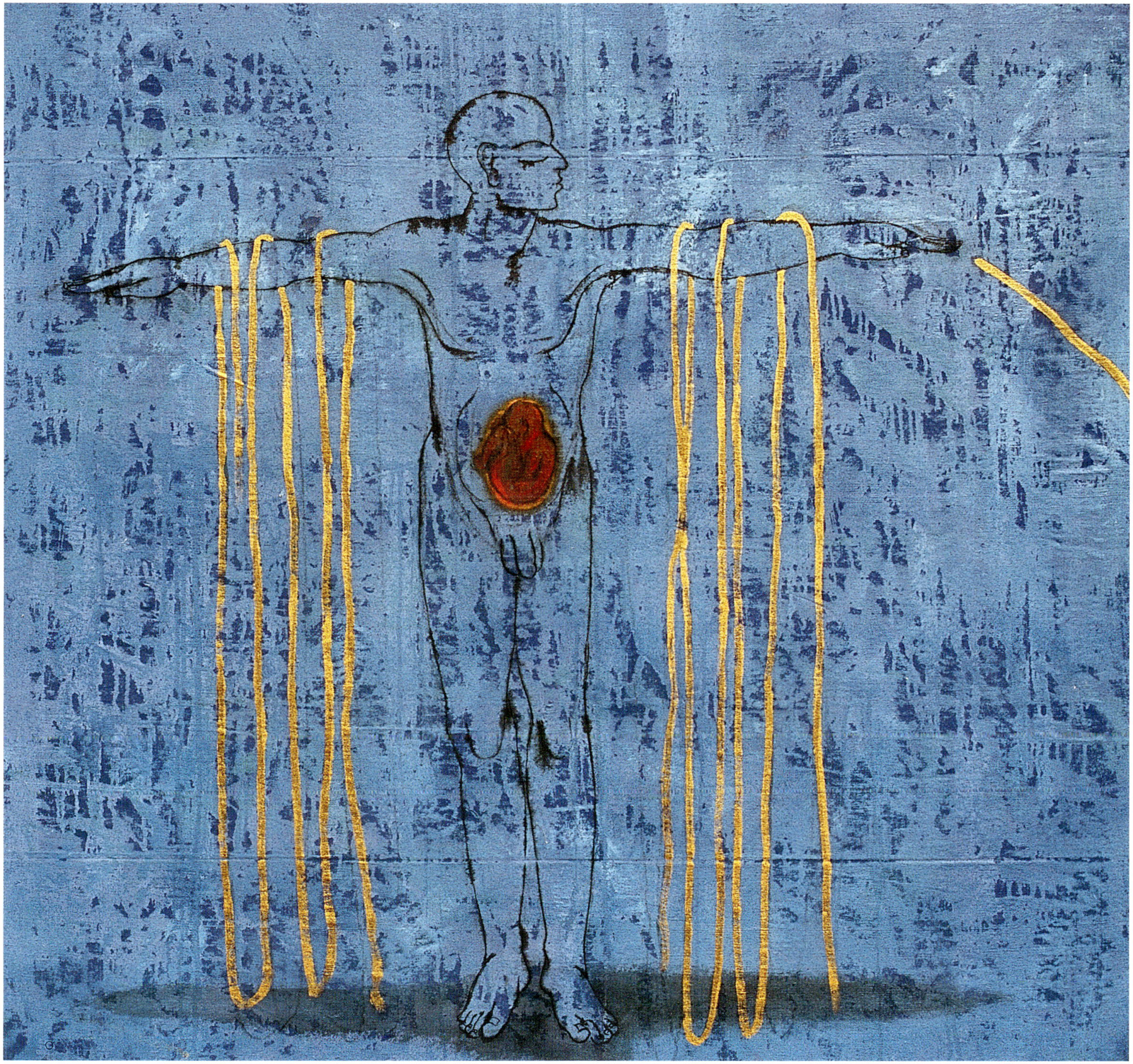

Womb and Man, acrylic on tarpaulin, 66x52", 2004

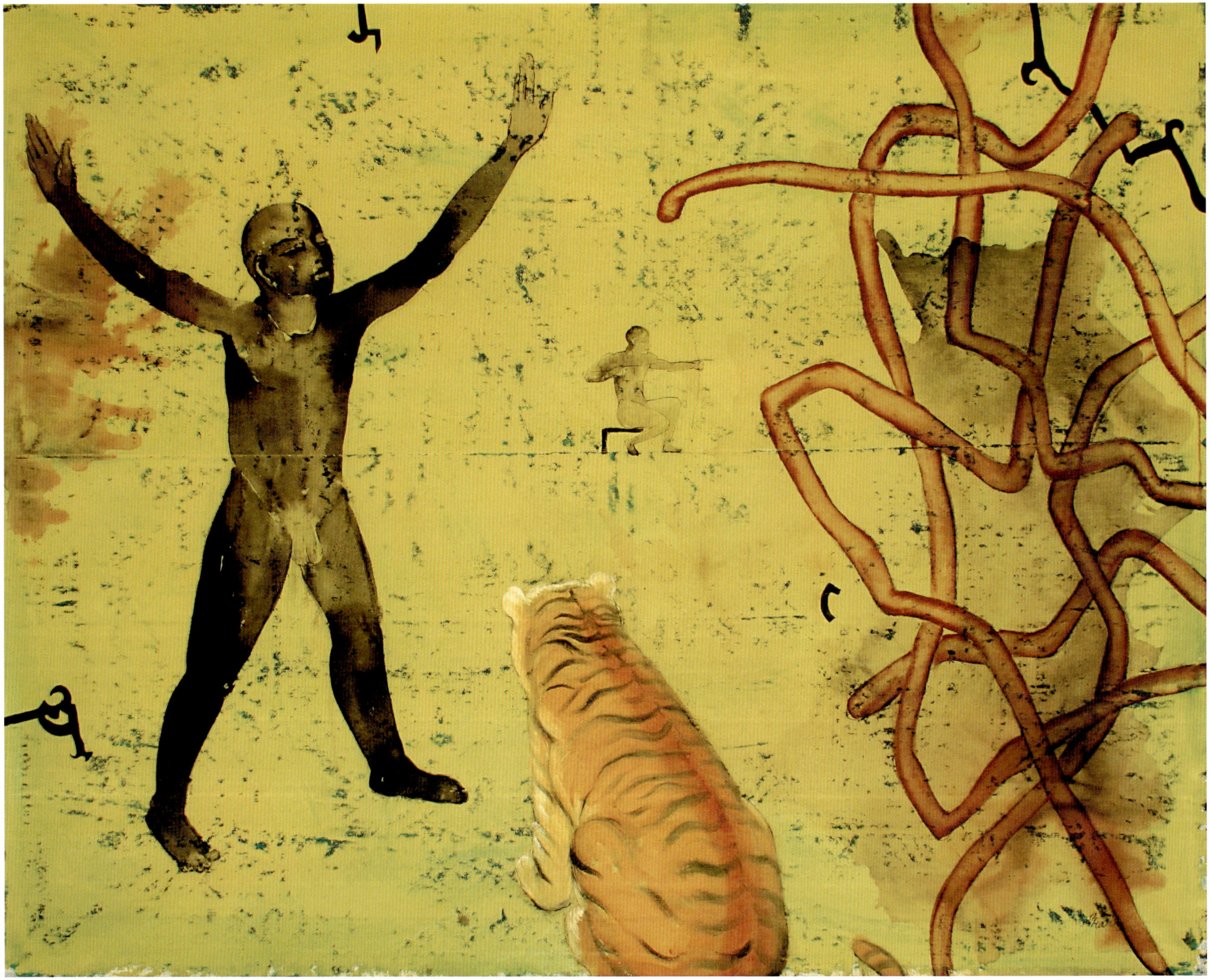

Shadow Hunter, acrylic on tarpaulin, 54x54", 2006

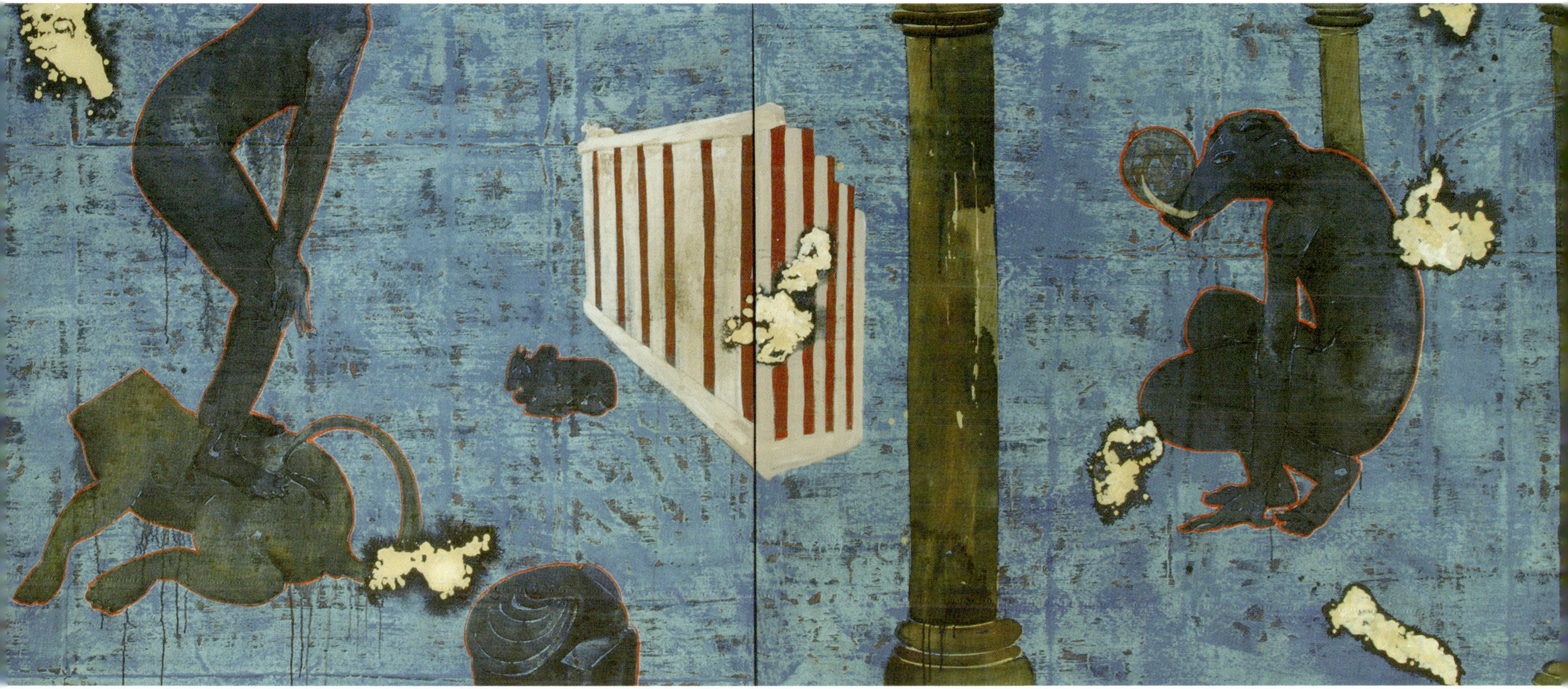

Broken Fort, acrylic on tarpaulin, 108x66", 2006

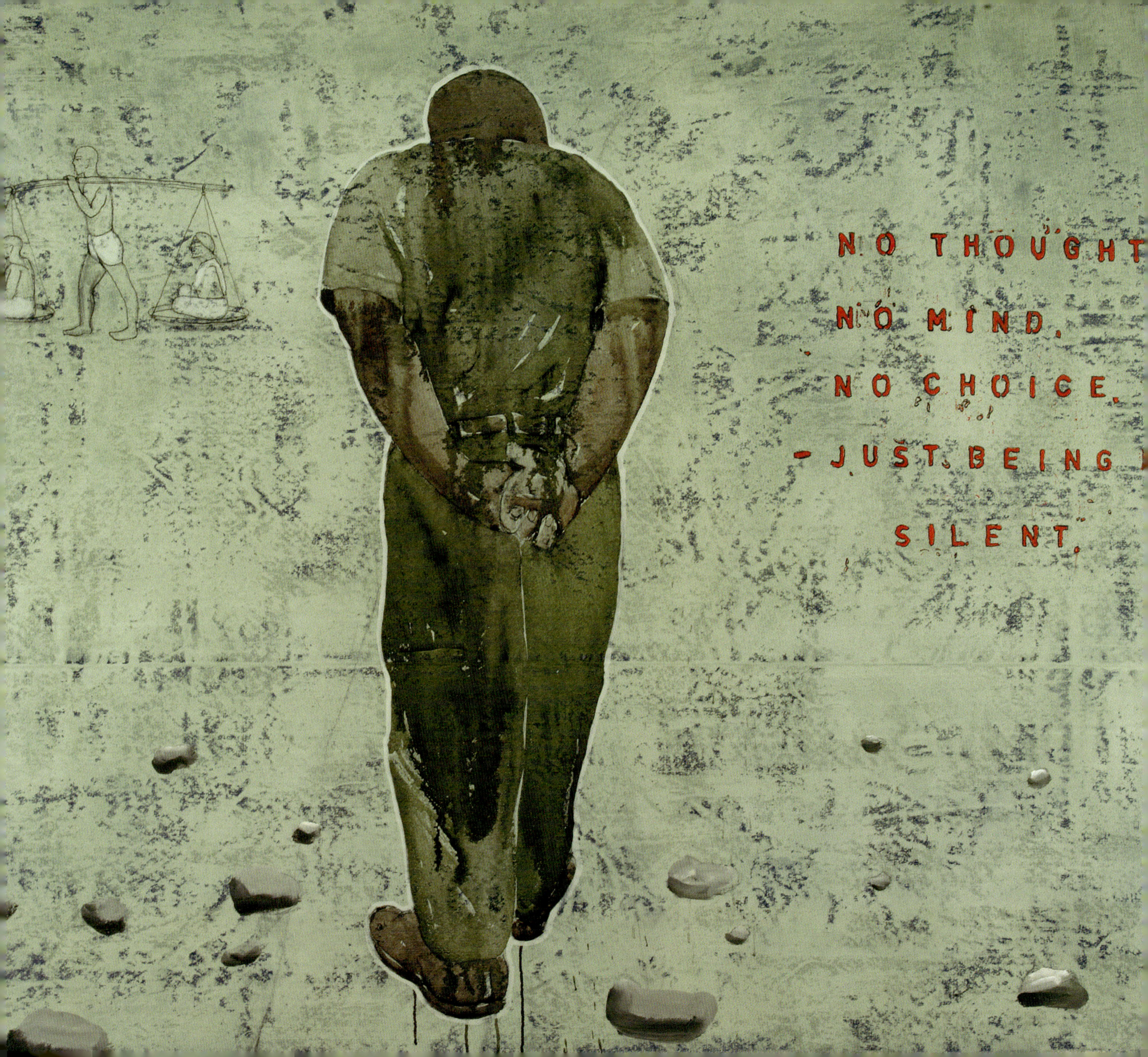
NO THOUGHT
NO MIND,
NO CHOICE,
- JUST BEING
SILENT.

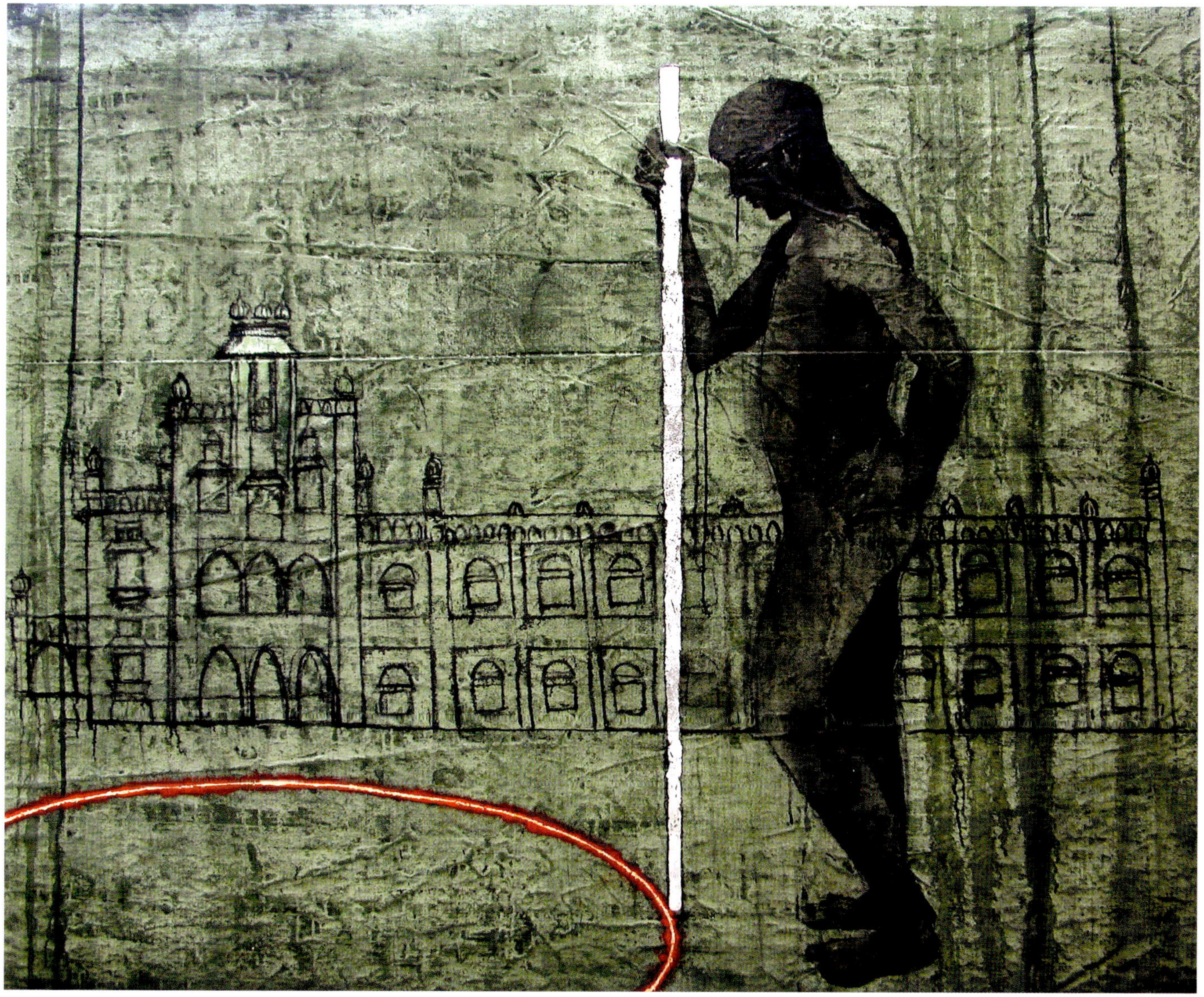

King and Kingdom, acrylic on tarpaulin, 66x54", 2004

Opposite page: *Walk for Peace*, acrylic and tarpaulin, 66x52", 2006

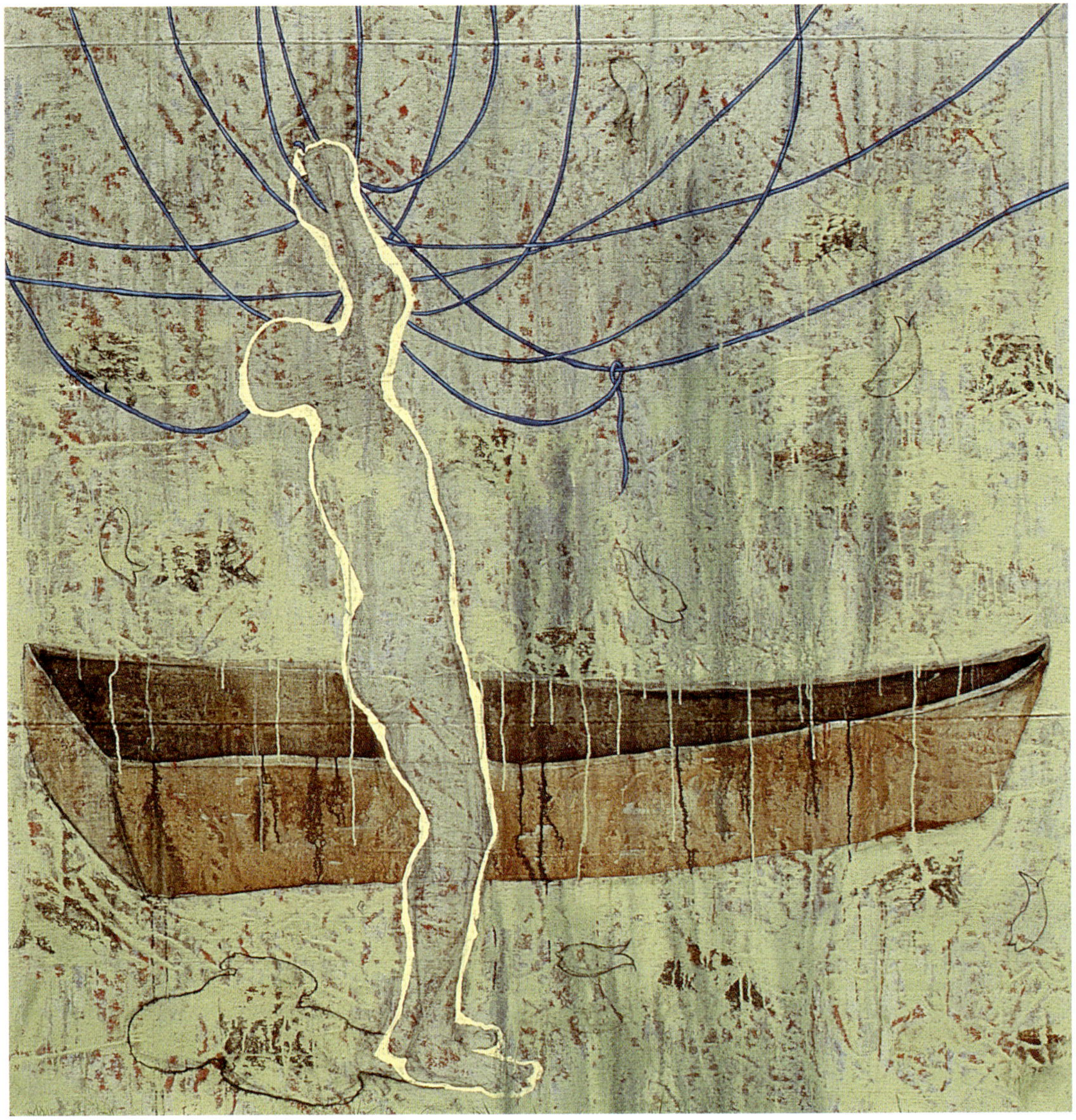

Knotting Water, acrylic on tarpaulin, 66x66", 2004

Opposite page: *Prayer - II*, acrylic on tarpaulin, 66x52", 2006

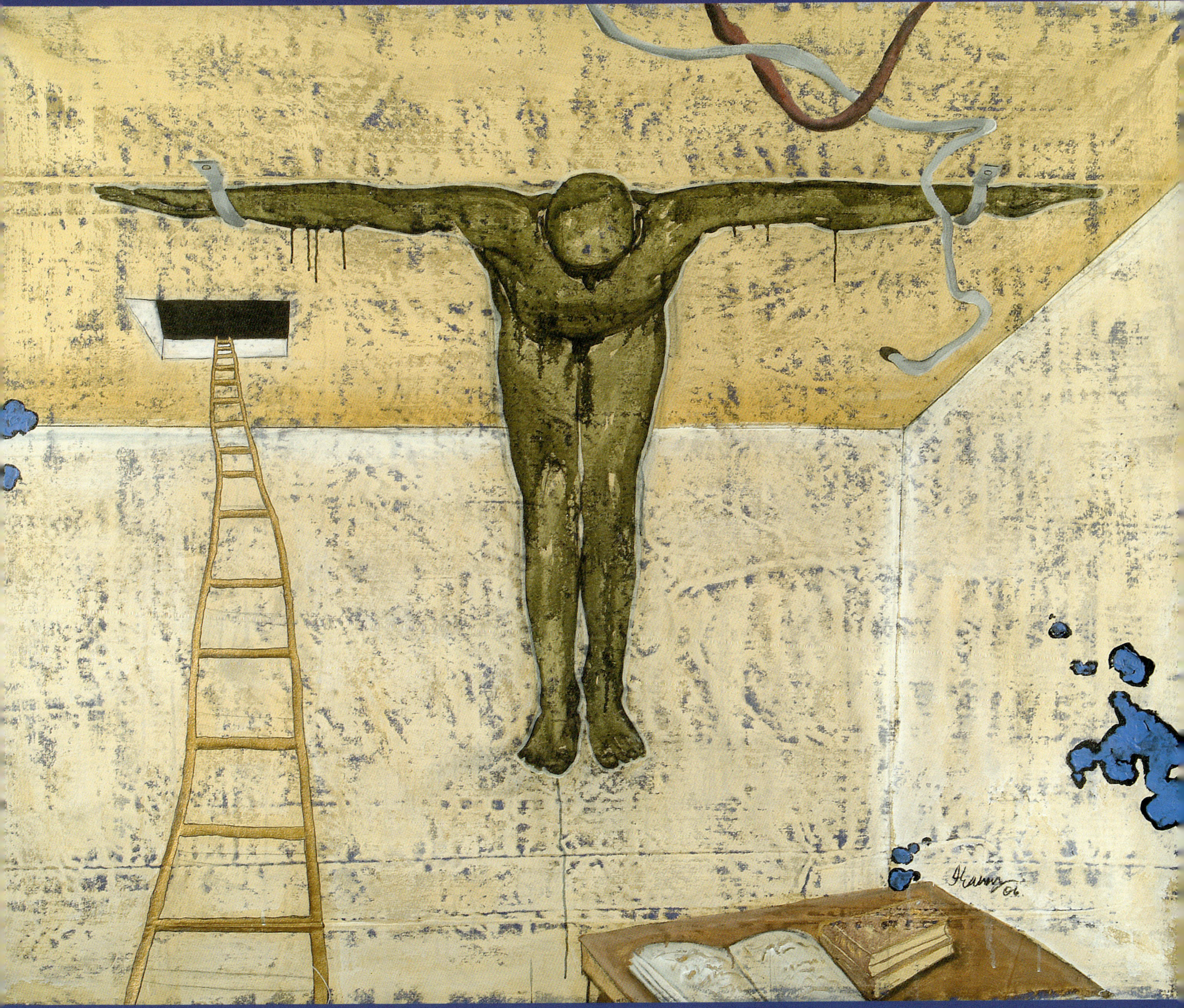

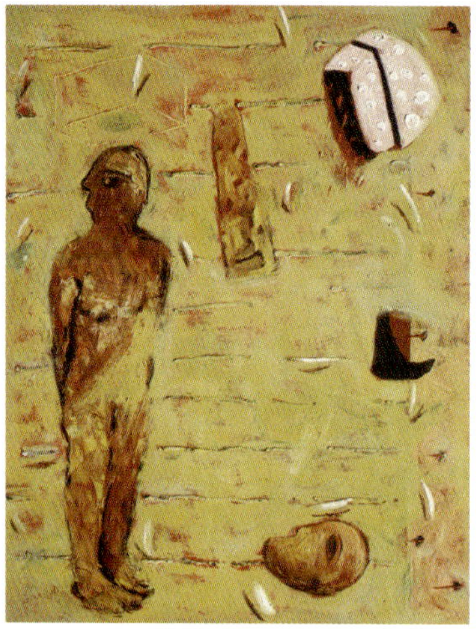

Oil on canvas, 48x62”, 1995

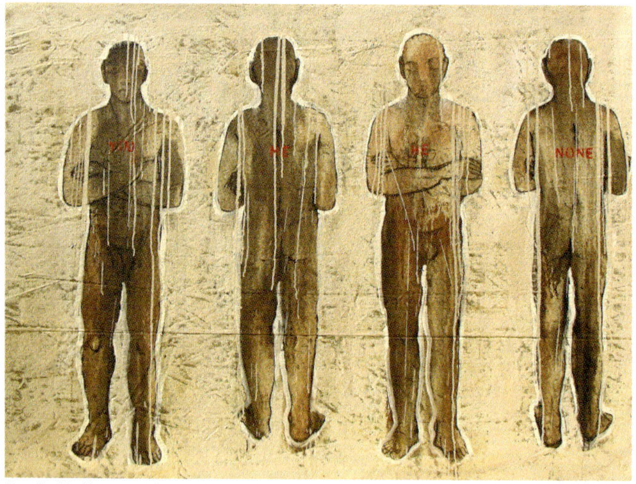

You Me He None, acrylic on tarpaulin, 66x48”, 2005

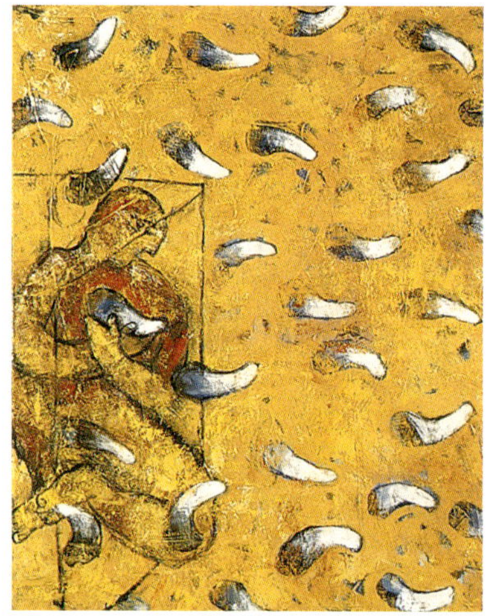

Oil on canvas, 42x48”, 1996

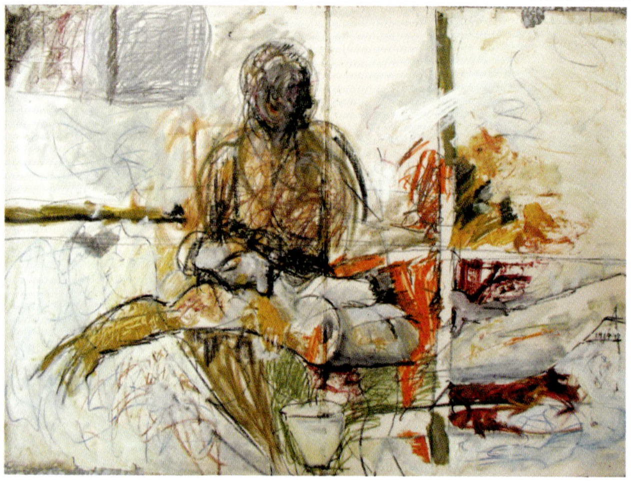

Oil on paper, 60x44”, 1993

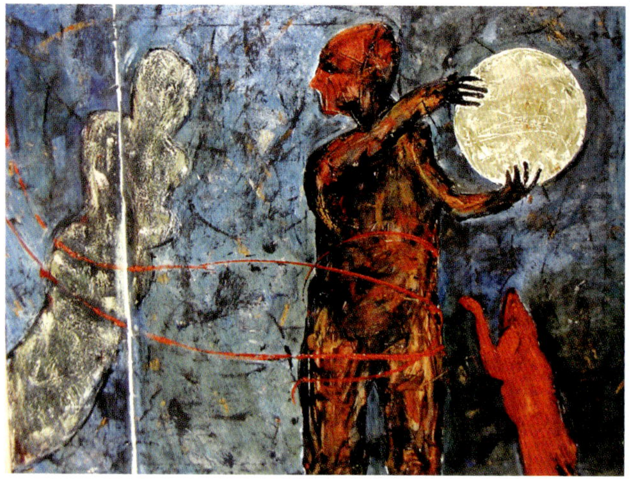

Oil on canvas, 56x42”, 1996

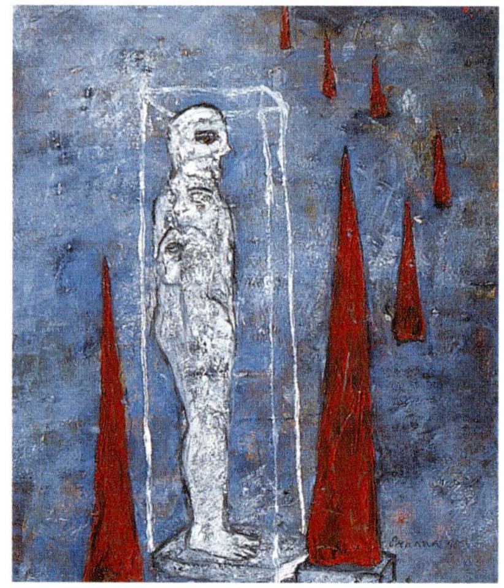

Oil on canvas, 42x56”, 1996

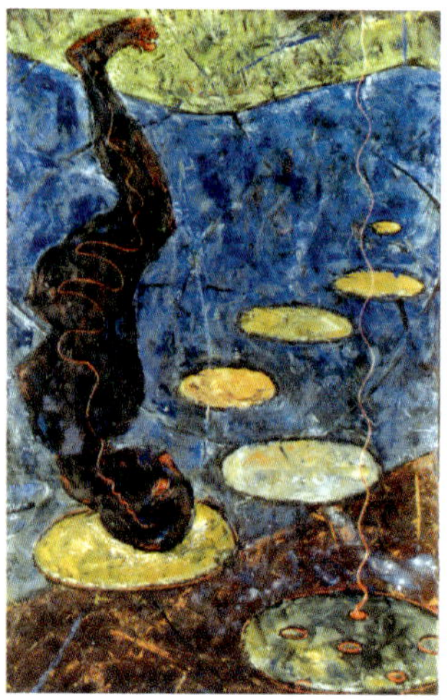

Oil on canvas, 48x72”, 1994

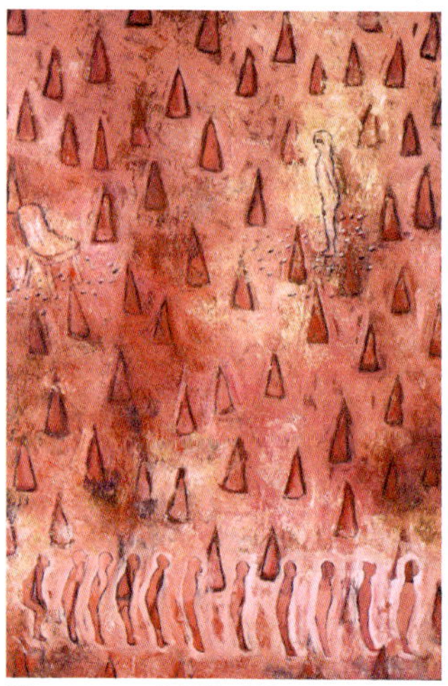

Oil on canvas, 48x72”, 1997

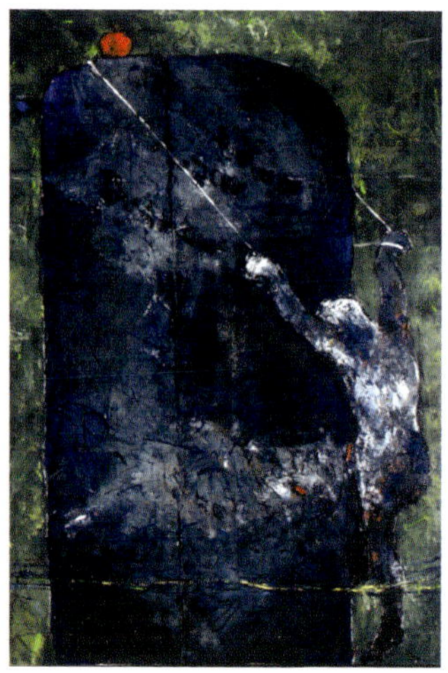

Oil on canvas, 48x72”, 1993

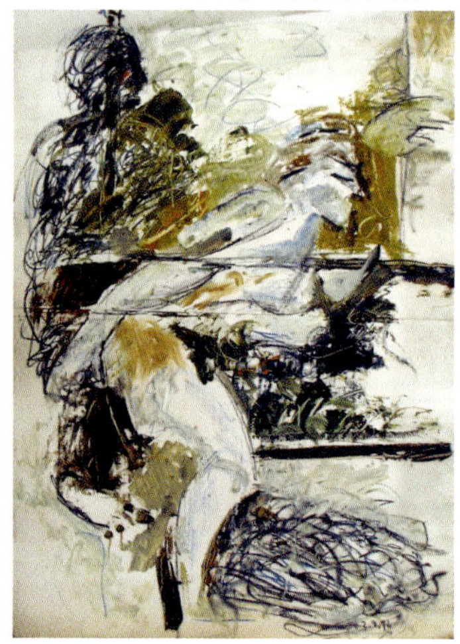

Oil on paper, 44x60”, 1994

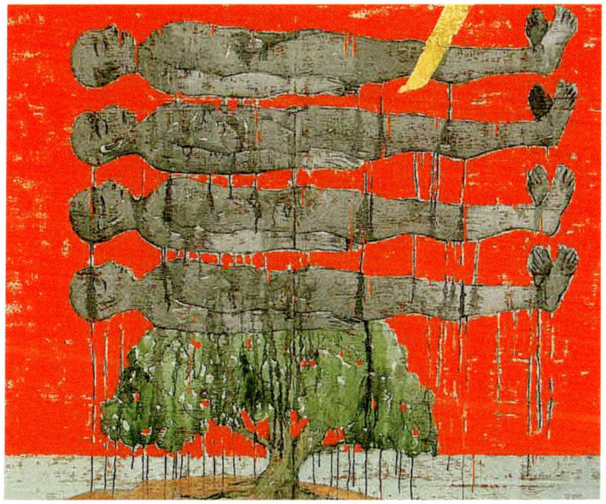

Acrylic on tarpaulin, 66x48", 2005

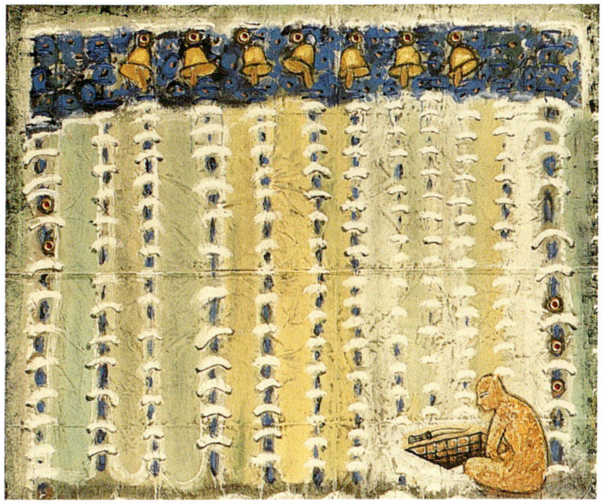

Oil on tarpaulin, 54x68", 1997

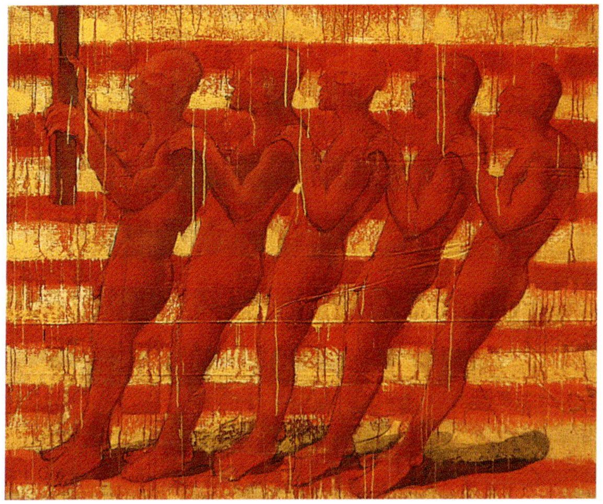

Acrylic on tarpaulin, 66x60", 1999

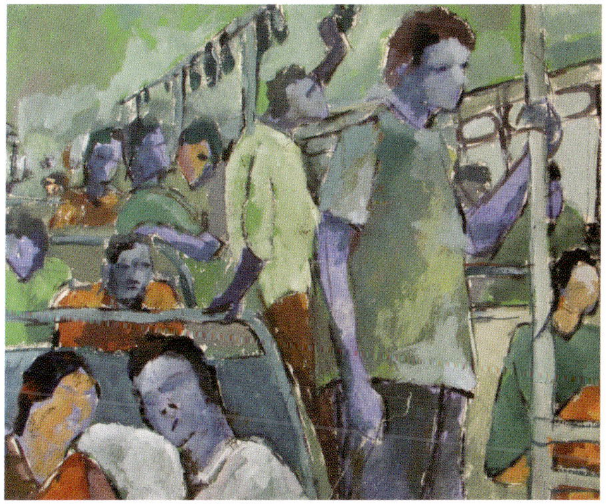

Poster colour on paper, 30x22", 1988

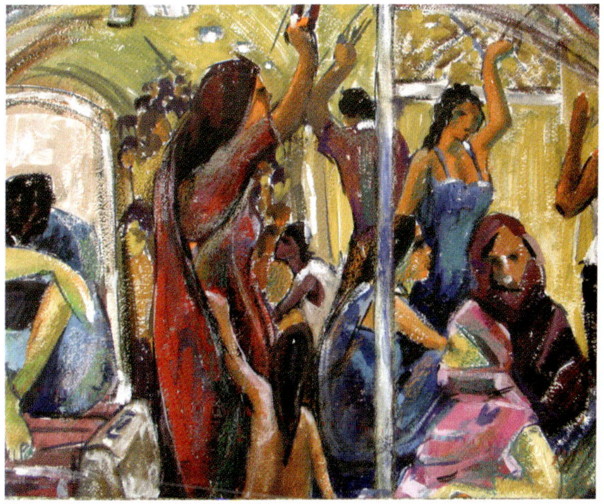

Poster colour on paper, 30x22", 1989

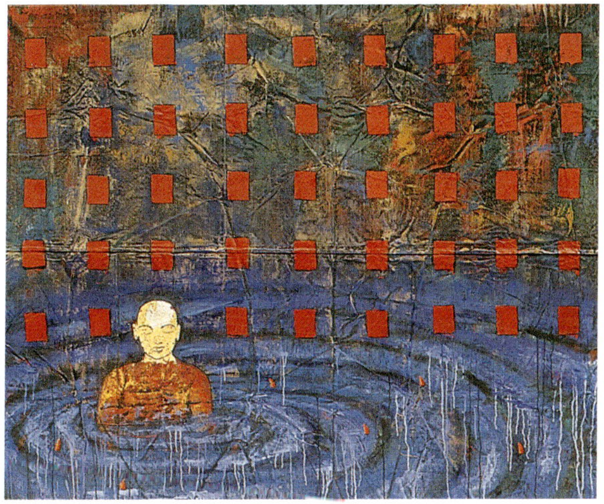

Acrylic on tarpaulin, 90x66", 1998

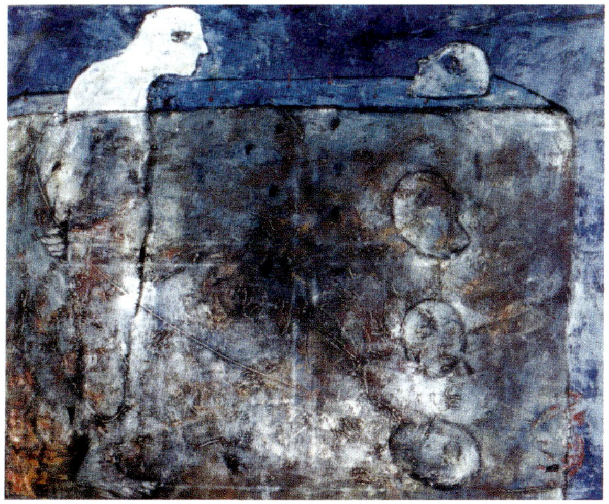

Oil on canvas, 66x60", 1995

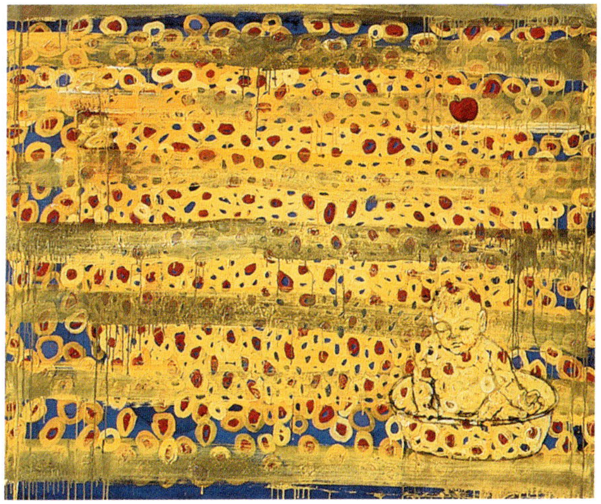

Acrylic on canvas, 66x52", 2001

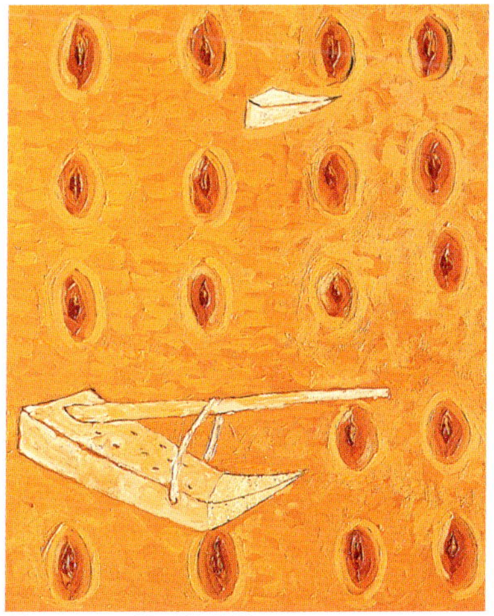

Oil on canvas, 36x48", 1998

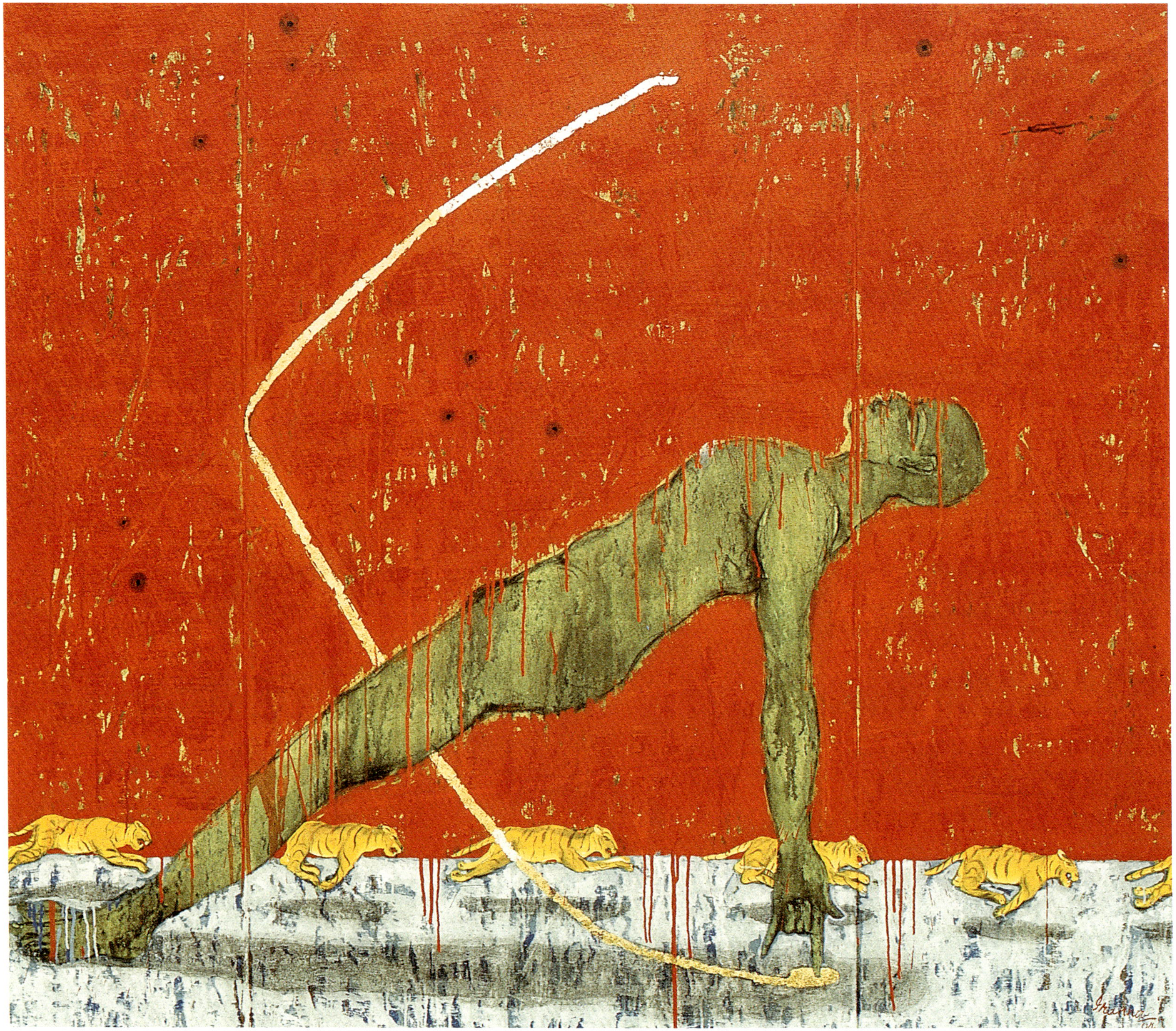

Untitled, acrylic on tarpaulin, 88x80”, 2004

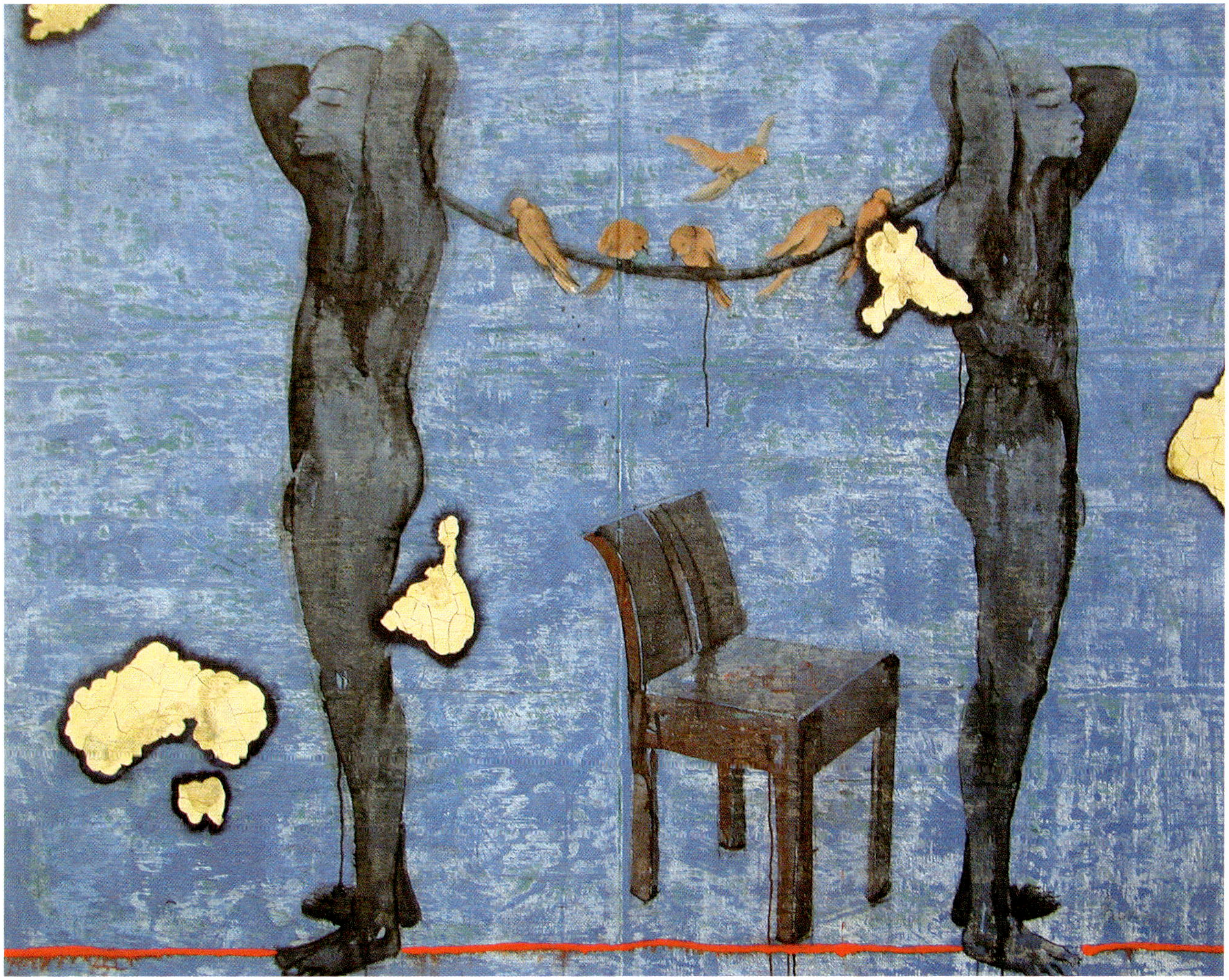

Untitled, acrylic on tarpaulin, 66x52", 2005

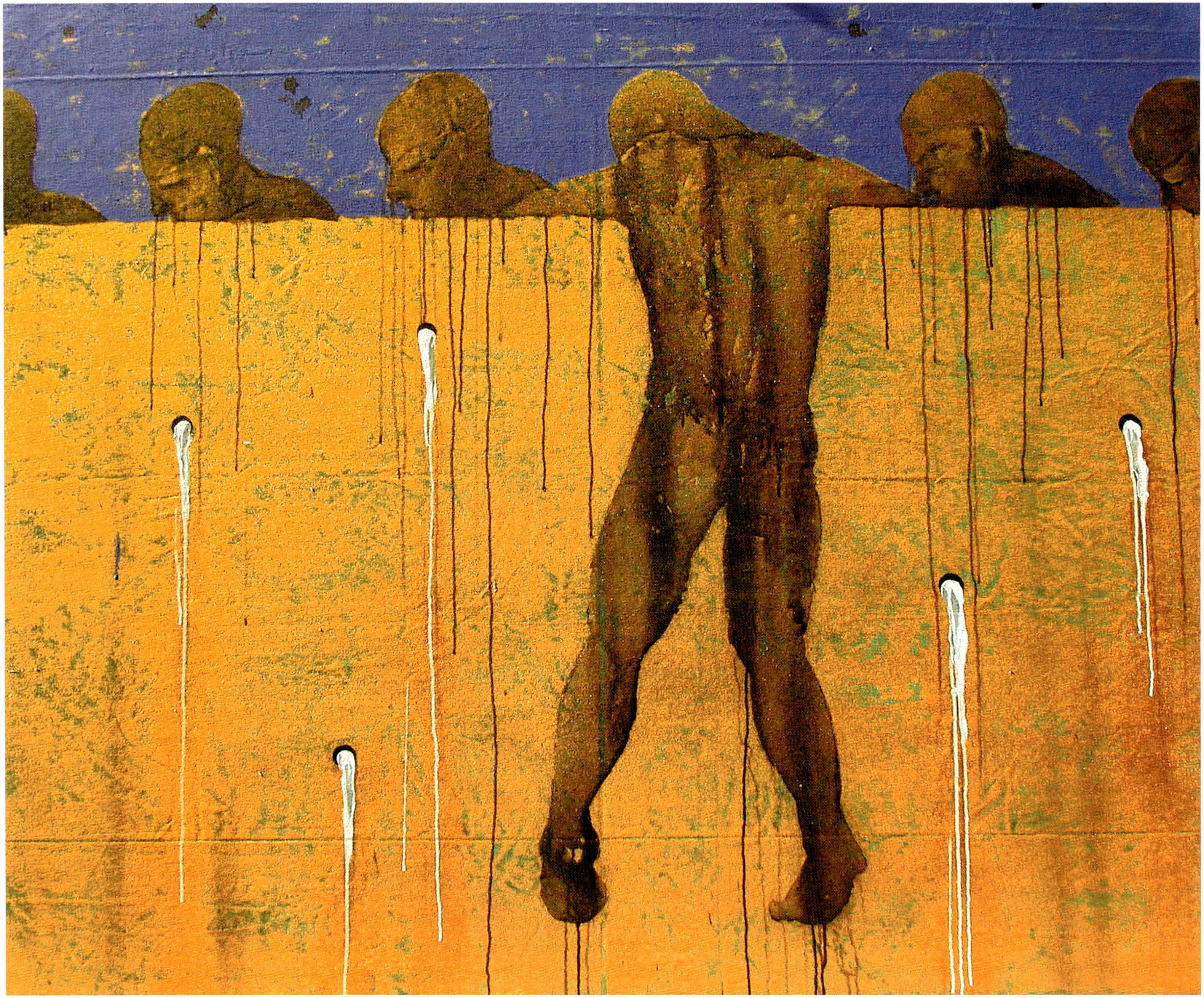

Untitled, acrylic on tarpaulin, 66x52", 2005

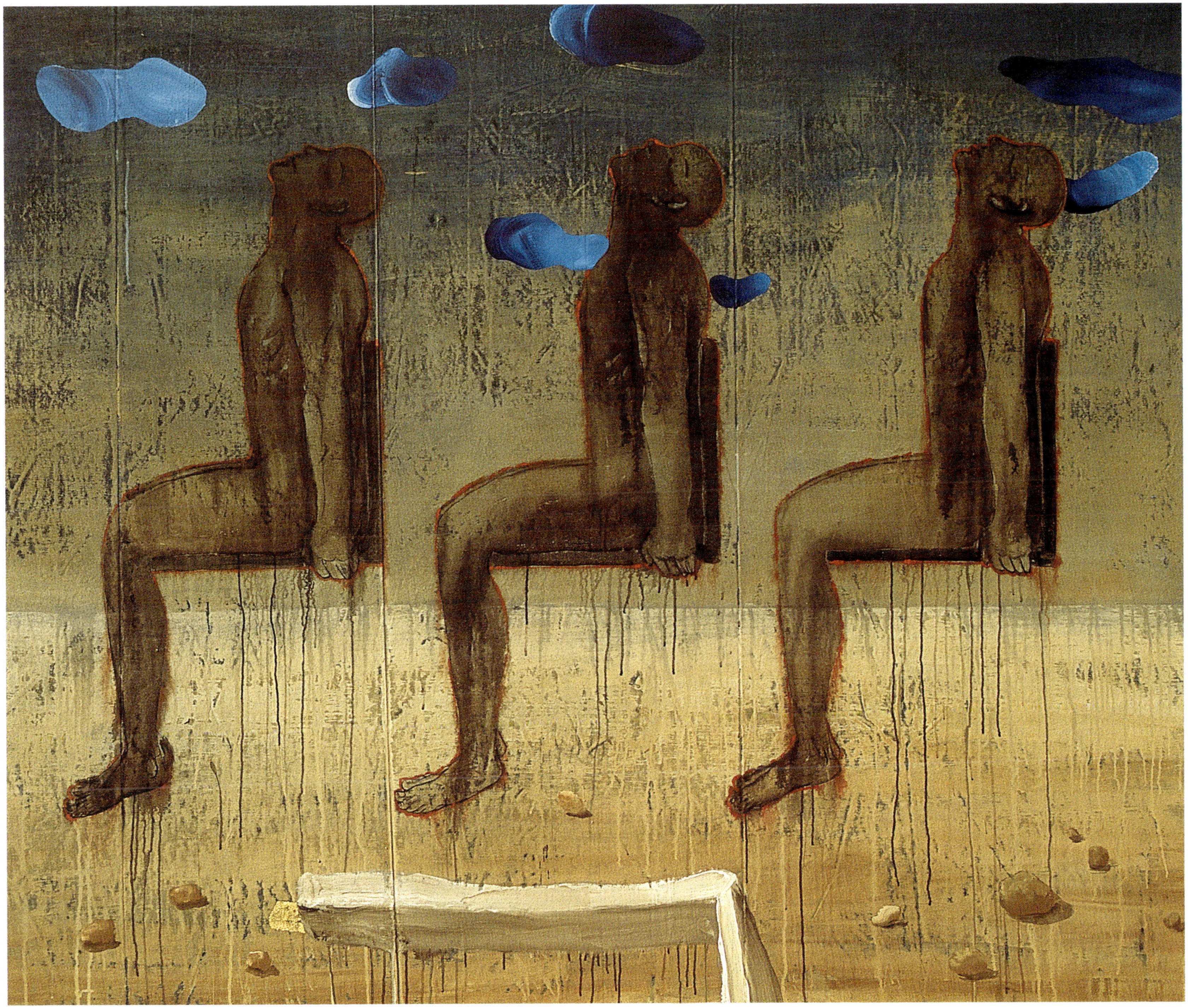

Untitled, acrylic on tarpaulin, 80x66", 2005

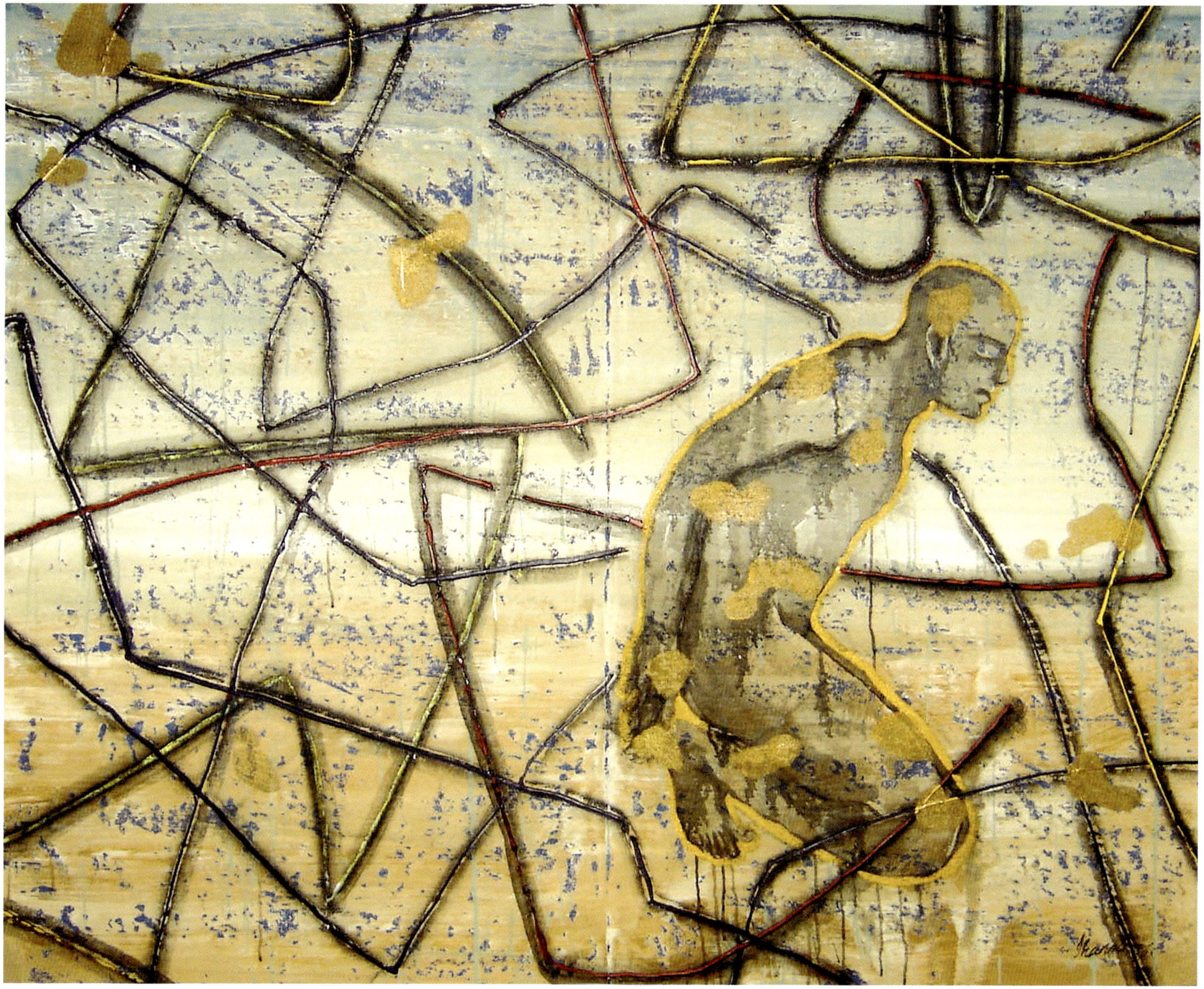

Untitled, acrylic on tarpaulin, 66x52", 2005

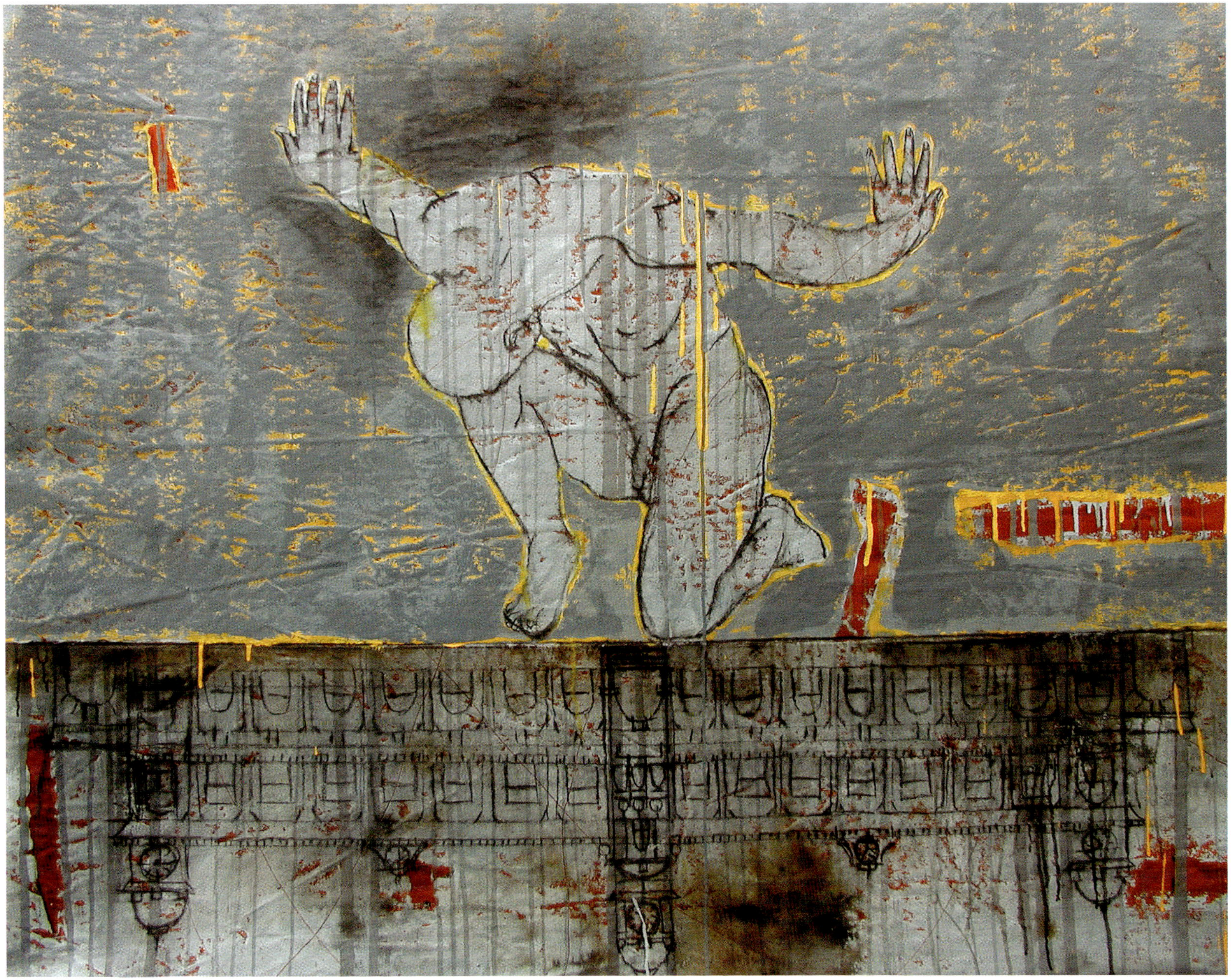

Untitled, acrylic on tarpaulin, 62x52", 2005

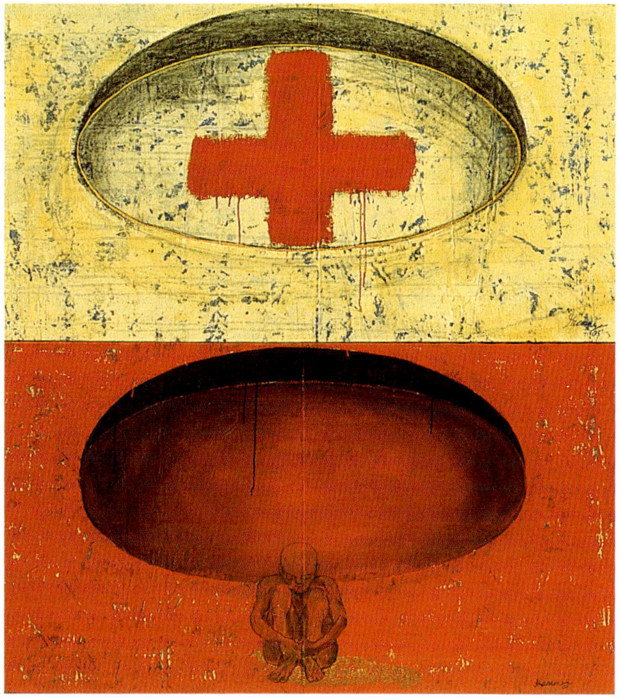

Untitled, acrylic on tarpaulin, 66x80”, 2005

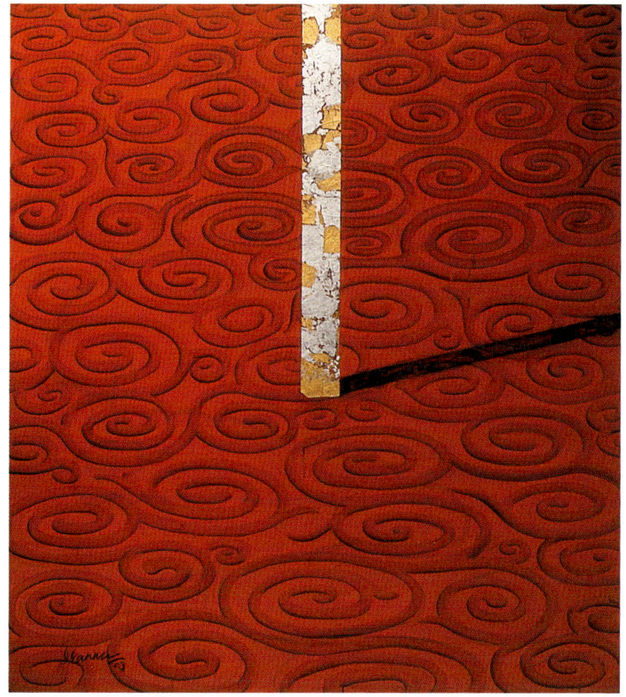

Acrylic on canvas, 60x72”, 2002

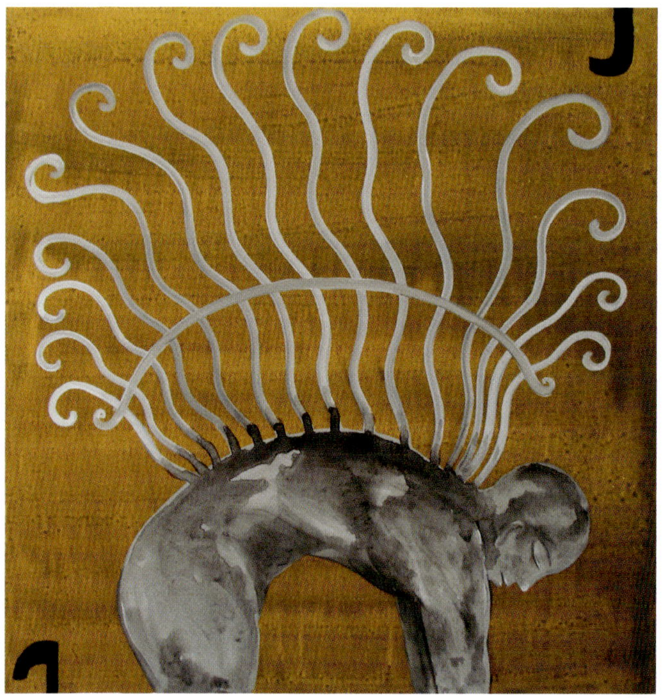

Untitled, acrylic on canvas, 30x30”, 2006

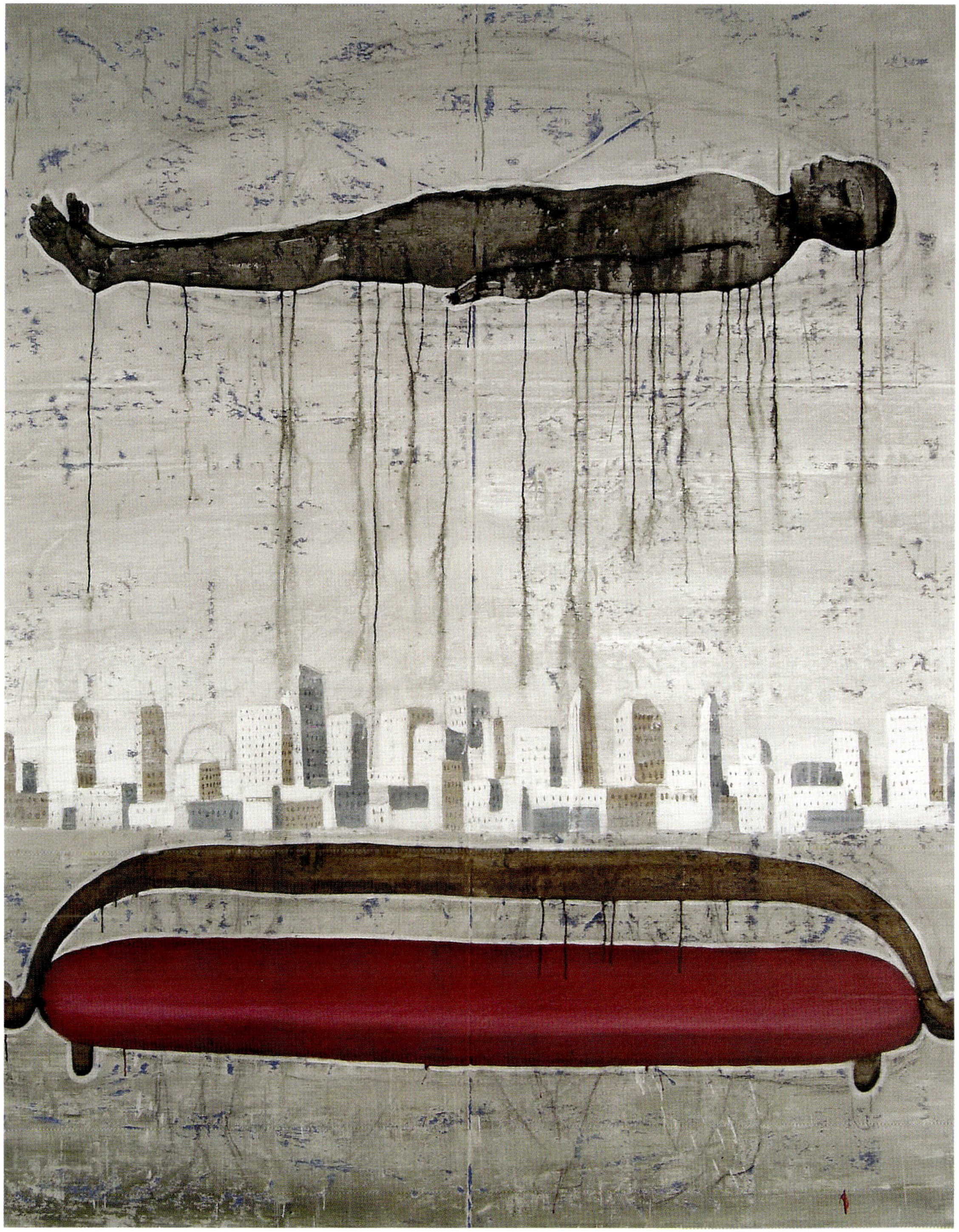

Eternity, acrylic on tarpaulin, 66x84", 2005

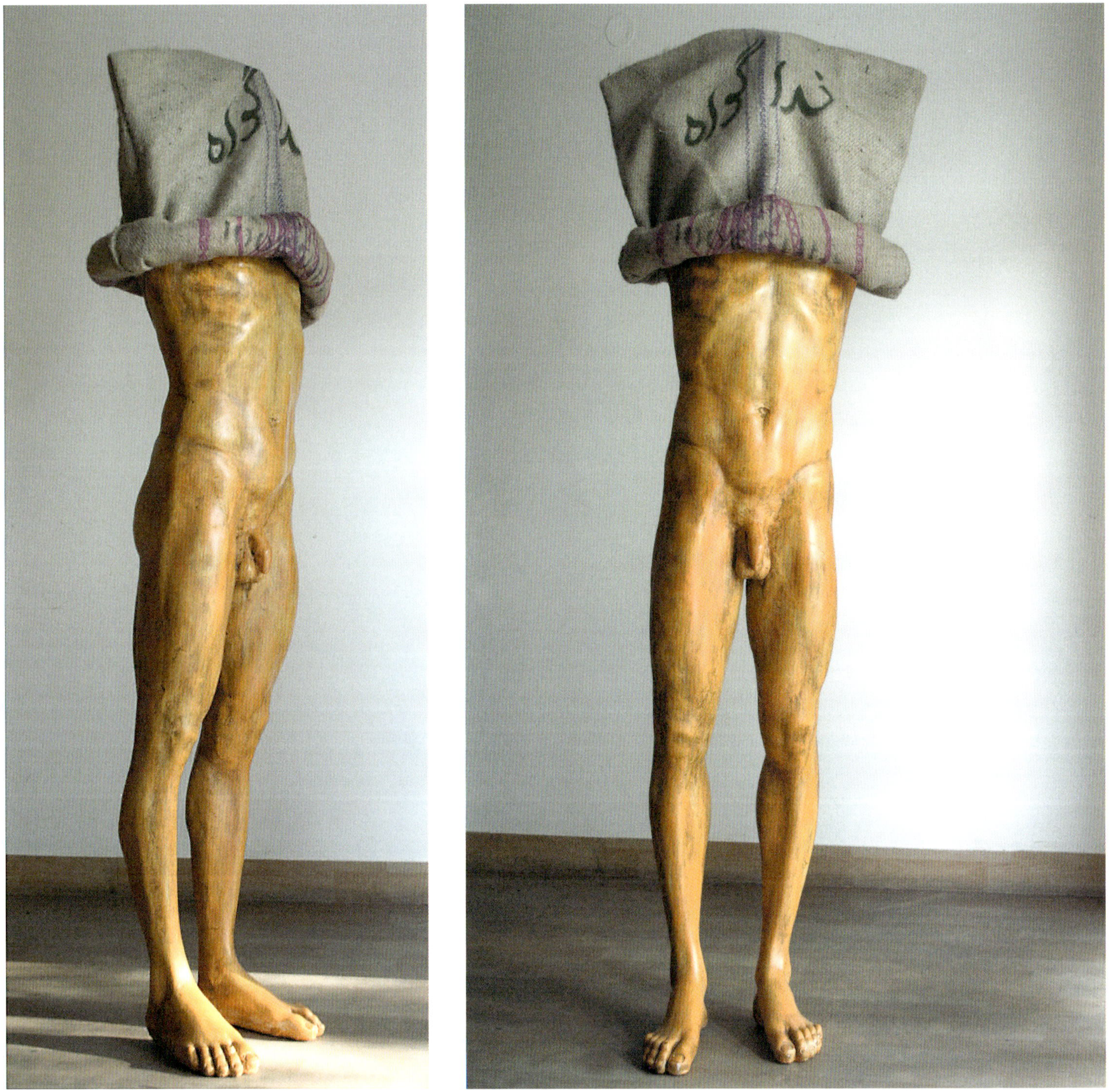

Make Sure You're Breathing, acrylic on fibreglass, jute bag, 72x24x24", 2006

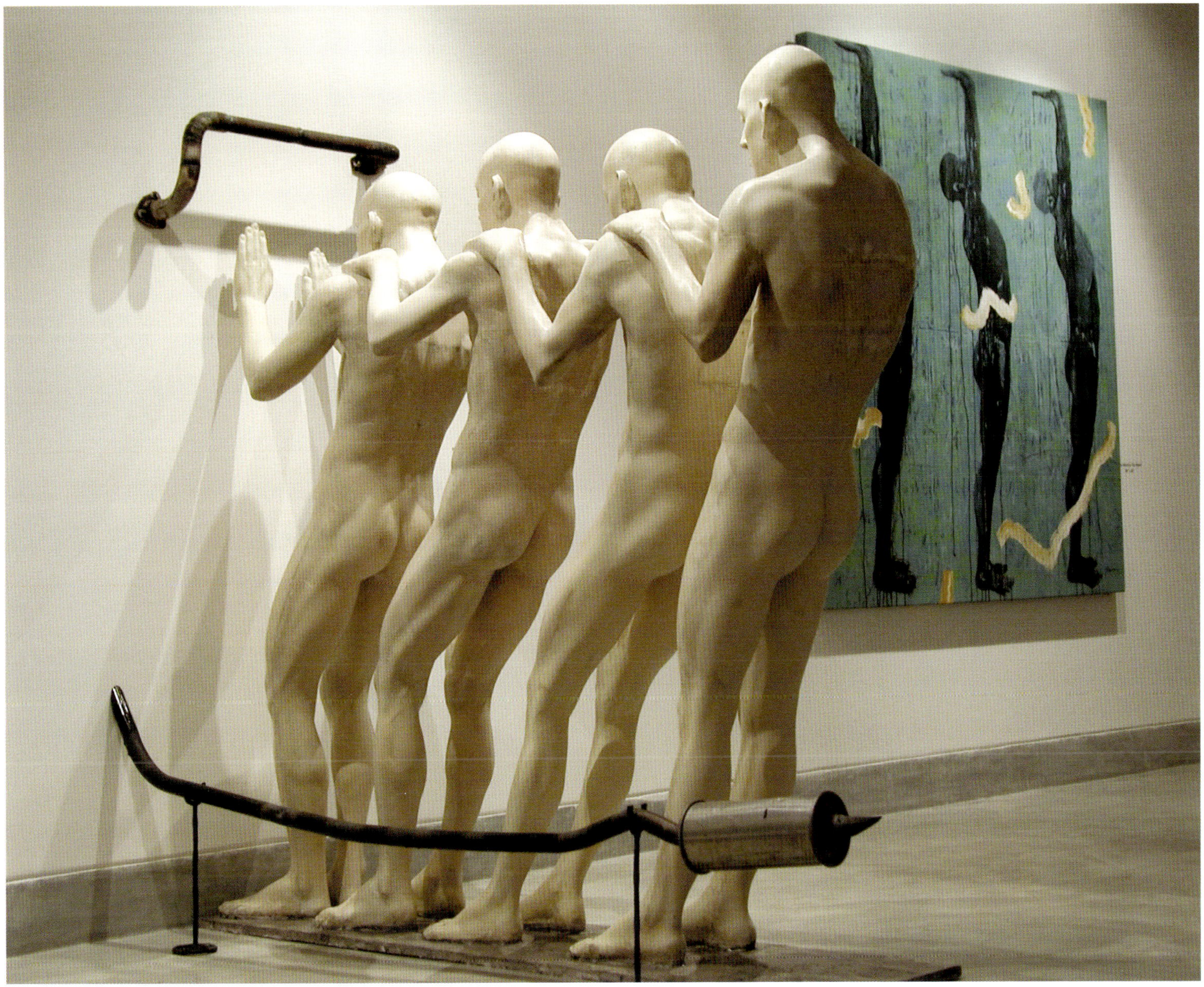

The Silencer, fibreglass and iron, 72x84x30”, 2005

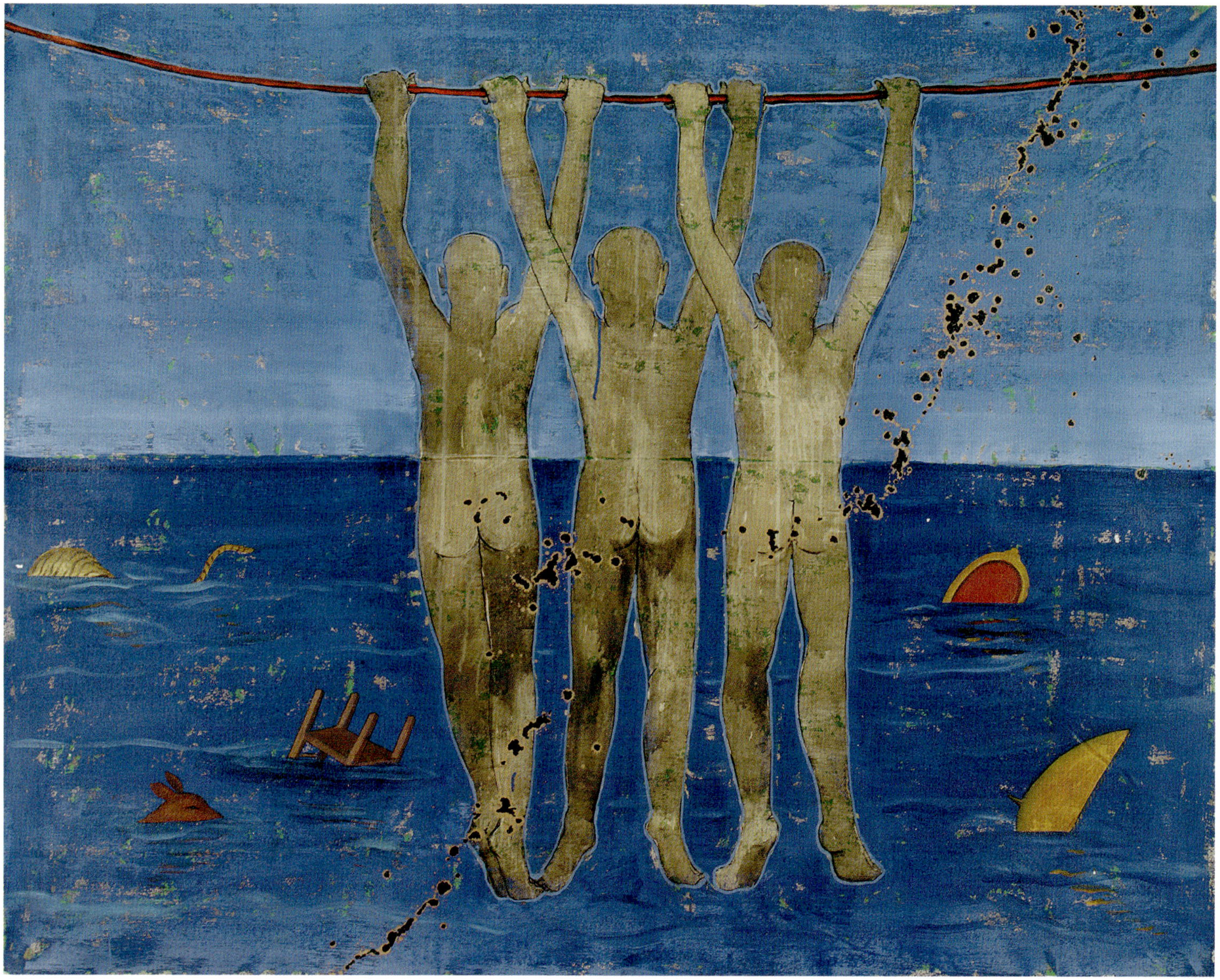

Untitled, acrylic on tarpaulin, 66x52", 2006

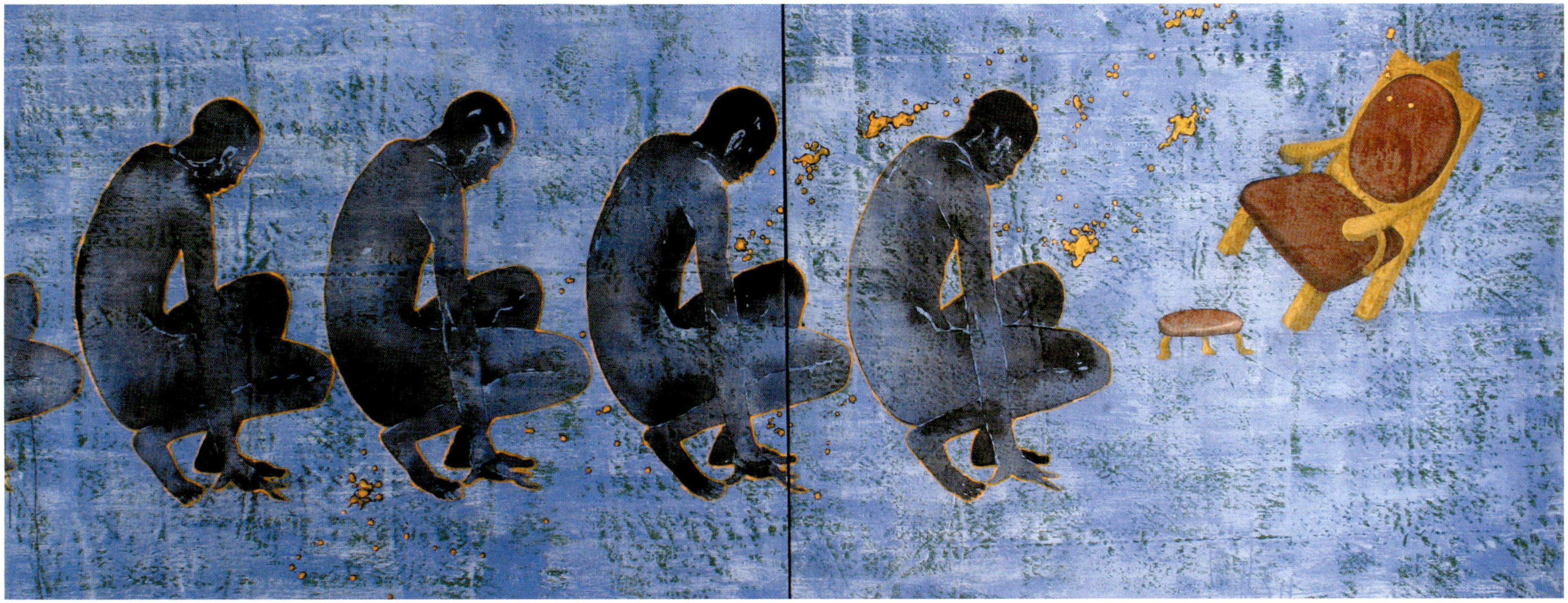

The Story of Five Gentlemen, acrylic on tarpaulin, 132x52", 2006

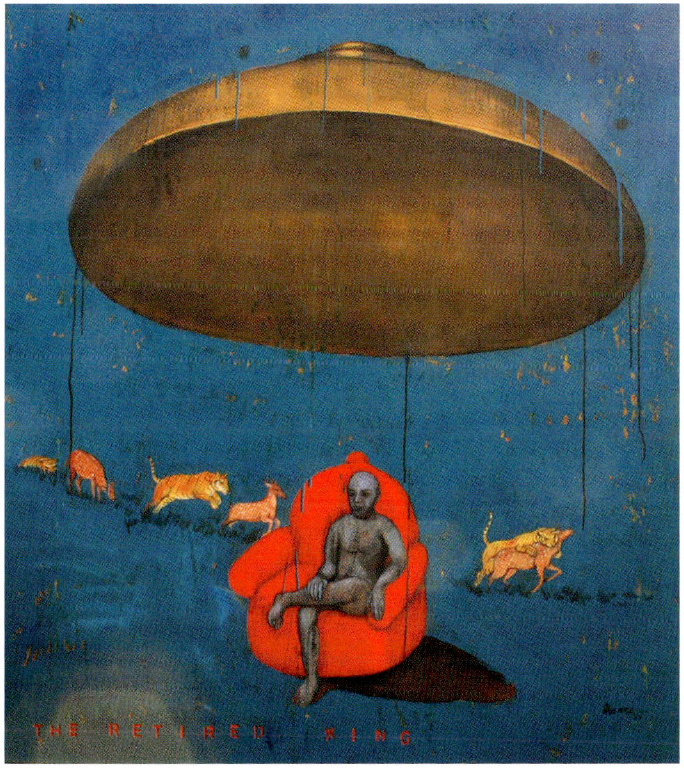

The Retired King, acrylic on tarpaulin, 52x66", 2006

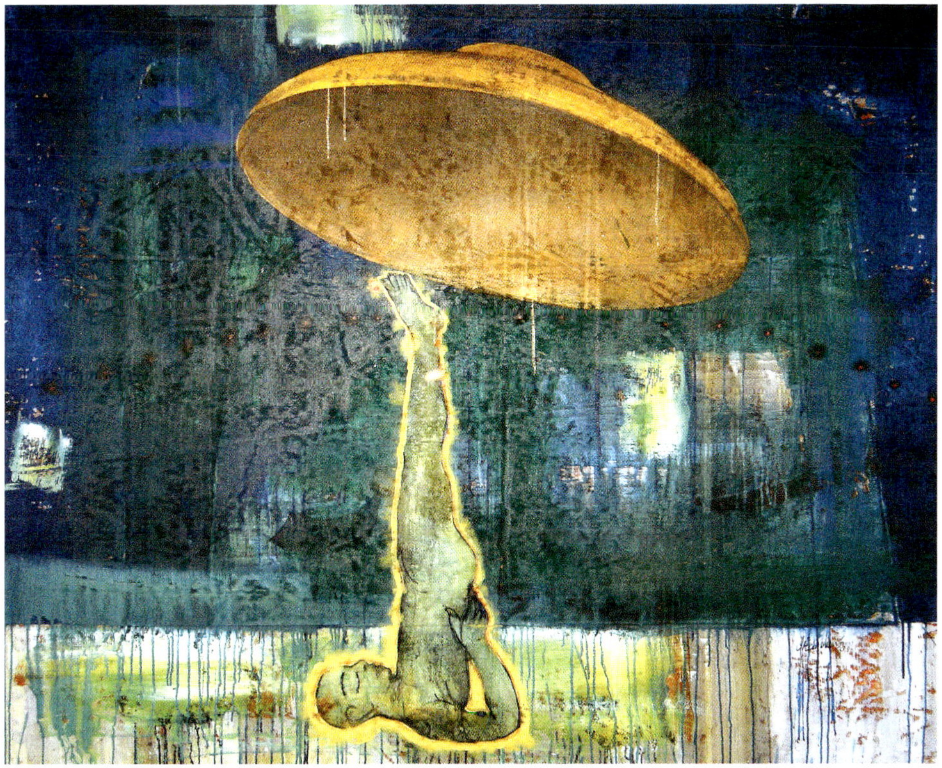

Untitled, acrylic on tarpaulin, 66x48", 2005

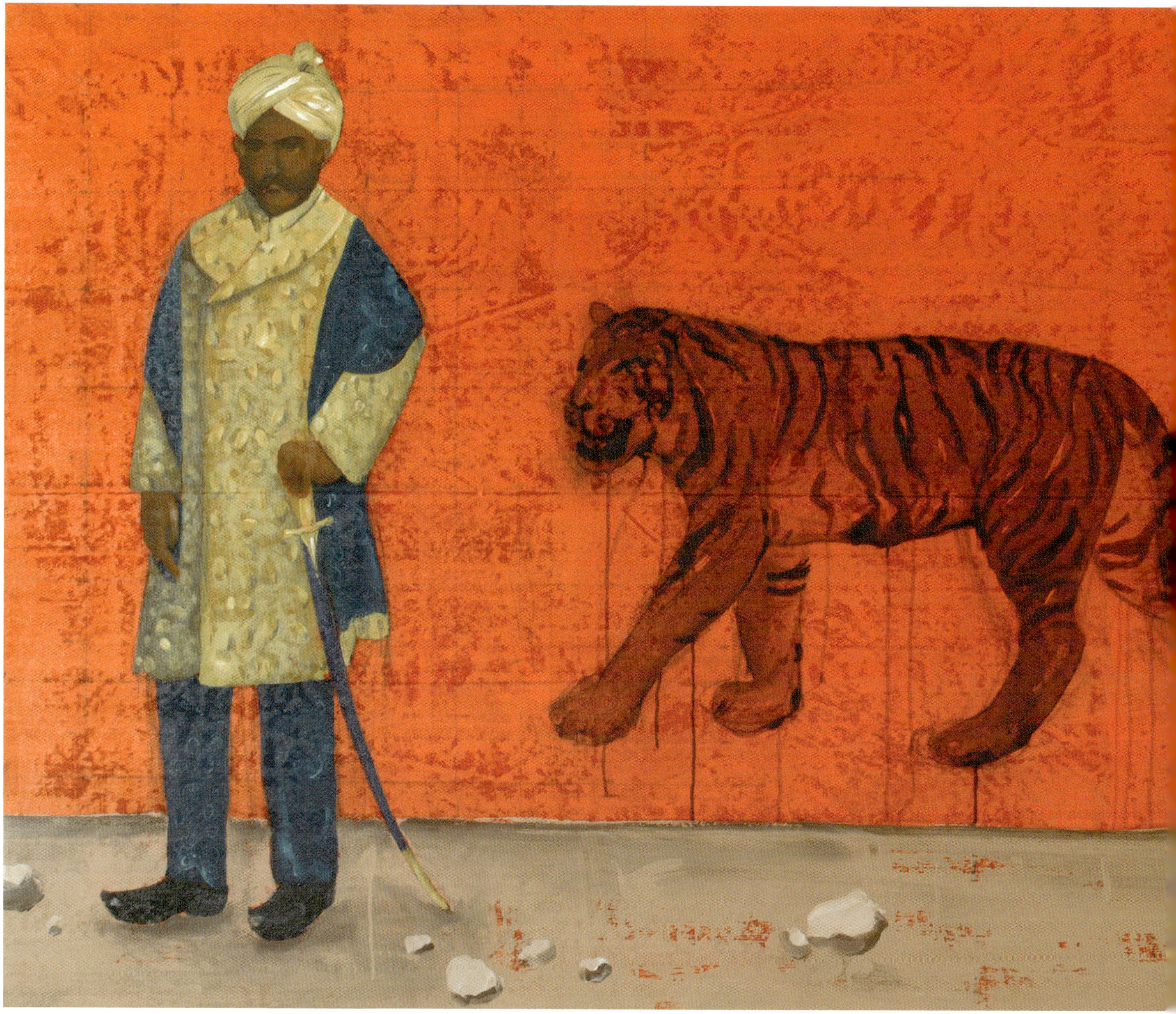

The Retired King, acrylic on tarpaulin, 132x52", 2006

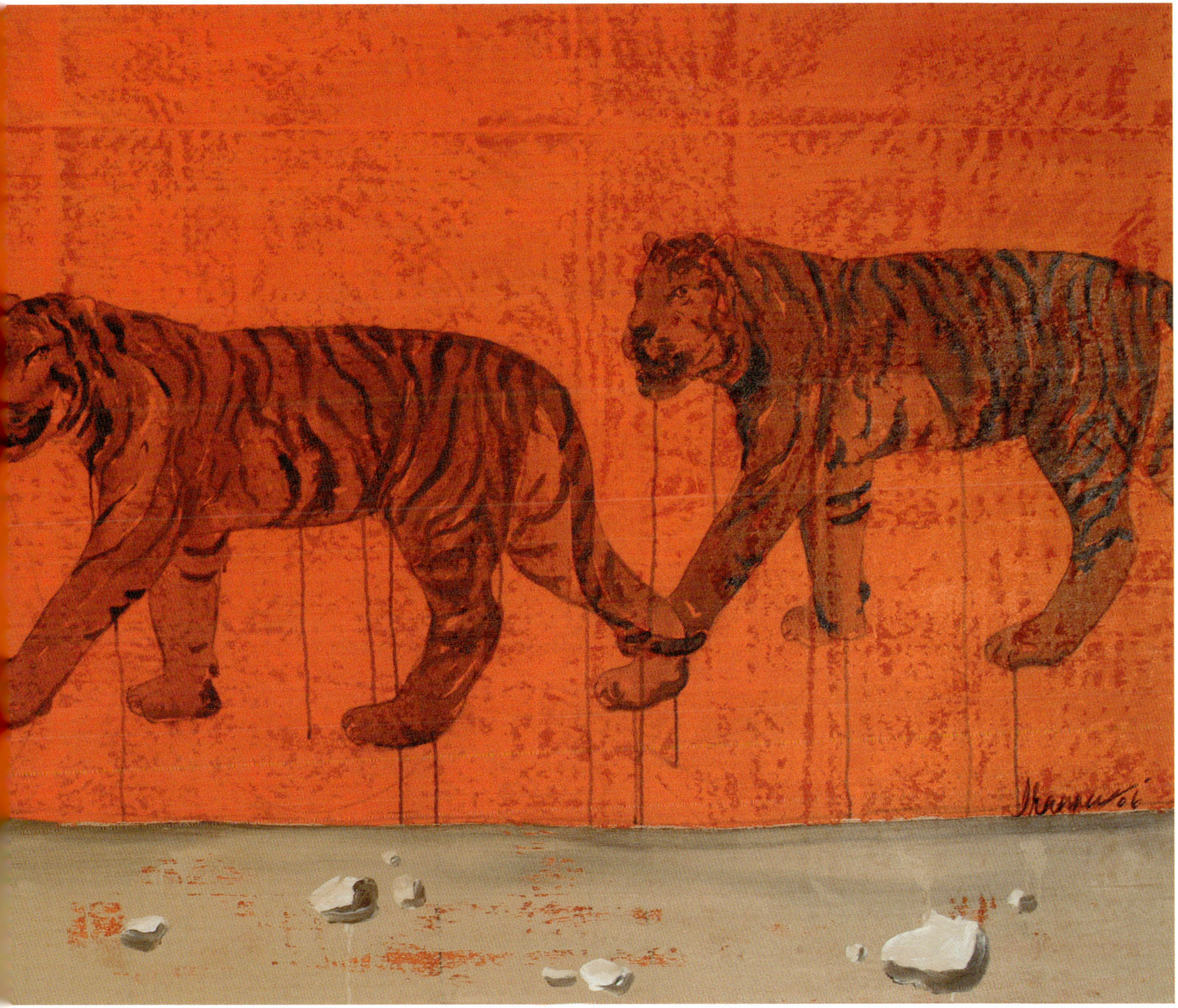

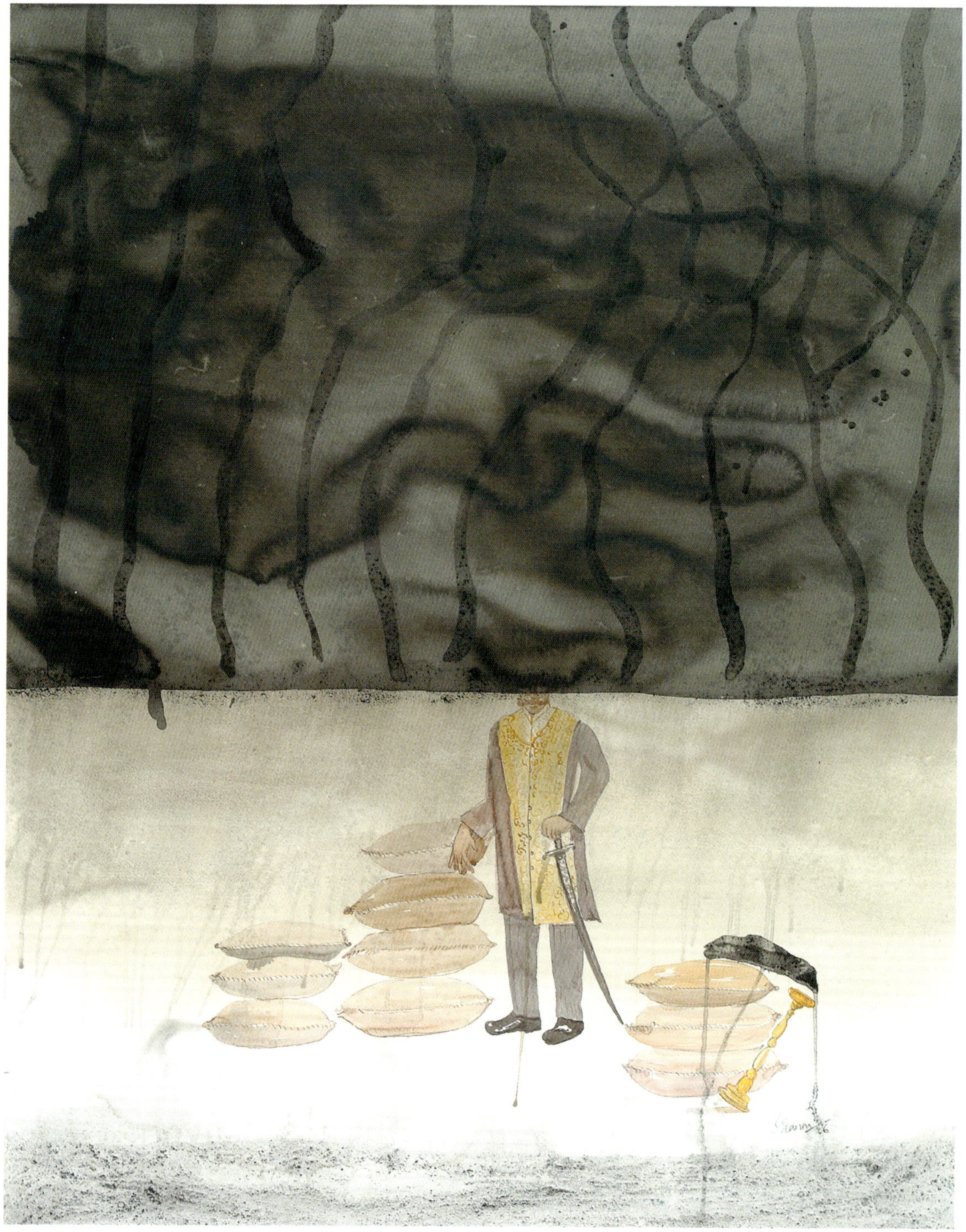

Masked King, watercolour on paper, 42x60", 2006

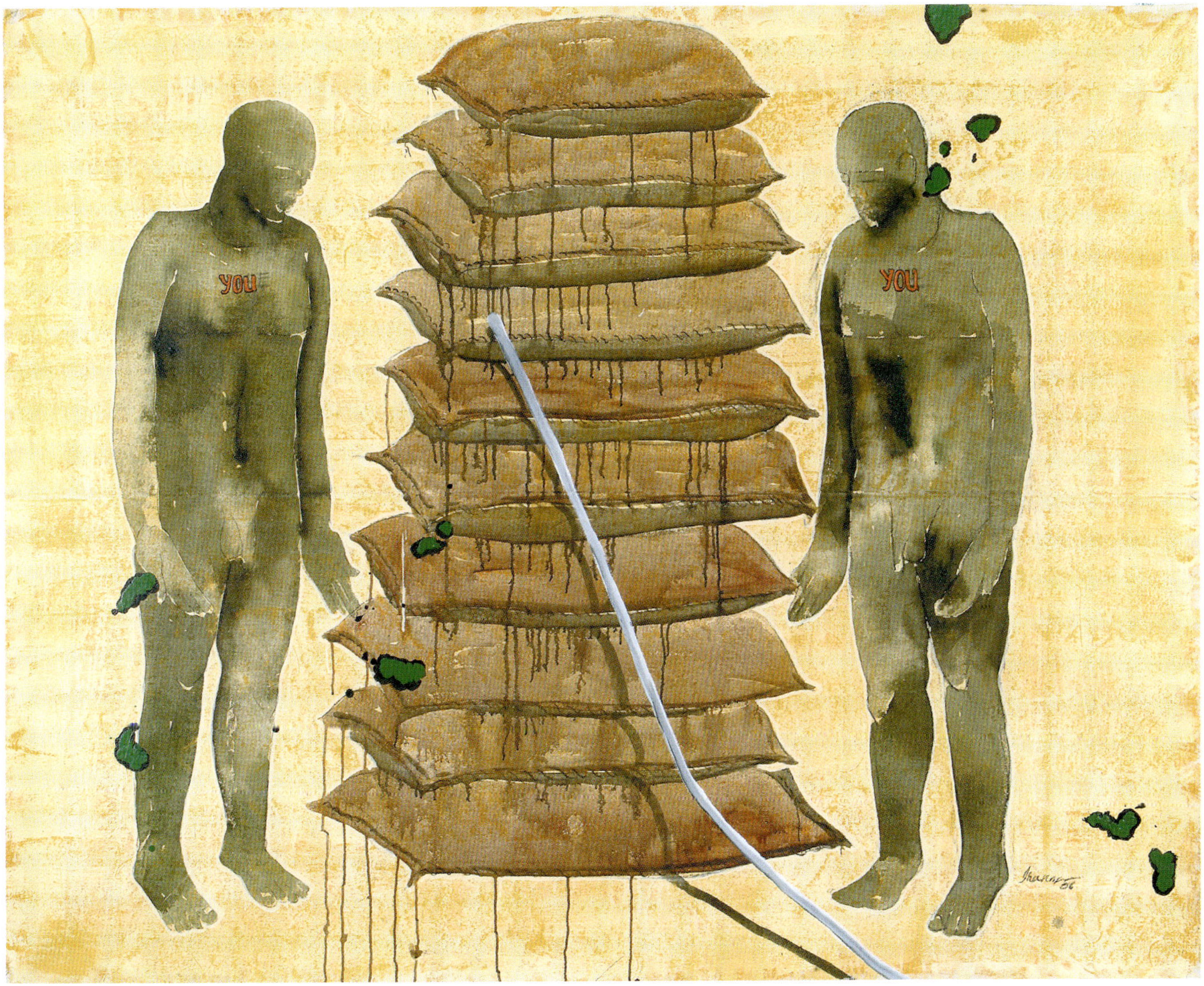

You and You, acrylic on tarpaulin, 66x52", 2006

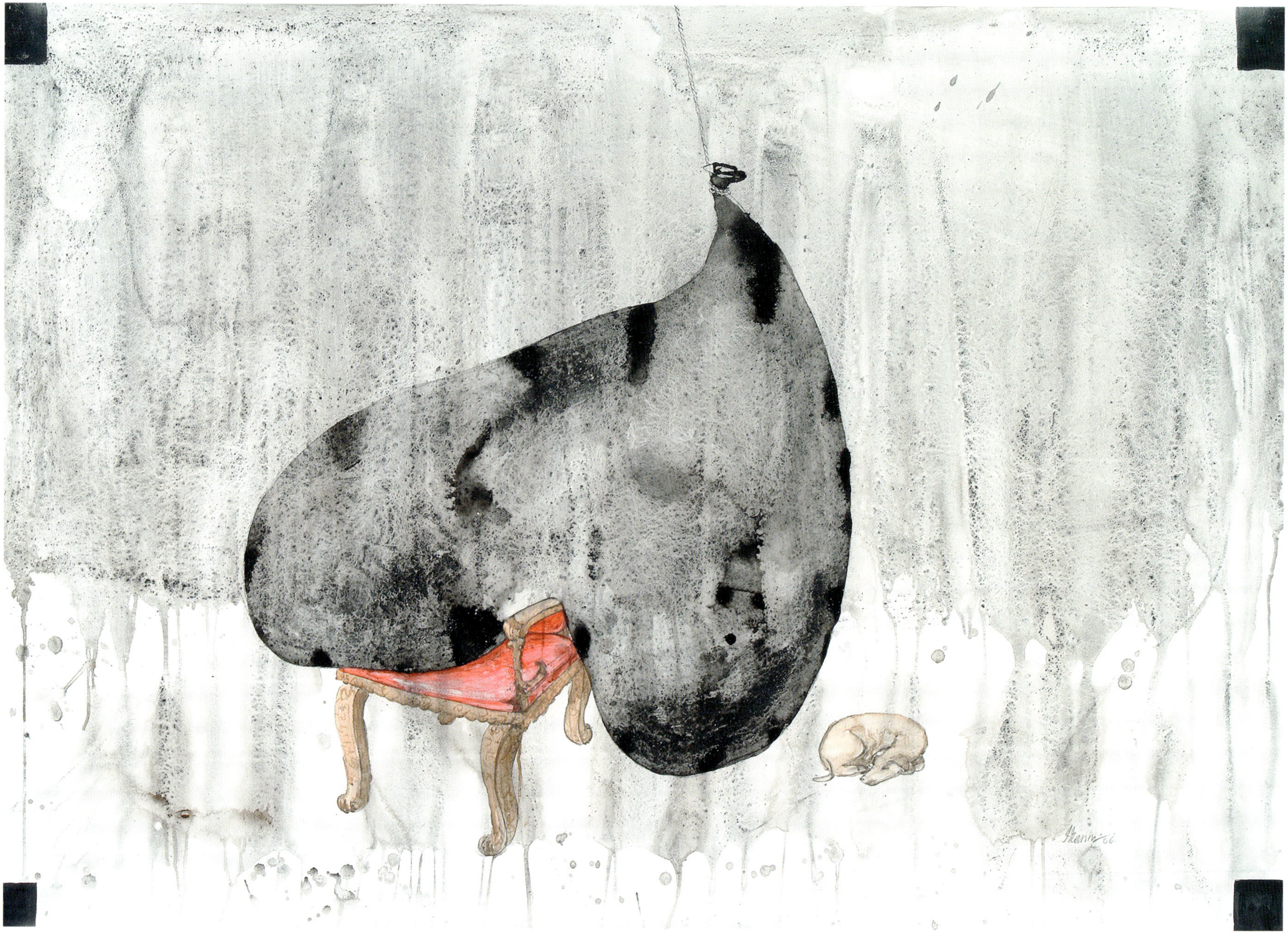

Breathe, watercolour on paper, 60x42", 2006

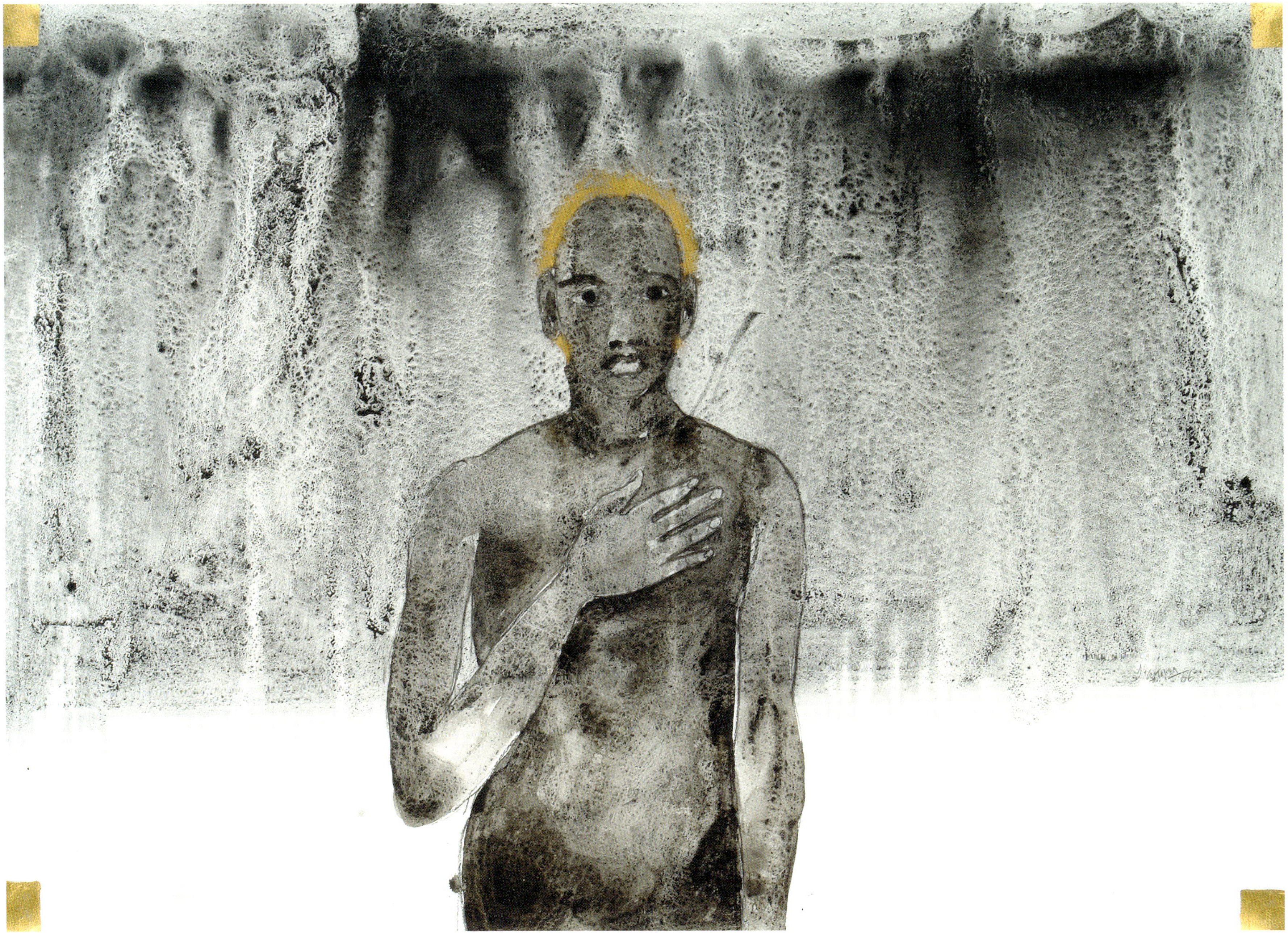

Promise, watercolour on paper, 60x42", 2006

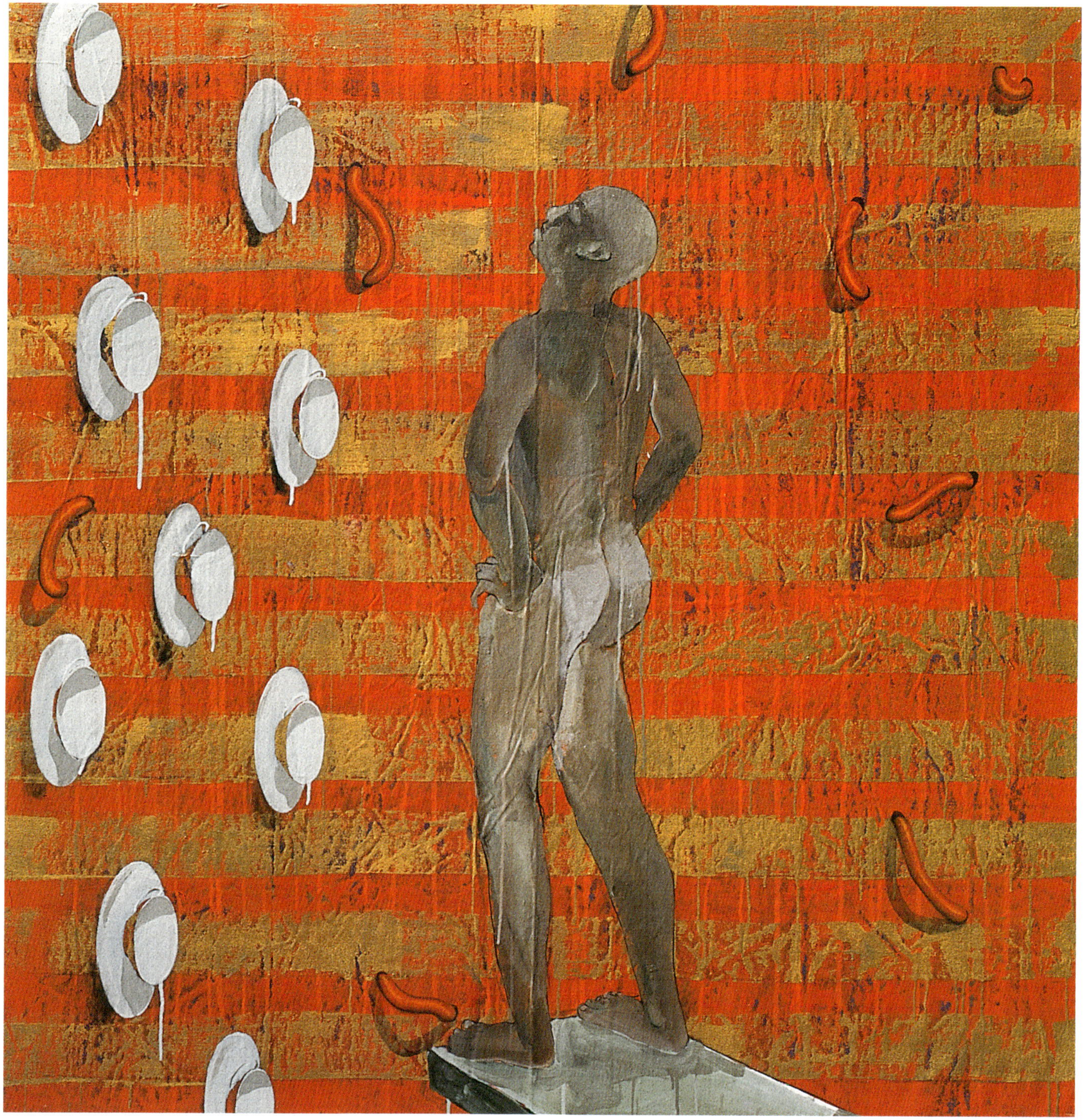

Untitled, acrylic on tarpaulin, 66x66", 2003

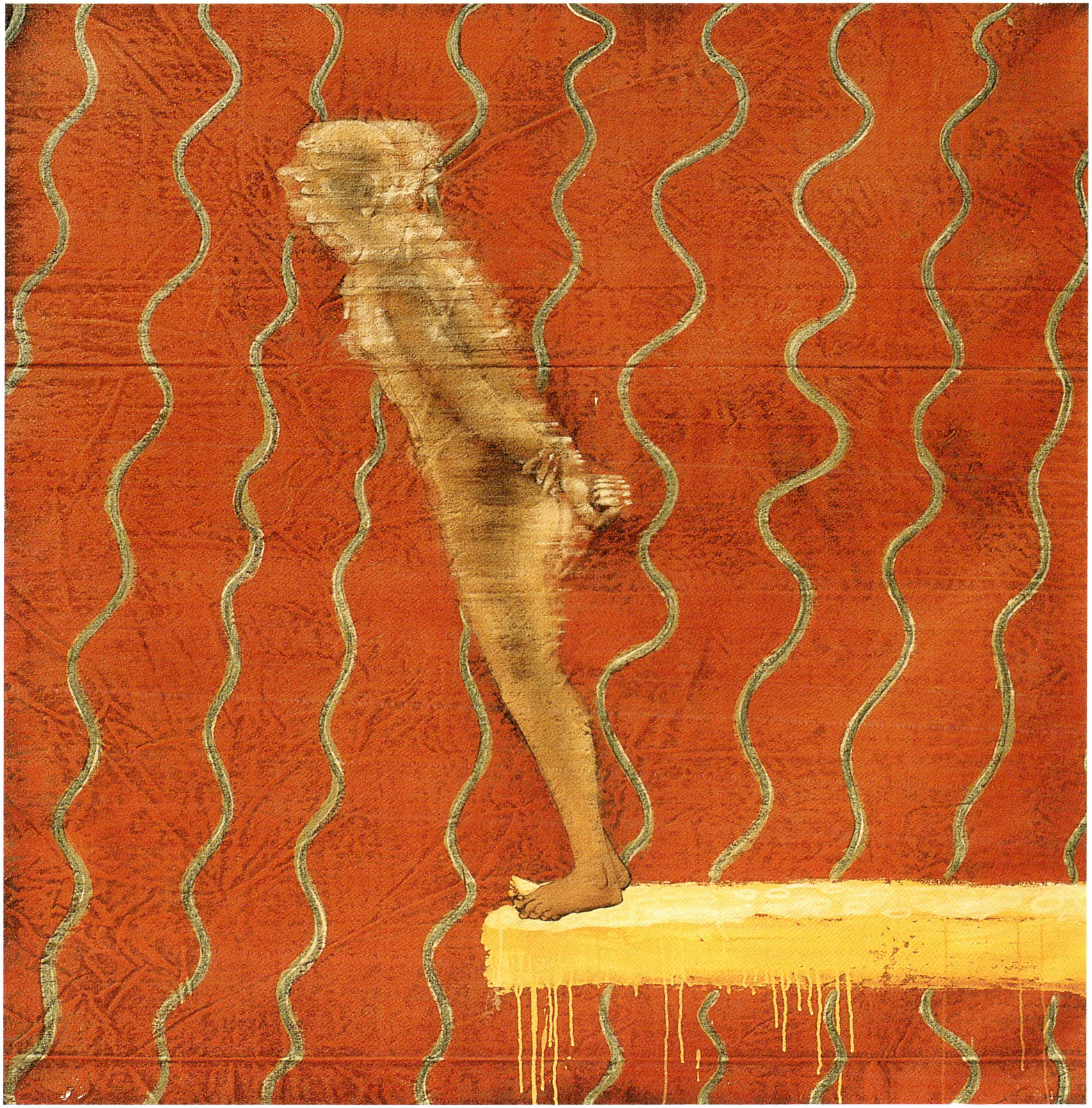

Untitled, acrylic on tarpaulin, 66x66”, 2003

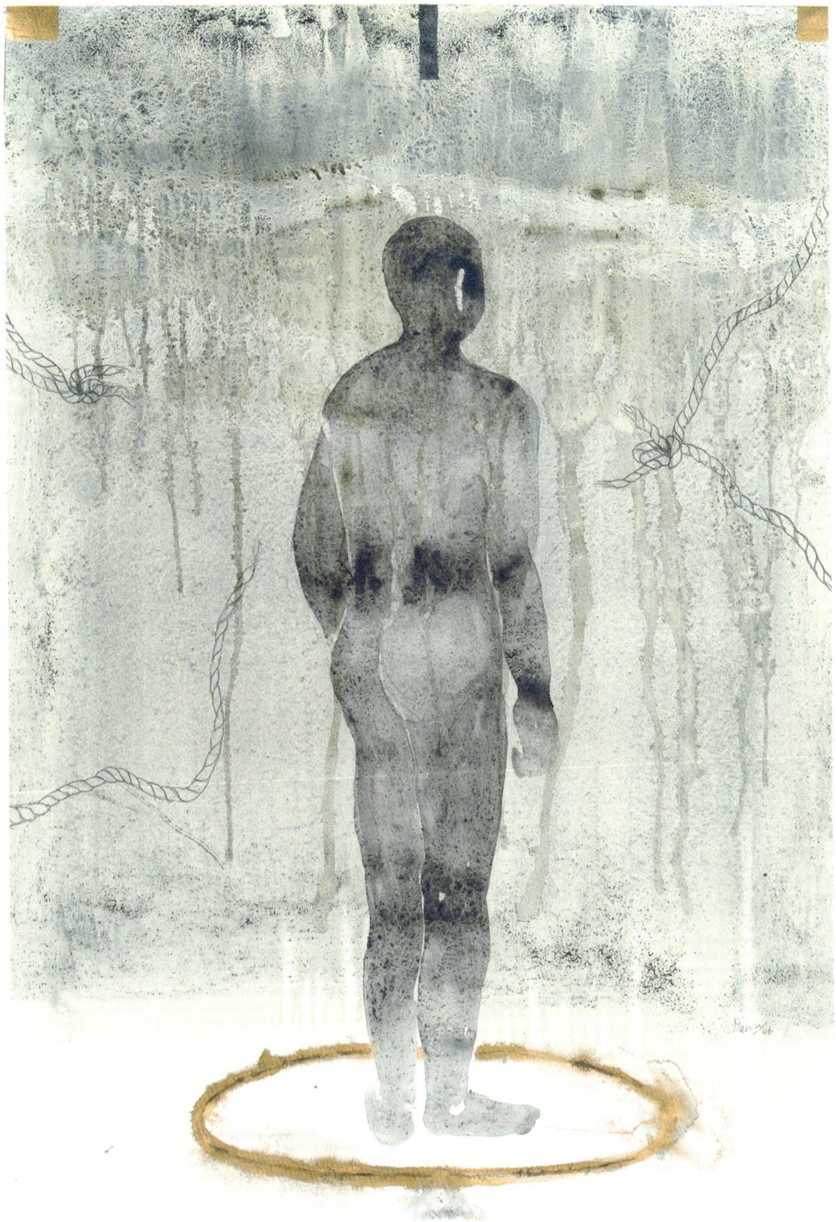

Barricades, watercolour on paper, 42x60", 2006

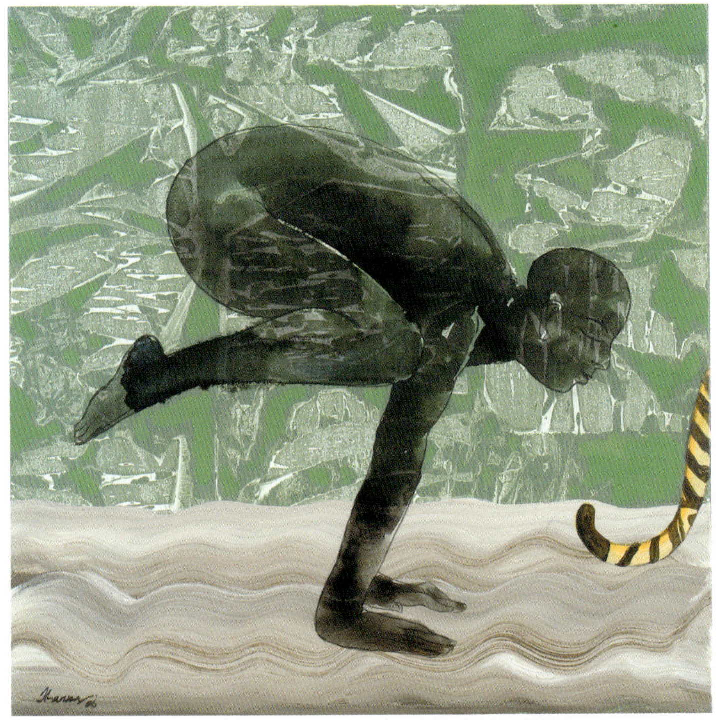

Untitled - III, acrylic on tarpaulin, 30x30", 2006

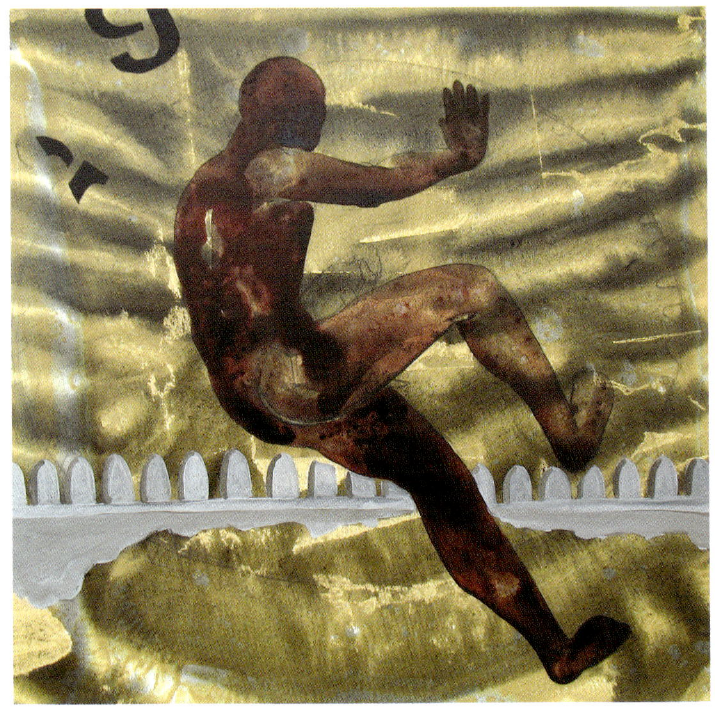

Untitled, acrylic on canvas, 30x30", 2006

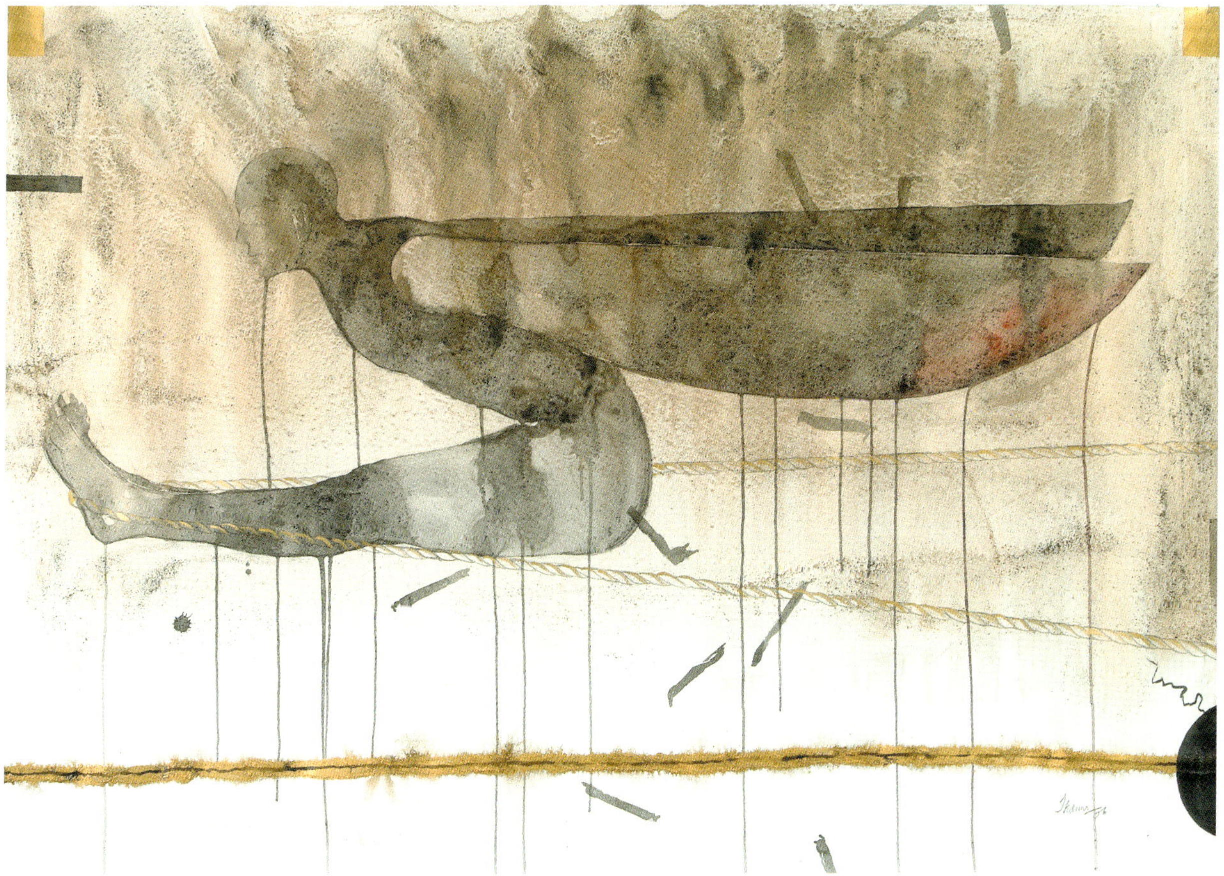

Wings, watercolour on paper, 60x42", 2006

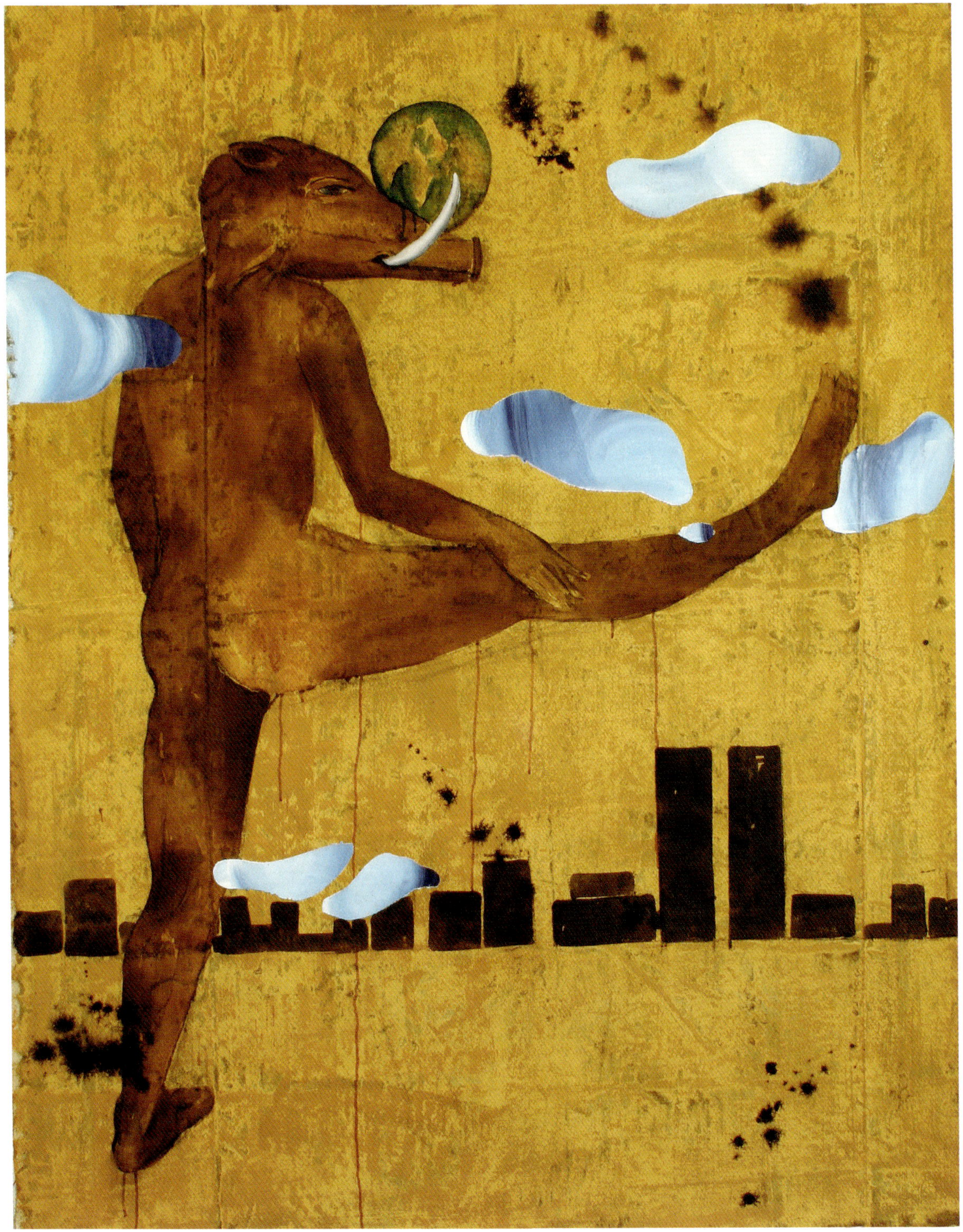

The King, acrylic on tarpaulin, 42x60", 2006

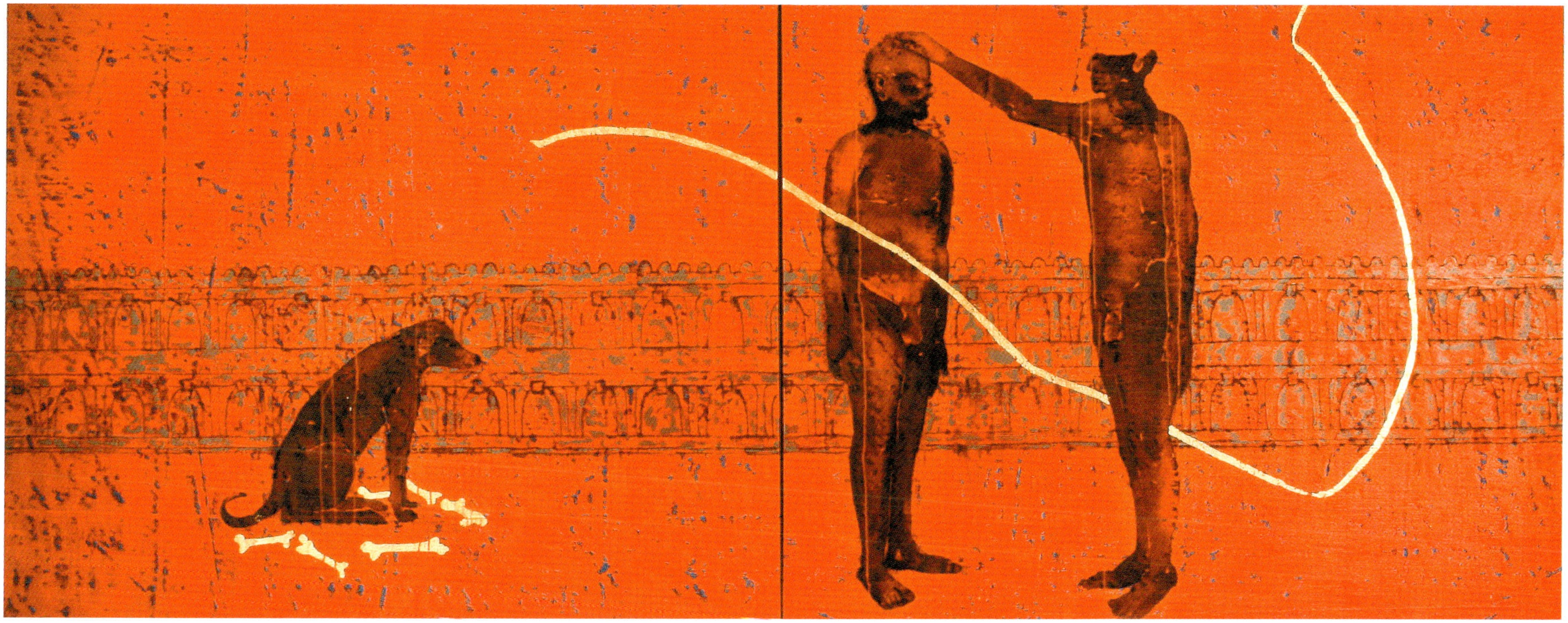

The Bones of Gold, acrylic on tarpaulin, 132x52", 2006

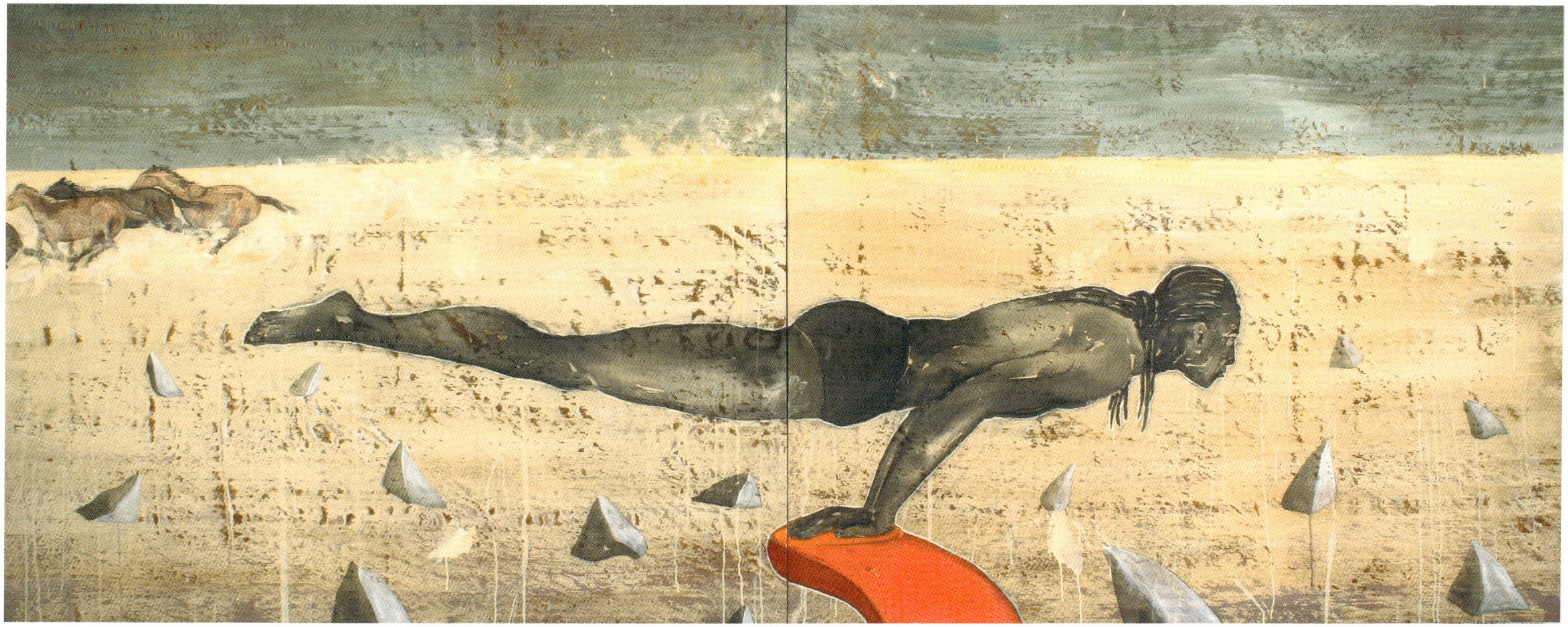

The Field, acrylic on tarpaulin, 132x52", 2006

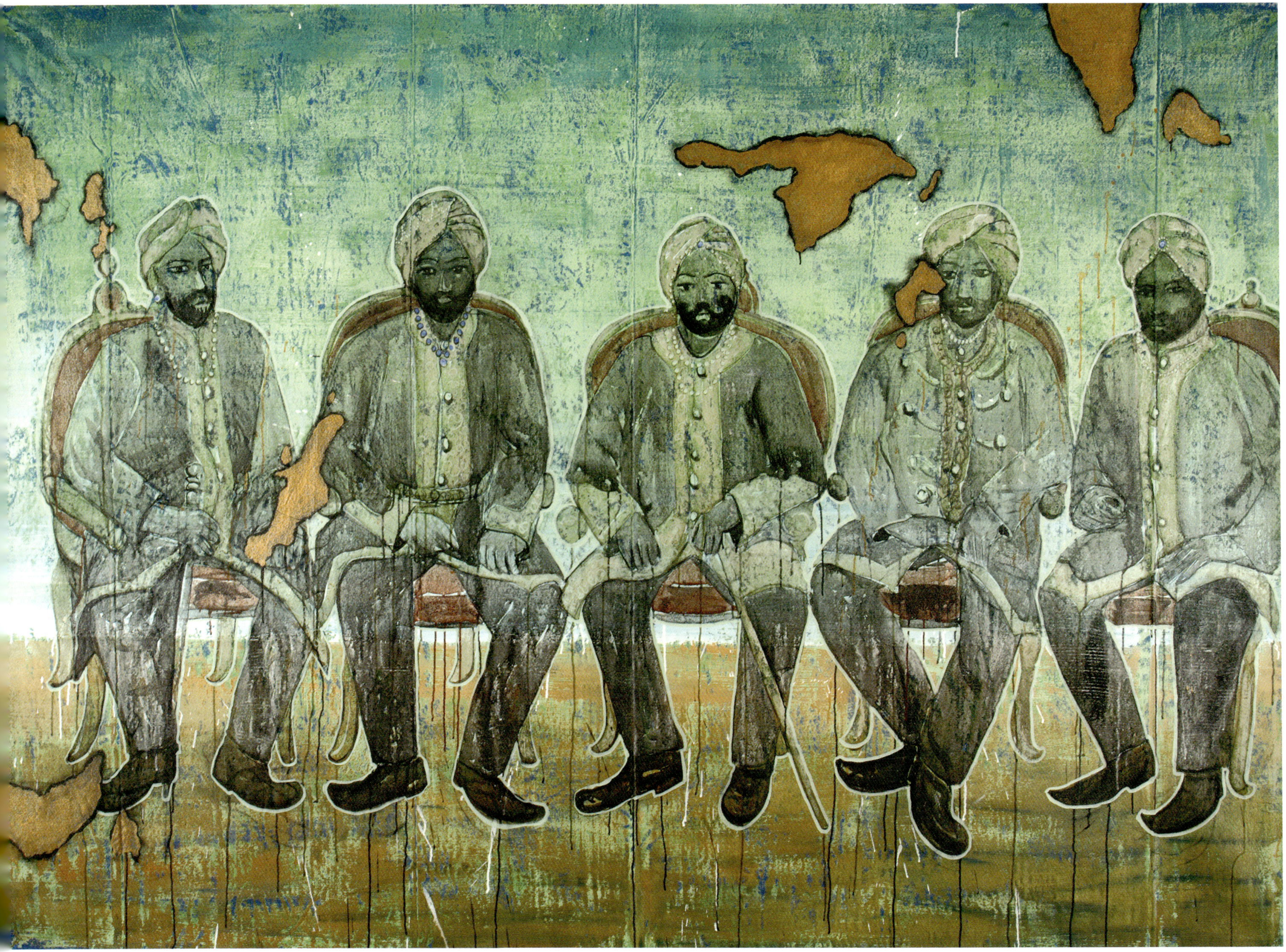

Photoshot for Land, acrylic on tarpaulin, 98x66", 2006

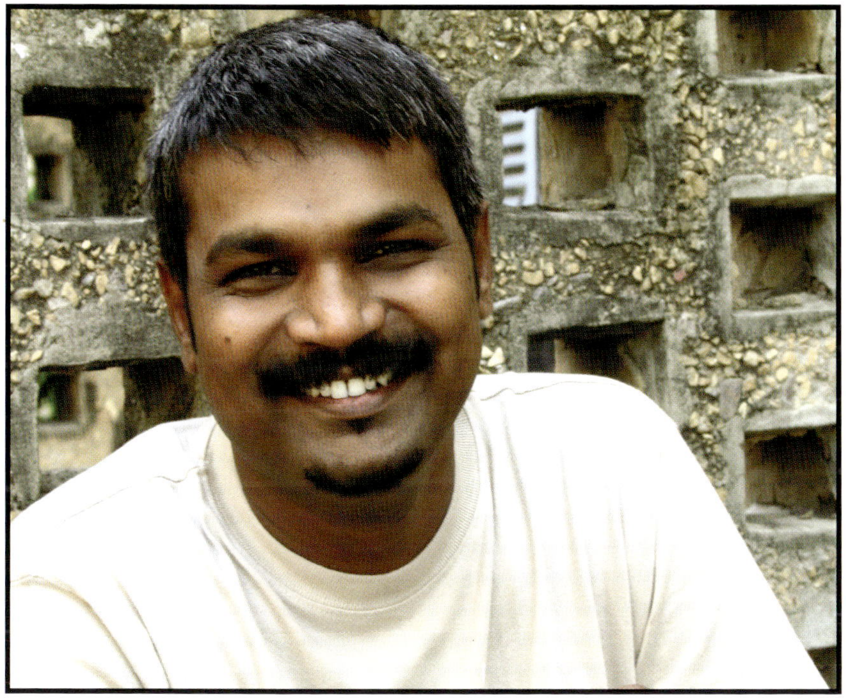

Chronology

Iranna GR

1970 Born in Sindgi, Bijapur, Karnataka (India)
1994 MFA in Painting from College of Art, New Delhi
1999-2000 Artist-in-residence at Wimbledon School of Art, London

Solo Exhibitions
2006 King of Clay, Gallery ArtsIndia, New York and California
2006 Early Works, Gallery Muller and Plate, Munich
2005 Threads of Humanism, Bodhi Art, Delhi, Singapore
2003 Dream and Perplexity, Chitrakala Parishath, Bangalore
2002 Artist of the Month (May), Saffronart, www.saffronart.com
2001 The Enigma of Departure, British Council and Guild Art Gallery, Mumbai
2000 Gallery Espace, New Delhi
2000 Maulana Azad Centre for Indian Culture, Cairo, organized by the Indian Embassy in Cairo
2000 Foyer Gallery, Wimbledon School of Art, London
1999 In the Shadow of Buddha, Gallery Martini, Hong Kong
1998 Shadows of the Real, Shridharani and Gallery Espace, New Delhi
1995 Edge Dynamics, Delhi Art Gallery, New Delhi and Jehangir Art Gallery, Mumbai

Residency
2003 Residency, George Keyt Foundation, Dambola, Sri Lanka
1997 Ninth Triennial India 1997 International Artists' Camp, Lalit Kala Akademi, New Delhi
1993 International Painting and Sculpture Symposium, Gulbarga

Attended numerous camps at the national level throughout India

Collections
National Gallery of Modern Art, New Delhi
Bharat Bhawan, Bhopal
Lalit Kala Akademi, New Delhi

Personal collections at Mumbai, Delhi, Hong Kong, Germany, Holland, Austria, Croatia and Chester Herwitz in USA

Group Exhibitions

2006 The Human Figure, Threshold Gallery, Delhi
2006 Contemporary Istanbul Art Fair, Istanbul
2005 We Are Like This Only, Vadhera Art Gallery, New Delhi
2005 Paths of Progression, Bodhi Art & Saffronart, Delhi, Mumbai, Singapore, New York
2005 Arad Bienalle, Romania
2004 Untitled, Gallery Espace, India Habitat Centre, New Delhi
2004 Peter Muller Gallery, Munich, Germany
2004 Gallery 27, Oslo, Norway
2002 Words and Images, National Gallery of Modern Art, Mumbai
2002 Modern and Contemporary Indian Paintings, Auction-cum-Exhibition, Bowring's Fine Art Auctioneers, Mumbai
2002 Jehangir Art Gallery Golden Jubilee Show, Jehangir Art Gallery, Mumbai
2002 European and Modern and Contemporary Indian Paintings, Auction cum Exhibition, Bowrings Fine Art Auctioneers, New Delhi
2001-02 Palette, Visual Art Gallery, India Habitat Centre, New Delhi
2001 Apparao Galleries, Madras
2001 The Human Factor, Guild Art Gallery, Mumbai
2001 Kaleidoscope, ISU International Art Gallery, Singapore
2001 Engendering - Images of Women, Guild Art Gallery, Mumbai
2000 Black and White, Art Today, New Delhi
1999 The Creative Process, Guild Art Galley, Mumbai
1999 Icons of the Millennium, Gallery Lakeeren, Mumbai
1999 Edge of the Century, Delhi
1998-2005 Harmony Show, Nehru Centre, Mumbai
1998 Vedanta Art Gallery, Chicago, USA
1998 Guild Art Gallery, Mumbai
1998 Gallery Espace, New Delhi
1997 Four Artists, Diverse Talents, Guild Art Gallery and Jehangir Art Gallery, Mumbai
1995 Schoo's Gallery, Amsterdam, Holland
1994 Shridharani Art Gallery, New Delhi
1994 Jehangir Art Gallery, Mumbai
1992 Award Winners' Exhibition SCZCC Nagpur, Bangalore, Indore, Hyderabad, Pune
1990 Chitrakala Parishath, Bangalore

Participated in many national and international exhibitions

Awards

2004 Harmony Show, Artist of the Year Award, Mumbai
2002 KK Hebbar Foundation Award
2001 State Award, Karnataka Lalit Kala Akademi, Bangalore
1997 Fortieth National Academy Award, Lalit Kala Akademi, New Delhi
1997 Fifty Years of Art in Independent India, AIFACS Award, New Delhi
1993 In Search of Talent, MF Husain & Ram Kumar selection award, Vadehra Art Gallery, New Delhi
1993 Bansi Parmimu Memorial Committee, New Delhi
1993 Delhi College of Art, New Delhi
1991-92 College of Visual Art, Gulbarga
1991-92 All India Exhibition Mysore, Dasara, Mysore
1990 Fourth All India Exhibition SCZCC, Nagpur

Scholarships

1999-2000 International Scholarship, Charles Wallace India Trust, British Council
1996-97 National Scholarship, Ministry of HRD, Government of India
1995-96 Garhi Research Grant, Lalit Kala Akademi, New Delhi

Iranna GR lives in New Delhi.